Reflective Laughter

Anthem Russian and Slavonic Studies

Reflective Laughter: Aspects of Humour in Russian Culture

EDITED BY LESLEY MILNE

Anthem Press

This edition first published by Anthem Press 2004
Anthem Press is an imprint of
Wimbledon Publishing Company
75–76 Blackfriars Road
London SE1 8HA

British Library Cataloguing in Publication Data
Data available

Library of Congress in Publication Data
A catalogue record has been applied for

ISBN 1 84331 119 4

Designed by Abe Aboody
Typeset by Alliance Interactive Technology, Pondicherry, India

Printed in India

1 3 5 7 9 10 8 6 4 2

CONTENTS

NOTE ON TRANSLITERATION

The transliteration system used is based on that of the Library of Congress, with the following exceptions.

In the main text for proper names the ending -ii is rendered throughout as -y. There are some names of persons which have become standardised in English according to different systems and for these in the main text the standardised form is used. They include such names as Beria, Yeltsin, Meyerhold, Tchaikovsky, Yagoda. The soft-sign′ has also been eliminated from proper names throughout the main text. Examples include: Ilia Ilf, Gogol, Kozma Prutkov, Pogorelsky, Soloviev. In all the above cases, however, in footnotes the complete transliteration system is used.

NOTES ON THE CONTRIBUTORS

Natalia Ashimbaeva is Director of the Dostoevsky Memorial Museum, St Petersburg. Her research interests are the history of Russian literature in the late nineteenth – early twentieth century. Her main publications are devoted to the works of Dostoevsky and Innokenty Annensky and include the edited volumes I. Annenskii, *Kniga otrazhenii* (Moscow, 1979) and *Vlastitel' dum: Dostoevskii v russkoi kritike kontsa XIX-nachala XX veka* (St Petersburg, 1997).

Craig Brandist is Senior Lecturer in the Bakhtin Centre and Department of Russian and Slavonic Studies at the University of Sheffield. He is the author of *Carnival Culture and the Soviet Modernist Novel* (Macmillan, 1996) and *The Bakhtin Circle: Philosophy, Culture and Politics* (Pluto, 2002), and co-editor (with Galin Tihanov) of *Materializing Bakhtin: The Bakhtin Circle and Social Theory* (Macmillan, 2000) and (with David Shepherd and Galin Tihanov) of *The Bakhtin Circle: In the Master's Absence* (Manchester University Press, 2004). He is currently director of the major research project 'The rise of sociolinguistics in the Soviet Union 1917–1938: Institutions, ideas and agendas'.

Gregory Carleton is Associate Professor of Russian at Tufts University and an associate of the Davis Center for Russian and Eurasian Studies at Harvard University. He is the author of *The Politics of Reception. Critical Constructions of Mikhail Zoshchenko* (Evanston, 1998) and *Sexual Revolution in Bolshevik Russia* (Pittsburgh, forthcoming).

Evgeny Dobrenko is Professor in the Department of Russian and Slavonic Studies, University of Nottingham. He is the author of many books, articles and essays. His most recent major publications are *The Making of the State Reader: Social and Aesthetic Contexts of the Reception of Soviet Literature* (Stanford, 1997) and *The Making of the State Writer: Social and Aesthetic Contexts of Soviet Literary Culture* (Stanford, 2001). He is editor (with Thomas Lahusen) of *Socialist Realism Without Shores* (Durham, 1997); (with Hans Günther) of *Sotsrealisticheskii kanon* (St Petersburg, 2000); (with Marina Balina and Nancy Condee) of *Endquote: Sots*

Art Literature and Soviet Grand Style (Evanston, 1999); and (with Eric Naiman) of *The Landscape of Stalinism: The Art and Ideology of Soviet Space* (Seattle, 2003).

J.A. Dunn is Senior Lecturer in the Slavonic Studies section of the School of Modern Languages and Cultures, Glasgow University. He is interested in all aspects of the mass media in post-Soviet Russia and is writing a book on the history of Russian television since 1991. Some of his recent publications have examined the language of the media (especially the consequences of linguistic globalisation and fragmentation for the maintenance of standard languages), while others have attempted to place the structure and content of the media within a pan-European context.

Ivan Esaulov is Professor in the Department of Theoretical and Historical Poetics, Russian State University for the Humanities (RGGU), Moscow. He is the author of numerous articles and five monographs, of which the most recent are *Kategoriia sobornosti v russkoi literature* (Petrozavodsk, 1995), *Spektr adekvatnosti v istolkovanii literaturnogo proizvedeniia* (Moscow, 1997), and *Mistika v russkoi literature sovetskogo perioda: Blok, Gor'kii, Esenin, Pasternak* (Tver, 2002). He is editor of the journal *Postsimvolizm kak iavlenie kul'tury* (1995–). His main area of specialism is in the poetics of Old Russian and Russian literature and the philosophy of religion.

Galina Galagan is a senior research fellow at the Russian Academy of Sciences Institute of Russian Literature, St Petersburg (Pushkinsky Dom). She is deputy editor of the journal *Russkaia literatura* and participated in the 28-volume *Collected Works* of Turgenev and the 30-volume *Collected Works* of Dostoevsky. She is the author of numerous articles on Russian literary history, editor of L.N. Tolstoi, *Ispoved'. V chem moia vera?* (Leningrad, 1991), and author of the monograph *L.N. Tolstoi: Khudozhestvenno-eticheskie iskaniia* (Leningrad, 1981).

Annie Gérin is an art historian and art curator. She teaches art history, art theory and cultural studies at the University of Regina, Canada. Her research interests revolve around unexpected encounters between non-specialised publics and public art. She publishes in the areas of Soviet monumental art and material culture, public art in Canada, and art on the World Wide Web.

Seth Graham is a lecturer in Russian at the University of Washington, Seattle. He recently defended his dissertation, a cultural analysis of the Russo-Soviet joke, at the University of Pittsburgh. His other interests include Russian and Central

Asian film, contemporary prose, and popular culture. His translation of Valeria Narbikova's novel *Day Equals Night* was published in 1999.

Edythe C. Haber is Professor of Russian Emerita at the University of Massachusetts, Boston, and also center associate at the Davis Center for Russian and Eurasian Studies at Harvard University. She is the author of many articles and the book *Mikhail Bulgakov: The Early Years* (Harvard University Press, 1998), and is currently working on a book on Nadezhda Teffi.

Efim Kurganov is Assistant Professor of Russian Literature at the University of Helsinki. He is the author of several monographs including the following *Literaturnyi anekdot pushkinskogo perioda* (Helsinki, 1995), *Anekdot kak zhanr* (St Petersburg, 1997), *Pokhval'noe slovo anekdotu* (St Petersburg, 2001) and *Anekdot: simvol i mif* (St Petersburg, 2002).

Lesley Milne is Professor of Russian and Slavonic Studies at the University of Nottingham. She has published books and articles on Bulgakov, including *Mikhail Bulgakov. A Critical Biography* (Cambridge, 1990) and *Bulgakov. The Novelist-Playwright* (Harwood Academic Publishers, 1995). The current focus of her research is the culture of humour in Russia in the twentieth century. A book *Zoshchenko and the Ilf-Petrov Partnership: How They Laughed* was published by Birmingham Slavonic Monographs in 2003.

Karen Ryan is Professor of Russian Language and Literature and Associate Dean of the Arts, Humanities and Social Sciences at the University of Virginia in Charlottesville, Virginia. Her work has appeared in a wide range of scholarly journals and her major publications include *Satire under Glasnost: the Journalistic Feuilleton, Contemporary Russian Satire: A Genre Study* and *Venedikt Erofeev's 'Moskva-Petushki'*. Her current research is a book-length project of images of Stalin in Russian Satire.

Marietta Tourian is a member of the St Petersburg Union of Writers and the Russian Academic Group in the USA. She is the author of articles and studies on V.F. Odoevsky, Pushkin, Dostoevsky, Turgenev, Antony Pogorelsky and the problems of Russian 'fantastic realism'. She prepared the editions V.F. Odoevsky, *Pestrie skazki* (in the 'Literaturnye pamiatniki' series) and a volume of selected works of Antony Pogorelsky.

Vladimir Tunimanov is a senior research fellow at the Russian Academy of Sciences Institute of Russian Literature, St Petersburg (Pushkinsky Dom) and is a member of the St Petersburg Union of Writers. He is on the editorial board of the journal *Russkaia literatura* and is the Vice-President (Russia) of the International Dostoevsky Society. He is the author of numerous articles and the monographs *Tvorchestvo Dostoevskogo 1854–1862* (Leningrad, 1980), *A.I. Gertsen i russkaia obshchestvenno-esteticheskaia mysl' XIX veka* (St Petersburg, 1994), *Kavkazkie povesti L. Tolstogo* (Sapporo, 1998).

Valentina Vetlovskaia is a senior research fellow at the Russian Academy of Sciences Institute of Russian Literature, St Petersburg (Pushkinsky Dom). She participated in the 30-volume *Collected Works* of Dostoevsky and is author of the monographs *Poetika romana 'Brat'ia Karamazovy'* (Leningrad, 1977) and *Roman F.M. Dostoevskogo 'Bednye liudi'* (Leningrad, 1988). Her most recent book is *Analiz epicheskogo proizvedeniia: problemy poetiki* (St Petersburg, 2002). She has published numerous articles on the history and theory of literature and has lectured on these subjects in universities in Russia and world-wide.

ACKNOWLEDGEMENTS

THE British Academy awarded a grant to support the conference 'Two Centuries of Russian Humour and Satire', held in July 2000 at the University of Nottingham, where some of the papers in this volume were first presented. The Institute of Russian, Soviet, Central and East European Studies of the University of Nottingham also supported this event and assisted with costs in the preparation of the present volume.

Quotations from the translation of Pushkin's 'Tsar Nikita and His Daughters', published in *After Pushkin: Versions of the poems of Alexander Sergeevich Pushkin by contemporary poets* (London: The Folio Society, 1999), are reproduced here with kind permission of Ranjit Bolt.

1

INTRODUCTION

Reflective laughter: Aspects of humour in Russian culture

LESLEY MILNE

In his book *Seriously Funny: From the Ridiculous to the Sublime*, Howard Jacobson makes reference to 'national expectations of comedy', as described by the Russian clown, Slava Polunin.[1] These 'national expectations' are based on Polunin's own experience of audiences and are expressed in artistically sweeping generalisations. In England, for example, humour is declared to be 'intellectual. People like intricacy there.' In France it is 'the fate of the character'. In the USA it is 'the holiday that counts; there they go to the theatre simply to be distracted and to forget', while for the Russians 'compassion is all that matters'. These statements are, of course, all wide open to challenge as 'national characteristics'. It would, however, be true to say that they usefully enumerate a gamut of responses, all of which could be found, in addition to others, in all the 'national traditions' of Europe. They can certainly all be found in the Russian culture of humour in the last two centuries, which is the topic covered by the chapters in this volume. In the first chapter of *Seriously Funny*, Jacobson had already hinted at aspects of humour that present problems for its reception across different cultures, namely its complexity and its exclusivity, observing that 'nothing is more frequently denied the foreigner than a capacity to understand or make [comedy]'.[2] It is therefore the aim of this book to breach that exclusivity and illuminate that complexity.

The time span of the articles is confined to the nineteenth and twentieth centuries, not because humour did not exist in Russia before then, but because it was only in the nineteenth century that it emerged into a culturally sophisticated literature of world stature. Russia did not have its Boccaccio, its Chaucer, its Rabelais or its Shakespeare. Russia was cut off from the European experience of the Renaissance and, until the time of Peter the Great, printing in Russia was a Church monopoly, which inhibited the emergence of a secular literature. What Russia had instead of Rabelais, as the scholars Likhachev and Panchenko pointed out, was a highly developed culture of the 'holy fool' (*iurodivyi*), whose actions or utterances appeared comically 'foolish' only to those who did not comprehend their inner spiritual significance.[3] This particularity of the Russian historical experience survives in what Jacobson refers to as 'Russia's great tradition of clowns and fools and holy innocents and *idiots savants*' and may underlie Polunin's assertion that for Russians 'compassion is what matters'.[4]

Among the first examples of secular literature in Russia were the so-called 'satirical tales' of the seventeenth and early eighteenth century. They gave expression to popular grievances and attitudes and, with their roots in the oral tradition, these tales marked the moment when Russian folklore took on permanent form for the first time.[5] Humour and satire were practised by the writers of the eighteenth-century Russian Enlightenment: the verse satires of Dmitry Kantemir; the fables of Ivan Krylov, with their epigrams and proverbs; the classical comedies of Denis Fonvizin. The first masterpiece of Russian nineteenth-century theatre was a comedy, Aleksandr Griboedov's play in verse, *Woe from Wit (Gore ot uma)*, which has its antecedents in the classical French tradition of Molière. Although completed in 1825, it was not passed by the censorship for the stage, and was printed only in part in an almanac. It was, however, the period of literary salons, at which the play was read out by its author to 'all Moscow' and 'all Petersburg'.[6] Written in verse, it is a cascade of aphorisms, and virtually every other line has entered the Russian language. Thus Griboedov's comedy and its reception can be said to exemplify the conditions in which intellectual humour thrives the world over: conviviality, an element of subversion, memorable formulation, and word-of-mouth transmission. The subversive factor of the play lies in the worldview embodied in its hero, Chatsky: he is full of wit, idealism and youthful energy, which are all undirected, except against the selfish banality of the world around him. Thus we have, at the outset, an illustration of a point made by Jacobson: 'Whenever we try to make an art that conforms to our inner world, it becomes protest'.[7] This dictum may in fact provide a key to a specific feature of Russian culture through most of the past two centuries: a particularly acute awareness of the difference between the 'inner world' of the artist and the public world of literature as censored, sponsored, or controlled by the state.

After the Russian Revolution, the reception of Russian humour and satire became heavily politicised. In the field of humorous writing, the enhanced sensitivity to the 'protest' element led to a persistent requirement of all humour that it should be 'serious' in the sense that it could be interpreted as satirical in intent. First émigré , then Western scholarship in general, appreciated and interpreted Russian humour chiefly as a critique of 'the absurdities of the Soviet regime' or its antecedents. Satire was regarded as the higher form, and humour that did not aspire to, or could not be pressed into, this purpose was devalued as 'empty'. Meanwhile, from the point of view of the sponsoring state, a similar elevation of satire over humour occurred. In official Soviet culture, humour was co-opted into the great task of building socialism. Again it was valued only in its satirical function: as a corrective, 'scourging', 'lashing' or otherwise castigating 'relics of the bourgeois past', which were impeding the development of the new, healthy socialist society. This demand was then retrospectively directed at the pre-revolutionary literary legacy. These polarised perceptions meant that whole areas of humour became culturally invisible. With the ending of the Cold War, the way has opened for new approaches: the focus has become much less fixed, widening the range of points for study, and extending the probe beyond the political surface. The aim of the present collection is therefore to present a fresh overview of the role of humour and laughter in the formation of Russian culture and counter-culture.

The title *Reflective Laughter* has been chosen because of its multiplicity of meanings and combined applications. The word reflective, as a synonym for 'meditative', or 'thoughtful', suggests the engagement of the mind in crafting ironies and paradoxes. Indicating a mirror that gives back an image of an object, it encompasses the idea of parody. The concept of throwing back something that strikes or falls on the surface can refer to the way that art, in this case its comedic forms, reproduces an aspect of the world it inhabits. All these different meanings are operative, in various ways and to differing degrees, in the essays that make up this collection. The collection cannot be complete, for the comedic culture in Russian tradition offers an infinite number of topics and a book can only be so long. But the treatments of the theme on display here offer sample approaches and sample 'sites', allowing readers to fill in the gaps according to their taste and experience.

The book starts with the major authors of the Russian classic literary tradition of the nineteenth-century. In her essay on Pushkin's poetic drama 'The Covetous Knight' Valentina Vetlovskaia analyses the inherent ironies and paradoxes that permeate Pushkin's poem, which Pushkin himself styled a 'tragicomedy'. In Pushkin's poem we have the simultaneous operation of two logics, the comic and the tragic, with the reader recognising the 'gloomy comedy' in this portrait of a warring father and son, where 'neither has recognised in the other a trait they have already lost or not yet acquired'. Vetlovskaia demonstrates how Pushkin transposes the traditionally comic theme of 'the miser' into a plot and treatment that reach the heights of tragic grandeur, but still retain a comic essence in the process of unmasking vice. This unmasking occurs not in an explosion of laughter but as a result of intellectual reflection, illustrating Nietzsche's maxim that 'the cleverest authors provoke the least perceptible smiles'.

There is, however, another, very different, aspect of Pushkin's 'cleverness', to which attention should also be drawn. His comic range encompasses what could be called 'the open laugh' or 'the laugh outright', examples of which introduce an element vital to any study of humour, namely the bawdy and erotic. For sheer, unmediated, enjoyment of this aspect of Russian humour, readers are referred to Pushkin's ballad 'Tsar Nikita and His Forty Daughters', brilliantly translated by Ranjit Bolt in a form that retains the short lines of insistent and ingeniously rhyming couplets. The forty daughters are perfect specimens of enchanting womanhood in all but one respect:

> One thing was missing...'Is that all?'
> I hear you cry. 'Twas, oh, so small –
> Scarcely a problem – nonetheless,
> For all its negligibleness,
> It *was* still missing... How the Hell
> Am I explicitly to tell
> My readers what this one thing was?
> I'm not sure if I can because
> That pompous, pious, pea-brained dunce
> The censor would explode at once...
> Between their legs – oh, dear dear dear!
> No, even that is far too clear –
> Much too indecent – let me see,
> A little more obliquity –
> Let's find a more circuitous route
> To lead you deftly, gently to't – [8]

How the daughters were each furnished with that crucial 'one thing missing' is spun into a wonderfully absurd tale, wittily told in a parody of the ballad style. 'Tsar Nikita' shows the superabundance of comic poetic energy in Pushkin's 'juvenalia'. As might be expected, it was not published in its time, and, along with his bawdily blasphemous *Gabrieliad* (a parody of the Annunciation), caused trouble for Pushkin, who destroyed the manuscript. Both poems circulated, however, in numerous copies that were preserved in the private archives of his contemporaries.[9] This is an example of the 'protest' of the 'inner world' of cheerful eroticism that flourishes beneath social veneers and defies the proprieties. The greater the constraints, of course, the greater the delight in defying them. It seems no coincidence that Pushkin's 'Tsar Nikita' was written during the Lenten period of fasting.[10]

The second essay in this collection deals with Gogol, the nineteenth-century Russian master of mystification and the absurd. The paradox of Gogol's art was most famously defined by the author himself in chapter VII of *Dead Souls* as 'laughter through tears', a definition that was to become almost prescriptive for Russian humour in general (which had the effect of further inhibiting responsiveness to 'empty merriment'). Efim Kurganov, however, approaches from a new perspective, that of Gogol's oral narratives and anecdotes, accounts of which have survived in the reminiscences of contemporaries. Where Pushkin's 'private' humour was bawdy verse, Gogol's was the risqué or indecent tale. As Kurganov shows, other literary luminaries of the 'Golden Age' of Russian literature also took great pleasure in such anecdotes, in particular the scatological. This element of comic degradation reflects the persistence of the motif of excrement in the anthropology of laughter, demonstrated by the frequency of references to it in Jacobson's *Seriously Funny.* Smut and scatology are present in the great carnivals and festivals of regeneration, or the British tradition of Christmas pantomime, or the performance of a street-theatre puppet-booth, where the audience of adults and children guffaw and shriek with delight at the marvellous impropriety of it all. In these contexts, comic indecency is traditional and expected. The point about Gogol's anecdotes, however, is that they were always told in maximally inappropriate social situations. Efim Kurganov sees here a domestic arena in which the great verbal conjurer could practise his techniques of comic surprise. Where others who tried to tell similar tales would be halted mid-way through, or ostracised afterwards, Gogol always managed to narrate the anecdote to its punch-line, frequently escaping censure altogether. These acts of what Jacobson calls 'social sabotage'[11] are seen by Kurganov as part of the Gogolian mission to expose the falsehoods of society, and also as showing a literary personality at play in social situations, using devices that reflect his literary techniques of ambushing the reader with the comically unexpected.

One of the most brilliant stars in the firmament of nineteenth-century Russian comic literature is the 'writer' 'Kozma Prutkov', invented by A.K. Tolstoi and his cousins, the brothers Aleksei and Vladimir Zhemchuzhnikov. Between 1853 and 1863 they published, under this pseudonym, satirical, humorous and nonsense verse and prose. They also furnished Prutkov with a spoof biography, combining two incongruous métiers: Prutkov fancies himself a romantic poet, while being in essence a most loyally conformist civil servant, director of the assay office in the ministry of finance. Prutkov's complacent aphorisms and plodding verse turn banality into a high art form and are an enduring part of the Russian comic treasury. In her chapter on Prutkov's 'ancestry' Marietta Tourian defines her aim as a contribution to the debate as to which of Prutkov's creators was pre-eminent. She suggests that it was A.K. Tolstoi who played the role of initiator and instigator, although the Zhemchizhnikov brothers were the more prolific. In pursuing this precisely defined aim, however, she gives a larger picture, which is a depiction of a literary culture in which pranks, polemics and parodies flourished among the literary elite. This started in the second decade of the nineteenth century, with the literary circle 'Arzamas', of which Pushkin was a member and to which A. K. Tolstoi's uncle belonged. Parody, the aesthetics of nonsense, comic eroticism and bawdy all flourished in the 'group behaviour' of this environment. It is Marietta Tourian's argument that these traditions, cultivated by the uncle, were passed on to the nephew who subsequently became co-creator and prime animator of the splendid Prutkov. Thus the laughter of the literary elite in one generation was reflected in the 'group behaviour' of the next.

The name of Dostoevsky returns us to the realm of the tragi-comic. Known for his 'cruel talent', he none the less had a genius for parody, irony, satire and buffoonery, although never without a tragic colouring. His forte is comic ugliness and comic dissonance, in which the comic and tragic co-exist and interact. The 'purest' example – if one may use such a word – of this intermix is to be found in Prince Myshkin in *The Idiot*, the supreme literary manifestation of Russia's great tradition of holy innocents. In her essay Natalia Ashimbaeva analyses the two levels of artistic interaction in the Prince's character: the sacred and the practical. The Prince is simultaneously both holy and ridiculous, embodying the principle of Dostoevskian poetics articulated by Bakhtin as the ability to reflect contradictory interrelationships 'in the cross-section of a single moment'.

Whereas there is an extensive literature on comedy in Dostoevsky, readers of Lev Tolstoi would be hard put to it to recall a profusion of comic moments in his works. Natasha's perception of the opera in Part VIII, Chapter IX of *War and Peace* might qualify, but the reader's smile at this defamiliarised perspective quickly vanishes. The humour is too ruthlessly subordinated to Tolstoi's moral purpose, which is to expose the grotesque falseness of this art form and the society that sustains it. Galina Galagan, however, takes a productively oblique approach, through Tolstoi's reading of a work of literature in which the humorous, ironic strain is dominant. We thus see the reflection of one author's laughter in the (at first sight very different) work of another, the reflection of one book in another author's path of development. The young Tolstoi enthusiastically reads Laurence Sterne's *A Sentimental Journey*, and then incorporates its devices into his own search for an authentic personal morality. The Sternian irony thus takes root on the ground of Tolstoi's own merciless self-analysis. Galagan shows us the moment when Tolstoi, terrified of appearing ridiculous, observes himself looking at himself in the mirror and perceives this itself as ridiculous. The reflective laughter here is ours as we recall our own experience of youth's obsession with its imagined physical imperfections. We also derive an ironic pleasure of self-recognition from the honesty with which youth's vanity is so mercilessly dissected. As Tolstoi said in his diary, 'We know about human weaknesses from ourselves and in order to illustrate them in a believable way it is necessary to express them in oneself.' Thus his self-irony generates the imaginative generosity of his art, which is always greater than the moral 'purpose' to which he subjugated it.

An author missing from this collection, whose name should none the less be included in this introductory overview, is the great nineteenth-century satirist Mikhail Saltykov-Shchedrin. His laughter exemplifies the type defined by Bakhtin as 'laughter that does not laugh'.[12] In the novel *The Golovlev Family*, the comic element is entirely absent, replaced by a rage of revulsion and contempt. *History of a Town* is an allegory, a parody of Russian history of the eighteenth and early nineteenth centuries, which is used as a vehicle to discuss Russia's historical legacy and political mentality. The device of grotesque exaggeration generates a darkly comic effect in the contrast between the brutal stupidities described, and the matter-of-fact manner of their narration. In the Russian tradition the book can stand as the epitome of 'closed laughter': rationalist, dry and mocking.

In her chapter on Nadezhda Teffi, Edythe Haber takes us into the pre-revolutionary twentieth century. Teffi was one of the core contributors to *Satirikon*, which was enormously influential in the humorous journalism of the epoch. A satirical weekly published from 1908 to 1918 (from 1914 to 1918 under the title *Novyi satirikon*), it concentrated not on direct political comment but on topical issues of everyday life. Its editor was Arkady Averchenko, who emigrated after the Revolution, as did Teffi. Through Teffi, Edythe Haber addresses the question of 'women's humour', arguing that in terms of attitude and topic, humour can be associated with intellectual aggression, assertiveness, superiority, the bawdy and the obscene. There is an alternative 'minority' humour of the outsider or underdog, but this is not available to women as long as they are at the centre of home and hearth, and therefore insiders. Only when women gain a measure of independence and stand outside the home does a situation arise that will foster 'women's humour'. Such a situation prevailed in early twentieth-century Russia. The humour of Teffi, an independent woman and a professional writer, reflects these social shifts. But Teffi's humour, Edythe Haber points out, is feminine rather than feminist, observing the foibles of both sexes with 'ladylike condescension'. The limits of her humour are defined by her social class as a member of the metropolitan urban elite. The sharpness of her eye and pointed elegance of her wit are, however, shaded by sympathy for the characters she portrays, as they try to find their style in the pre-revolutionary world of department stores and flamboyant fashions. This world, and its values, was about to be swept away. The humour of Teffi, and *Satirikon* in general, represents the confident dominance of an intellectual elite and its culture, and as such is a swan-song. After the Revolution, this cultural dominance was shattered. The members of the intelligentsia who remained in Russia were forced into reassessment of the mission of Russian literature and the role they were to play in it. All the subsequent chapters in this collection deal with this post-revolutionary period of Russian culture.

The chapter by Ivan Esaulov on the important Russian comedic traditions of holy foolishness and buffoonery summarises the history of these phenomena and examines them as two variants of unofficial cultural behaviour, strategies deployed in different eras as a means of polemic with the dominant culture. While elements of holy foolishness can be seen in the work, and the behaviour, of such writers as Gogol, Tolstoi and Dostoevsky, it is the post-revolutionary era of emergent totalitarianism that provides the focus for Esaulov's analysis. He illustrates his study with examples not only from artistic literature but also from academic writing. Thus Ilf and Petrov are seen as operating the strategies of buffoonery, as does the critic Viktor Shklovsky. The religious philosopher Aleksei Losev, unable to engage directly with Marxist-Leninism, is viewed as resorting to holy foolishness as a mode of polemical scholarly discourse. The work of the poet Maksimilian Voloshin then represents an interim stage, reflecting the problems of coming to terms with the destruction and violence of the Russian Revolution by displaying an ambivalent cross-contamination of these two modes of buffoonery and holy-foolishness.

The tradition of buffoonery is viewed by Esaulov as essentially Western. On this basis he takes issue with interpretations of Mikhail Bulgakov's *The Master and Margarita* that analyse the novel from the Western perspective of the 'noble buffoon', without taking into account specifically Russian Orthodox influences that enrich and transform this Western tradition. My own chapter continues this 'Western European' approach, suggesting that certain ideas, conceived 'from the outside', in English rather than Russian, might none the less be productive in generating an framework for the analysis of works of Russian literature. The concepts of the innocent, the rogue and the joker are offered as categorising three different types of comic hero and three correspondingly different authorial standpoints, as writers position themselves in relation to the ideals and the reality of the society in which they live. They also represent three different types of authorial fate. The three models in the first decades of Soviet power are Zoshchenko, the writing partnership of Ilf and Petrov, and Bulgakov. For its last decades, covering the period from the post-Stalin Thaw to the last year of the century, the authors are Voinovich, Iskander and Pelevin. These three categories of innocent, rogue and joker are seen as reflecting three different modes of response to given historical situations that are characterised by social, economic and political upheaval.

Mikhail Zoshchenko is a pivotal name in the culture of Russian laughter in the twentieth century. Writing for the satirical journals of the 1920s, he exemplifies the difference between them and their pre-revolutionary predecessor, *Satirikon*, in that Zoshchenko's chosen audience was the untutored proletarian reader. His characteristic device was to adopt the perspective and voice of the 'common man', struggling with the new concepts and language introduced by the Revolution, trying to find his feet in this new society. This is exaggeration, stylisation, parody, and as such appealed as much to the intellectual elite as to the nominally primary addressee, the 'man in the street'. Zoshchenko was popular also among the émigré intelligentsia, who read his works as satirical exposures of the 'absurdity' of post-revolutionary Russian reality. Herein lies a dangerous vulnerability to interpretation as 'anti-Soviet', which is the question analysed by Gregory Carleton in his chapter on the reception of Zoshchenko's work from the 1920s to the end of the century.

Carleton points out that appreciation of works of humour and satire is conditioned by the ideological pre-suppositions of the reader, and also that the context in which a work is presented has a bearing on whether it is perceived as 'anti-Soviet'. For example, a sketch written in 1934, if it appears in an anthology containing satirical works written in that period but not published until much later, will also be read as 'unpublishable in its time' – even though the sketch in question was in fact published in no less a place than *Pravda.* Carleton demonstrates that 'there was much more circulating in the Soviet literary environment of the 1920s and 1930s than we commonly assume' and that we suffer from 'a binary perception' in which works have to be received as either pro- or anti-Soviet. Zoshchenko was a classic victim of such a binary reading. In 1946, Andrei Zhdanov, Stalin's cultural lieutenant, attacked Zoshchenko as 'anti-Soviet', destroying his livelihood and reputation and turning him into a martyr. But this famous attack does not, in itself, mean that Zoshchenko was an 'anti-Soviet' writer, either in effect or in intention. The end of the Cold War should have removed such automatic reflex responses, but they have proved remarkably tenacious, fostered by the current predilection for reading works as 'transgressive' or 'subversive'. Thus, Carleton argues, our laughter is merely a reflection of our own times and our own prejudices, unless we can imaginatively enter into the competing, complex and confusing literary world in which the works themselves were produced.

There were, however, 'clear cut examples of writing openly directed against the state or the system', as Carleton reminds us, naming Zamiatin as one such writer. Vladimir Tunimanov reads Zamiatin as a dedicated ironist, reacting against the symbolist poet Blok's rejection of 'the laughter demon' as 'destructive'. Faced with the choice between two responses to the state of the contemporary world – the tragic or the ironic – Zamiatin declared himself firmly on the side of the latter. His novel *We* is shot through with irony at every level. Irony is the response of the individual, the 'I'; it is anti-dogmatic, and in that sense 'anti-religious'. *We* was written between 1920 and 1921 and is a high lampoon of contemporary trends in early post-revolutionary Russia, taken to their logical extreme. Its subtly taunting laughter reflects – and anticipates – the efforts of the new state to inspire, or impose, faith in a new political and social doctrine. But, as Vladimir Tunimanov points out, the 'heretics' in the novel, led by the charismatic I-330, display the same dogmatic ruthlessness of purpose. The liberating power of true irony transcends this position, and is a state of intellectual clarity achieved by none of the novel's characters. As a summary of the function of Zamiatin's 'reflective laughter' we could perhaps cite an aphorism from the Western European intellectual elite: Elizabeth Asquith Bibesco's famous maxim that 'Irony is the hygiene of the mind'.[13]

We customarily regard such 'cleansing' laughter as in essence subversive, but this fails to take into account the uses to which laughter can be put by the state, when it wishes to mock its ideological enemies. In the West we have been inclined to approach the anti-religious propaganda of the militantly atheist Soviet state through the perception of Bulgakov's *The Master and Margarita.* The publication in 1989 and 1990 of Bulgakov's diaries for the period 1922–25 revealed that in 1925 he had paid a visit to the editorial offices of the journal *Bezbozhnik* ('The Atheist', literally 'The Godless'). There he collected a set of back numbers, and was so shocked by the negative depiction of Jesus Christ that the first inception of the idea for *The Master and Margarita* can be seen as dating from this moment.[14] Annie Gérin, however, introduces us to this same thematic material from the perspective of *Godless* itself, demonstrating how the anti-religious propagandists used caricature to combat the power of the 'old' religions, both Christianity and Judaism, and their clergy. She reminds us that *Godless* could call upon the service of talented artists, and we see how irony became a tool for confronting superstition. The 'new reader' of *Godless* would learn to laugh at his mistaken assumptions of the past, and the visual caricature was of particular importance in reaching a newly literate, or barely literate, audience. The cartoons in *Godless* allow us to enter into imaginative collusion with the post-revolutionary propaganda that they reflect.

Cinema was a powerful new tool in the education of the masses, and Evgeny Dobrenko illustrates in his chapter how in the Stalinist 1930s the film genre of musical comedy created an image of the masses as the state power wanted to see them, as an expression of the national 'popular spirit'. The classical musical heritage was alien to the experience of the 'new consumer' who entered the theatres and concert halls after the Revolution. Through an analysis of three musical comedies of the 1930s Evgeny Dobrenko reveals a model of the Socialist Realist project, its process towards a synthesis of 'high' and 'popular' culture, by which each was absorbed into the other and the 'classical heritage' became 'the property of the wide working masses'. Furthermore these film musicals reflect 'state laughter', the fixed function of 'Soviet satire' as always 'an image of what is announced today by the authorities as being "of yesterday".'

Laughter, however, need not always be a tool. It can be a by-product, as Craig Brandist shows in his examination of *Parnas dybom* (Parnassus Upside-Down) in the context of 'scientific parody' in early Soviet Russia. This chapter reflects the enormous creative energy of Russian literary scholarship in the second two decades of the twentieth century, the passion for systematisation as a path to objective study of a work of art, expressed as the sum of its 'devices'. A parody of a text is an exercise in isolating its distinctive stylistic devices, thus facilitating critical analysis. *Parnas dybom* appeared in 1925 in the wake of such theorists as Shklovsky, Tynianov and Viktor Vinogradov. It contained three short poems and tales, familiar to the reader from the nursery, but here rendered in the style of such authors as Homer, Julius Caesar, Dante, Shakespeare, and Anatole France. Although it was conceived as a textbook, a sample of scholarly exercises, its first edition was, however, anonymous, since its authors, all young lecturers at Kharkov University, thought it unfitting their rank to publish such frivolity. Readers, on the other hand, responded above all to its merriment and it became enormously popular. Although it lapsed into obscurity between 1927 and the late 1960s, on its re-emergence it regained its legendary status. Thus laughter, from the original by-product, became the means of transmission. The parodic mirror of *Parnas dybom* is of course the supremely reflective mode, here reduced to an imitation of stylistic essence. Craig Brandist goes on to examine parody in the theoretical constructs of the Bakhtin Circle, their indebtedness to German scholarship, and the evolution of Bakhtin's theory of carnival, in which the ideas of others are integrated into a philosophical cultural whole. Ideology, and not merely style, becomes an object for parodic dismemberment, and parody is incorporated as a tool for free creativity in a struggle between official and popular forms of culture.

If, as Evgeny Dobrenko's chapter shows, Stalinism itself aspired to synthesis of the official with the popular in the project of Socialist Realism, then Bakhtin can be viewed as seeking the constant regenerative, resistant element in popular laughter. Karen Ryan's article, 'Laughing at the Hangman: Humorous Portraits of Stalin' examines the ways in which authors from the 1960s onwards – Voinovich, Gladilin, Suslov, Iskander, Aleshkovsky, and Viktor Erofeev – 'reduce and diminish' the awesome figure and, by extension, his lengthy legacy. Within the period of Stalinism itself, such allegorical treatments as *The Dragon* by Evgeny Shvarts (1944), ostensibly an attack on Nazism, and Kornei Chukovsky's prototypical *Cockroach* (1923), allowed their readers to make similar inferences. The article argues that ironical humour born of terrible, tragic experiences reflects an important complex of socio-psychological needs, which involve 'coming to terms with questions of guilt and complicity', acquiring the perspective necessary to transcend them, and thus renewing faith in the essential soundness of the national culture.

Any Russian speaker who visited Russia from the 1960s through to the end of the Soviet period knows the importance of the *anekdot* or joke, usually political or else acquiring political significance because of its prevailing context of ironic play with a non-ironic official culture. As Seth Graham points out, the idea of arrests for telling *anekdoty* became part of Soviet popular consciousness. The jokes and joke-cycles were so ubiquitous that they cross-contaminated or became self-referential, to the point where reflexive 'jokes about jokes' evolved. The *anekdot* was an outlawed genre precisely because it was such 'an ideal medium for rapid, clandestine propagation of unvetted opinions'. Interestingly, one of Graham's anecdotes about Stalin is also cited in a literary version by Ryan. It could be inferred that the *anekdot* in Soviet culture fulfilled many, if not all, of the qualities and functions attributed by Ryan to ironic portraits of Stalin, but in a concentrated, condensed form. It might also be said that in its momentary life, endlessly repeated, the *anekdot* achieved the parodic dismemberment and subversion of official culture that represented for Bakhtin the ideal of popular carnival.

One aspect of contemporary popular laughter not covered in the present collection is 'sick' or 'black' humour, of which Arnold and Svetlana McMillin have provided a wonderfully no-holds-barred compendium.[15] This is the area of playground rhymes, and their (frequently obscene) adult counterparts, which achieve their humour through comic heartlessness. As a relatively innocuous illustration, one could cite two jokes, which demonstrate the equivalence of English and Russian culture in this respect.

English 'Mummy, mummy, why do I keep going round in circles?' – 'Shut up, or I'll nail your other foot to the floor.'

Russian 'Don't keep bumping into Daddy. That's no way to treat a man who's hanged himself.' (*Ne tolkai papu. Ne dlia togo on povesilsia.*)

Such examples remind us of what Jacobson describes as 'our inexhaustible capacity to evade the burden of sympathy and the compulsion to suffer'.[16] Humour here is enhanced by the explosive contrast between the content and the form, where tragedy, violence or obscenity are unexpectedly condensed into a quatrain or a joke. In this shrieking dissonance they are like the stories and novels of Vladimir Sorokin, which parade violence and depravity in a form that parodies the solemn cadences of the traditional Soviet novel. In post-Soviet Russia Sorokin is enormously popular among readers with stomachs for such strong meat; others turn away in disgust.

The last chapter in the collection, by John Dunn, examines humour and satire in post-Soviet Russian television. Prime among the examples of TV comedy shows is the *KNV*, which is also mentioned in Seth Graham's article on the *anekdot.* The letters represent the programme *Klub veselykh i nakhodchivykh* (rendered by

Graham as the Club of Jolly and Witty, and by Dunn as the Club of the Merry and Resourceful). Graham refers to the programme in the context of short comic pieces that were published or performed during the Soviet period on the variety stage or television. The *KNV* is described by Dunn as 'the flagship of Russian television comedy'. This programme started in 1961 and forms a line of continuity between the period of the Thaw, through part of the era of 'stagnation' under Brezhnev (when it was closed down, in 1971), and into the post-*glasnost* era of the latter half of the 1980s, when it was resurrected. Examining the main humorous and satirical TV programmes of the last fifteen years, John Dunn chronicles the steady breaking down of taboos of all sorts, political, linguistic, scatological and sexual. Significantly, perhaps, the only area where he suggests there may still be untrodden paths is in the direct travestying of senior clerics of the Russian Orthodox Church.

One interesting observation made by Dunn is that the format of *KNV* appears to be exclusive to the Russian tradition. No other national culture has an equivalent. A further important point is that *KNV* operates on the scale of the entire former Soviet Union, making it 'just about the last functioning Soviet enterprise'. This preservation of a particular comic tradition in *KNV* stretches even further. The format has been adopted among russophone communities in emigration, with international games, such as those between Israel and the C.I.S., being shown on Russian TV.[17] The programme thus provides a common language for the post-Soviet Russian diaspora. There are grounds for tracing its tradition of merry and resourceful wit back, through the 1960s, to that 'grammar of Soviet humour' provided by Ilf and Petrov in their perennially popular novels *The Twelve Chairs* (1928) and *The Golden Calf* (1931).[18] Thus, in terms of Russian humour and satire, the twentieth century ended on a note of affirmation both of cultural particularity (the format is unique to russophone communities) and cultural continuity (the intellectual wit of each successive generation still finds the same 'grammar of humour' productive).

One could go as far as to say that the 'club of the jolly and witty', so lumbering in translation and so neatly packed into its shorthand acronym *KNV*, expresses the essence of a 'group tradition' of intellectual humour that goes back to the early nineteenth-century literary circle of Arzamas, with its pranks and literary polemics. In different historical circumstances this witty intellectual resourcefulness has expressed itself in different genres and acquired different functions, reflecting the circumstances and psychological needs of the group at different periods. Their sustained reflections on the ironies and paradoxes of the always imperfect human condition found their genre in the philosophical and psychological tradition of the Russian novel, while the 'group activity' when sponsored by the state was coopted into the twentieth-century utopian project to create the perfect society.

Finally, in late Soviet and post-Soviet television comedy, the 'club of the jolly and witty' has discovered an essentially collaborative medium in which to flourish, although now, of course, it will have to reflect the new commercial demands of the market-place, controlled by the personal allegiances and tastes of powerful oligarchs. In such circumstances the merry resourceful wit simply finds new opportunities for intellectual reflection and group activity, or rediscovers old ones. It will be interesting to observe what these may be.

2

TRAGICOMIC PRINCIPLES IN PUSHKIN'S DRAMA 'THE COVETOUS KNIGHT'

VALENTINA VETLOVSKAIA

THE first of the 'little tragedies', written or completed by Pushkin in the autumn of 1830 in Boldino, was prefaced by the poet with the subtitle 'Scenes from Shenstone's tragicomedy: The Covetous Knight'. Experts and specialists have puzzled over the reference to this English source (and its mystifying character has not yet been fully explained), but the author's indication of the genre of the work ('tragicomedy') has not been given any particular or serious attention. An exception is the study by N. N. Minsky, who interpreted covetousness as a passion that is tragicomic by its very nature. According to Minsky, covetousness 'has its roots in the final tragedy of life, which is conditioned upon the impossibility of all hopes, the instability of every kind of happiness, the impossibility of all desires. . . . The miser exchanges reality for its reflection, from real things he turns to possible things, from happiness to symbols of happiness, but his relations to the symbols . . . is not disinterestedly contemplative, but rather lustful and bellicose. He continues to fight for the attainment of goods, which are not utilised by him, and in this way, falls into contradiction with his own self.'[1] Apart from Minsky's, other studies as a rule generally do not see any comedy whatsoever in Pushkin's drama.

In N. N. Skatov's recent research, which is full of profound and precise observations, the genre designated by Pushkin is unquestionably elucidated by the following justification: 'paradoxically, passion for the utmost self-enrichment here turns into the utmost self-limitation – both internal and external. For this reason 'The Covetous Knight' is the only one of Pushkin's 'Little Tragedies' to be called a tragicomedy'.[2] Unfortunately, Skatov does not go into details. And indeed it would be impossible to do so in a book that addresses the general problems of the poet's biography and work in all its scope and magnitude.

D. P. Iakubovich's extensive and detailed commentary to 'The Covetous Knight', which traces the comic (as fundamental) and tragic (very seldom encountered) treatment of covetousness in European literature, on which the poet could have based his own work, states that: 'In this term [tragicomedy] Pushkin can scarcely have included the substance imparted to him by the classics, as for them tragicomedy usually ends happily, and not with the death of the hero. Using the term as it is applied to early English drama (the tragicomedies of Robert Greene, George Peele, John Fletcher, John Heywood and others), Pushkin more likely had in mind a mixing of genres that is characteristic of Shakespeare and Romantic dramas'.[3] How this 'mixing of genres' manifests itself in 'The Covetous Knight' is not elucidated by Iakubovich, but following this reasoning (and, moreover, leading to it), he names the drama simply a tragedy. G. A. Gukovsky interprets the drama on the tragicomic (and only the tragicomic) plane. He writes:

> The victory of the principle of capital – this is in the plot of 'The Covetous Knight' a tragedy not only for the baron, but for the whole of Europe, drowning in the filth of financial insanity. The theme of comedy (Gukovsky has in mind the predominant treatment of base defects – V. V.) becomes the theme of tragedy. In fact, if you interpret the theme of covetousness . . . as a moral-psychological anomaly, it is above all ludicrous and stupid. A man has a pile of money and does not use it, does not spend it, but lives like a pauper and dies from hunger on his coffers of gold! Is this not utterly stupid? Does his absurd obsession . . . serve anything other than laughter? It is a different issue with Pushkin. Having understood covetousness as a perversion of human striving, as the necessary consequence of the dark and aggressive power of money, he could not laugh at it, as he saw in it the psychological manifestation of a principle that brings evil, suffering, debauchery, moral and social ruin to the world. In the theme of covetousness he saw a psychological focus for the historical drama of mankind. And as a drama it is all the more terrifying as it is inevitable, an historical law'.[4]

This, it is already clear, does not lead to laughter. But all the same (we note in parenthesis), one does not preclude the other: on the one hand it is a funny, absurd obsession, but on the other it is serious in its underlying causes or its results.

However, this research is correct to state that Pushkin uses a traditionally comic theme for the widest possible generalisations, and that these generalisations (we would add, not only, but primarily) relate to the tragic idea of the conflicts represented in the drama.

Coming from another direction, Vladimir Propp reaches the same conclusion. In his book on comic poetics he follows Belinsky by placing in opposition the characters of Gogol's and Pushkin's misers. Belinsky wrote: 'The passion of covetousness is not a new idea, but a genius knows how to make something new out of old cloth. There is a single ideal of the miser, but he can be found in limitlessly varied types. Gogol's Pliushkin is repulsive, repellent – he is a comic character;

Pushkin's baron is terrifying – and he is a tragic character. Both of them are frighteningly true. This is not like Molière's miser, who is the rhetorical personification of covetousness, a caricature, a figure from a pamphlet. No, these are frighteningly true characters, who make us shudder at the thought of human nature. Both of them are devoured by a single, vile passion, but all the same they are in no way similar to each other, because neither is the allegorical personification of the idea which they express; they are both living characters, in whom a common vice is expressed individually, personally.'[5] In the chapter on 'Comic Characters' Propp writes: 'The very same attribute which, if it is exaggerated moderately, can turn out to be comic, is, if it is taken to the level of a vice, tragic.' This is very evident in the comparison, for example, of two misers – Pliushkin in Gogol's *Dead Souls*, and the baron in Pushkin's 'The Covetous Knight'.[6] This study also enumerates the features which distinguish Pushkin's miser and raise him (in contrast to the worthless Pliushkin, who concentrates on wretched and petty skinflintiness) to the ranks of tragic heroes. In this schema, according to Propp, it is important that 'the covetousness of the baron reaches grandiose proportions'; that it is justified by the 'gloomy philosophy of the power of gold' and the potentially limitless power of the miser who possesses it; that for the baron this passion is combined with ambition and villainy; 'his covetousness is a vice, linked with the most terrible crimes'.[7] But crimes and serious vices (like the whole area of suffering), according to Propp, are outside comedy: He states, 'It is possible to laugh at man in almost all of his manifestations. The sphere of suffering constitutes an exception, as was noted by Aristotle'.[8]

Not only the character of the hero, raising a vulgar passion to unheard-of heights and even endowing it with the dimensions of tragic greatness (scene II, the miser's emotional monologue in the cellar), but also the confrontation lying at the heart of the drama (the mortal enmity of the father and son, which has an unhappy outcome) corresponds to the spirit of tragedy. Any such confrontation depicts suffering, but, as Aristotle explains, fear and pity in particular are awakened where 'suffering arises amidst those closest to one another – for example, if a brother kills or intends to kill his brother, or a son his father, or a mother her son, or a son his mother, or does something of that kind. . .'.[9] In the final scene of Pushkin's drama the father is ready to kill, and it is only by accident that he does not kill his son, but the son kills his father. Such a denouement is already sufficient. The tragedy here is obvious, and nobody denies it, and even Pushkin, as is well known, by calling his dramatic works of 1830 as a whole 'The Little Tragedies' (see the letter to P. A. Pletnev of 9 December 1830), had begun to count the drama we are addressing among them.

With the tragic aspect, then, everything is clear. It is quite a different matter with the comic. There is no doubt, generally speaking, that the tragic and the comic are in principle compatible. 'Certain situations . . . are possible', writes Propp, 'when a work is comic in its approach and style, but tragic in its substance. Gogol's *Diary of a Madman* and *The Overcoat* are two such works'.[10] The reverse can also happen. Indeed, laughter through tears[11] arises when in the amusing there can be perceived something serious, and when the serious hides something funny. The subtitle of Pushkin's drama, defining its genre as a tragicomedy, points to this final possibility.[12]

We should also note some stances from the general theory of comedy. According to Propp's observation, the comic is firmly linked with ridicule.[13] He writes, '. . . mocking laughter [and consequently, the comic itself – V. V.] is always provoked by the exposure of failings in the internal, spiritual life of man. These failings relate to the sphere of moral foundations, volitional motives and mental operations'.[14] Quite frequently (and it is thus with our current subject) all these aspects are combined.

Of failings of a moral nature, side by side with cowardice, vanity, boastfulness, falsity and others, miserliness is often ridiculed, as Albert's words about his father demonstrate:

> My father sees it [money] not as friend or servant,
> But master – serves it like some eastern slave,
> A dog upon a chain. He lives in squalor,
> He lights no fire, and feeds on crusts and water;
> He never sleeps at night, but runs and barks –
> The gold it is that sleeps. No more of this!
> One day I'll be master of that gold:
> That day it shall not sleep.[15]

In the son's words about his miserly father, aside from ridiculing vulgar feelings, it is easy to note the mockery of a will which is directed towards a preference for the most wretched, contemptible way of life (likening the miser to a slave or a chained dog) over all other, much more worthy and pleasant ways of passing the time.

Sometimes (as in the given example) the failings are obvious. As Propp observes: 'In order to begin to laugh, the comic object must be seen; in other cases it is necessary to give behaviour some sort of moral evaluation (the comedy of covetousness, cowardice and so on).'[16] But failings are often hidden and demand unmasking, as Propp observes: 'Laughter begins at the moment of unmasking, when what is hidden suddenly becomes obvious, as in other comic situations'.[17] Shortcomings which do not come to light, naturally, do not arouse laughter: '. . .laughter is provoked by the sudden discovery of any sort of concealed defect. When there are no such defects, or we have not yet spotted them, we will not laugh.'[18]

The unmasking can be unexpected and sudden, or it can occur only as a result of reflection and prior effort. From this there can be one or another reaction: from explosive laughter to a restrained smile. According to Nietzsche (who, as a philosopher, was able to offer a particularly useful evaluation of intellectual activity), 'the cleverest authors provoke the least perceptible smiles.'[19] It is precisely this sort of comedy that we are addressing for the most part in Pushkin's drama. The processes of intellectual reflection permeate the work as a whole, thus combining comedy organically with tragedy. For this reason an analysis of every aspect of this would signify an analysis of the work as a whole. We have to limit ourselves a little.

The tragic and comic principles of the drama have the same source: the choice the covetous knight makes which promotes gold and money to first place among any and all of life's values.

The choice is always free and granted to one's own understanding, which inclines man towards that which seems to him to be the good.[20] Therefore to whatever consequences it leads (fortunate or unfortunate, good or bad), they can be seen as deserved by those who made the choice, and a judgement as to whether they were right or wrong can be made.

For the miser the idea that gold is worthwhile is unarguable. It is unarguable to the extent that it becomes in his eyes the object of chivalrous duty (instead of the Beautiful Lady and in opposition to the love of the earth, which in the hero's opinion is undoubtedly a base passion). It also becomes an object of religious worship (in the form of idols and statues which are raised in place of God), as we see in the knight's behaviour in the cellar, in his confession, sacrifice and prayers, and his emotional exclamations:

Here is my Earthly bliss!
(*puts in more coins*)
So now,
Enough of chasing round the weary world
To serve the passions and needs of men.
Here you shall sleep the sleep of strength and peace,
The sleep of gods amidst the depths of heaven. (112, 70–4)

The cult of money replaces the ideas of devotion to a lady and respect for the divine. The fact that the baron relates to gold as to a loved one and as if he is worshipping an idol (which, it must be said, is a commonplace comedic comparison), was noted by Belinsky: 'Gold is this man's idol, he is full of pietic feelings towards it, talks about it in the language of goodwill, and serves it like a diligent and devoted priest. . . . He looks upon gold as an ardent young man looks at a woman with whom he is passionately in love, the possession of whom he bought at the price of a terrible crime, and who is all the more dear to him because of this. He would like to conceal her from *unworthy glances*; he is horrified by the thought that she will belong to someone else after his death.'[21] The cult of money is, however, in the view of the knight, fully justified: gold gives him power over the world and the possibility to realise any dreams. The love of money, covetousness, is here combined with feudal arrogance. The baron states:

> What is not
> Subject to me, to my demonic rule?
> At my desiring, palaces will rise,
> And nymphs come dancing through my splendid gardens;
> The muses will compete to bring me tribute,
> Genius abandon liberty, my slave,
> Virtue and never-resting labour humbly
> Await their due reward from me. I'll whistle,
> And shyly blood-stained crime will creep to me,
> And lick my hand, and look into my eyes
> To read in them some signal of my will.
> All things submit to me, and I to nothing;
> I am above desire; I am at peace;
> I know my power – all I need to know. (110–111, 21–37)

The covetous knight's reasoning seems irreproachable. So Belinsky thought, and as far as I know, he has not been contradicted. He wrote, 'Let us go into this cellar, where the skinflint feasts his eyes upon his gold . . . we will shudder at the tragic magnitude of the miser's foul passion; we will see that it is natural, that it has its own logic.'[22] The miser's choice of money and gold as the highest value of life seems correct.

But where there is a choice (and it is founded on reason) the possibility of mistakes also exists[23] – either tragic (if the hero does not recognise it and it leads to profound, irreparable misfortune), or comic (if it is revealed, unmasked, and is a cause for laughter).[24] In this case we have both at once. In accordance with the dual character of the mistake (as simultaneously both tragic and comic), two logics are at work in the drama.

One is the logic of the miser, certain of his rightness and acting in accordance with this. The other is the author's, who sees his error. And the comedy of the situation, we should also note, consists in part in the fact that this covetous knight, trembling over every last penny, barely knows how to count.

Between the one logic and the other a certain distance is created. It gives a place to both serious refutations, and to irony and paradoxes,[25] which serve the mocking, comic illumination of the hero, or even all the main characters and all their dramas.

The serious refutation is obvious in those fatal consequences and destruction which the miser's choice entails, the extent of which he himself does not understand. Moreover, in the final analysis, they also signify tragedy on an impressively wide scale. It is the tragedy of a family (insofar as money tears apart any familial bonds, even the closest, with the father opposing the son, and the son the father, in enmity). It is also a tragedy of the state (insofar as the power of money suffers no other, and above all else is the ruling power, secretly or openly taking over from other power-bases. Thus the baron does not need the duke, to whom he is subordinated as a vassal; he does not obey his orders; by keeping his son with him, he deprives his sovereign of a valiant warrior and a possible advisor and friend, that is, a reliable support for the ruling house). Finally, it is a tragedy on a universal level (since by elevating gold over and above God, the baron abolishes officially recognised religion, and all the written and unwritten codes blessed by tradition, which regulated relationships between people, the world around them and nature as a whole. He thus destroys forever the centuries-old order, offering nothing in its place apart from rebellion and chaos, to be suppressed by force). The negative consequences indicate the source of the evil, and the reasons for it, dethroning the miser and his entire philosophy.

Irony and paradox continue their dethroning on the comic plane. They reveal inadequacies of the intellect (stupidity) in place of apparently positive attributes; lies in place of truth; kinship in place of apparent hostility and separation; hostility and separation in place of apparent kinship; unwarranted pretension and emptiness in place of apparent greatness; destitution in place of wealth; weakness in place of strength – in a word, every possible substitution coming from the usual and most effective comic devices. Ridicule and refutation negate every single point of the miser's emotional speech, which extols the virtues of gold and its possessor, and appears at the compositional and ideational centre of the drama. Since I have already had occasion to write about this in some detail in another context (without reference to the poetics and problems of comedy),[26] I shall return to it here only briefly.

Thus, talking of the limitless power of gold and its ability to satisfy any needs and passions, the baron concludes with great arrogance:

> All things submit to me, and I to nothing;
> I am above desire; I am at peace;
> I know my power – all I need to know. (III, 34–7)

But this is funny: in the baron's abstinence there is decidedly no merit whatsoever. Since gold can wield power and satisfy any desire only when it is spent, the miser (according to his own words) cannot in fact satisfy a single desire; with the exception, it is true, of the one desire that he is not 'above' – the desire to descend into the cellar and 'pour his accumulated handfuls of gold' into his coffers. Indeed all the baron does is collect gold, advancing the idea that any profit increases his power and potential, and any loss reduces them. From this comes his personal asceticism, and the conviction that everyone who does not collect gold as he does (starting with his son) is wasting it. Willy-nilly the baron controls and rules the world precisely in his 'consciousness', and further than the limits of his own imagination he cannot go:

> At my desiring, palaces will rise,
> And nymphs come dancing through my splendid gardens. (110, 23–5)

And in fact, the baron can 'only desire', but is not capable of fulfilling anything. Declaring his absolute, autocratic will, he in vain gratifies empty arrogance. In spite of his wealth, the covetous knight is undoubtedly free in only one way – in his desires – but no further. And if this is so, he is no higher than the lowliest beggar, eating the same dry crust, who is also free in his desires (mansions... nymphs... muses... genius and so on) but achieves nothing.

However, even in his desires the covetous knight is free only with essential reservations. With one notable exception (his striving to accumulate every last penny), he steers his desires in a fixed direction – precisely in *not* allowing them to be fulfilled. And this is also how he 'rules' other people and the world. Having buried his own desires alive, he buries alive those of others as well.

But it is also an amusing paradox that the baron, without recognising it, also buries the gold he worships. Every 'poor' handful, sunk into the cellar, into his coffers, hardens there in eternal rest. And his entire 'hill', enclosed under a 'peaceful, dumb vault' and consisting of gold coins, is a burial vault, a tomb.

> Would I could hide
> This cellar from unworthy eyes! Possess
> The power to leave the grave, returning here
> A watchful spirit seated on a coffer,
> To guard, as now, my riches from the living! (113, 114–18)

Like a phantom watchman, the covetous knight sits on his coffers even now. Even if he leaves his cellar physically from time to time, he will never truly leave it: his soul, his shadow guards the treasure against the living all the time and everywhere. Deceived by his own passion, the baron does not notice that in his attention to the honour and glory of his idol which, in his opinion, is equal to the glory and honour of the divine powers, he is in fact with maniacal doggedness reducing the value of gold to the value of dust. Every handful, piled together by the knight in his cellar, and all his 'shining chests' in the end turn into just a more or less imposing heap of earth, collected little by little.

Erecting an edifice to this potent force exclusively in his 'consciousness', the baron is from the very beginning only occupied with constructing his mausoleum. However majestic the height of the hill he has raised seems to him, in fact it is no higher than the cellar vaults. In any case this is only the height of a grave, which the knight cannot appreciably augment even with a gravestone in the shape of his own shadow.

Now we will move on from the baron's monologue and briefly address the comedy lying at the heart of the conflict.

There is a widespread view that the conflict between the heroes of Pushkin's drama arises from the opposition of their characters (the miser and the spendthrift). In my opinion this interpretation is quite unfounded. I see it is a tribute to the literary tradition, out of whose framework Pushkin's tragicomedy certainly arose, but which it definitively transforms. 'The opposition of characters' Pushkin once noted, 'is in no sense art, but the vulgar spring of Fr[ench] tragedies'.[27] We would add 'and comedies'. Propp writes:

> In Molière there are usually figures from two generations: the old and the young. The older generation is represented by repellent, negative types (the miser, Tartuffe, the misanthrope), while the younger generation is positive. The young want to fall in love and marry, but the older generation do not allow them to do so. The younger generation's cheerful and cunning servants bring them to triumph and the older generation to disgrace with all their vices.[28]

In the full course of Pushkin's drama we do not see a single trace of spendthriftiness in Albert. On the contrary. The hero is thrifty. In relation to his 'heroism' in the duel with Count Delorzh he says:

> What prompted those heroics? Miserliness –
> Sharing a roof with a father such as mine,
> You can't avoid infection. (102, 36–8)

The battle horse, and the satin and velvet clothes which Albert lacks are for him not luxury items, but necessities; they are required by his rank:

> Last time, when all the knights
> Sat in their silk and velvet, only I
> Appeared in cuirass at the Duke's grand table.
> I had to say I'd come that day by chance.
> What shall I say this time? (101, 17–22)

It is true that in his conversation with the usurer he says:

> No more of this!
> One day I'll be master of that gold:
> That day it shall not sleep. (106, 107–8)

And:

> Ah yes indeed,
> Upon the baron's funeral-day we'll see
> More money flow than tears. (106, 109–10)

But it is probably only at the funeral that money will 'flow' without any limits. Indeed Albert has as much reason to hoard gold as to hate it. The young knight has learnt to recognise the value of money through years of enforced abstinence, which he terms 'fasting'. The value of money is distinctly augmented by the death of his father, in which Albert, as soon as he cools down a little, will perceive his own guilt and crime. Let us look at the baron's words before his coffers full of gold:

> Have I acquired all this
> From fortune's hand . . .
> Who could ever record the harsh privations,
> Restraints of passion, weighty calculations,
> And all the days of care and wakeful nights
> My gold has cost? Or will my son maintain
> My moss-grown heart has never known desire,
> And conscience never gnawed my vitals, conscience,
> The sharp-clawed beast that tears the heart out, conscience,
> The uninvited guest, unloved companion,
> Uncivil creditor – the awesome witch
> That makes the moon grow dim, the grave, confounded,
> Yield up its dead?. . . He who has gained his riches
> Through suffering – just see that unfortunate
> Waste what was won with blood. (113, 96–13)

Indeed, Albert prepares to put the gold into service, but this is before going down into the basement as the legal owner of the treasure. It cannot be ruled out that when he sees it, its brilliance will blind him as well. All the more so, as the duke has banned him from appearing at court, not to mention the next tournament:

> Out of my sight! And never dare come back
> Until I summon you. (119, 97–9)

Albert will thus have sufficient time to behold his wealth with his own eyes and understand its many and varied virtues. Then, following in the footsteps of the old baron, he can take the next step along that road and, having abandoned the idea of transient things, fall in love with gold itself. In the final analysis, Albert is his father's son.

The difference between the baron and Albert is mainly (and perhaps only) one of age. The baron has already lived through and forgotten his youth, which he spent in the duke's court, amidst banquets and chivalrous tournaments, which he enjoyed to the full – to the point of boredom and satiety. As the duke suggests: 'My court is not for you.' (115, 29) This is then confirmed by the baron:

> At court? You're young, and fond of tournaments
> And banquets. I'm not fit for them. (115, 30–33)

Albert, however, has not yet reached old age. That is why the baron, throwing down the challenge to his son, does not realise that he is condemning to death his own youth; and the son, taking up the challenge, does not realise that he is sentencing his own old age to death. Moreover, youth is a deficiency (in the father's eyes) or a virtue (in the son's eyes), which, as we know very well, passes rather quickly. The father's death sentence on the son, and the son's on the father, are directed not so much against each other as against themselves, as neither has recognised in the other a trait they have already lost or not yet acquired. That is the gloomy comedy inherent in this picture; gloomy because neither father nor son recognises it.

Answering his son's accusation of lies, the baron appeals to a higher justice, he demands punishment:

> Thunder never rolled
> Till now! Just God – the sword shall be our judge!
> (*Throws down a glove; his son immediately picks it up*). (119, 87–8)

Until this final moment the baron had not thought about God's truth, which is also God's mercy and love. The miser served and still serves different gods. But, as it turns out, for all their might, they are far from being able to help anyone. However, these gods are not averse to mocking those who take them too seriously. And that is what happens here. The father first and foremost finds himself being punished and mocked, and precisely when he is in no mood for laughter.

In connection with this it is not irrelevant to recall the roots of the tragicomic genre in the European tradition – Plautus's *Amphitryo*, which recast a Greek plot in Roman style. Addressing the audience in the play's prologue, Mercury calls it first a comedy, then a tragedy, then continues:

> Are you disappointed
> To find it's a *tragedy*? Well, I can easily change it.
> I'm a god, after all. I can easily make it a comedy.
> And never alter a line. Is that what you'd like?. . .
> But I was forgetting – stupid of me – of course,
> Being a god I know quite well what you'd like.
> I know exactly what's in your minds. Very well.
> I'll meet you half way, and make it a *tragi-comedy*.
> It can't be an out-and-out comedy, I'm afraid,
> With all these kings and gods in the cast. All right, then,
> A tragi-comedy – at least it's got one slave-part.[29]

However the tragicomic aspect lies not only in the characters in the play, but also in the plot. It was already very popular in the art of Ancient Greece,[30] and many centuries later, drew the attention of dramatists of the modern era (Molière, Kleist and others). The plot of the play revolves around the love of Jupiter for Alcmena, the wife of the Theban king Amphitryo. While Amphitryo, leading the Thebans, is taking part in a military campaign, Jupiter, having taken on Amphitryo's appearance, amuses himself with his wife Alcmena, who does not suspect the deceit. Mercury helps Jupiter, his father, in this amorous swindle, by taking on the appearance of Amphitryo's slave, Sosia. The real Amphitryo returns to find that he has been cuckolded in his absence, and bitterly reproaches his bewildered wife. After deliberately creating much confusion – and striking Amphitryo with a thunderbolt – Jupiter finally reveals the truth to Amphitryo. Alcmena meanwhile gives birth to twins – one child Amphitryo's, the other Jupiter's (the baby Hercules). Thus all is well at the end of this comedy of errors, where the comic effect lies in the substitutions and the confusion they cause. But serious and even tragic notes arise thanks to the idea standing behind the action: while the gods are laughing, the people cry (the cruelly deceived Amphitryo and Alcmena).

In Pushkin's work the situation is different: when people are too serious (relating to money as an idol), if the gods do not laugh, then the devil certainly does. But the 'Just God' to whom the baron made appeal never laughs, he always punishes with sorrow in his heart.

Translated by Sarah Young

3

GOGOL AS A NARRATOR OF ANECDOTES

EFIM KURGANOV

THE oral novellas of Gogol have never been collected together nor studied. What is more, they have not even been included in collections of the writer's prose (even though place could have been found for them in an appendix). The oral novellas of Gogol belong to high art, however, to the same extent as his plays, tales and the great unfinished 'poem', *Dead Souls.*

I

Gogol was an inimitable narrator, with his own style and special repertoire of plots. He knew how to demolish the expectations of listeners, how to amaze them with a story that could explode the flow of a conversation, making it risqué and witty. In the early stage of his life, when he was giving private lessons, Gogol was already literally cramming these lessons full of anecdotes:

> Gogol told lots of anecdotes at every possible opportunity . . .; he performed his tales of ancient history with such inexhaustible gaiety and inspiration! I cannot help smiling when I recall his anecdotes about the wars of [the Egyptian pharaoh] Amasis, about the origins of civil societies and so on. His tales were extremely funny.[1]

Anecdotes were exactly those flashes that lit up Gogol's speech when he was among friends:

> Gogol's Malorussian oral tales and his reading (he was known to be an amazing reader and a first-class narrator) made a strong impression on Belinsky . . . At that time Gogol often allowed himself to become animated in the circle of his old comrades and friends

who did not belong to high society; he would prepare Italian macaroni (which he loved) himself in their kitchen, and entertain them with his tales.[2]

In conversations with his high-society friends also, Gogol knew how to astound them with his inimitable oral novellas. Here is one that the writer told A. O. Smirnova-Rosset:

> The Emperor Nicholas I gave the order that indecent surnames be changed. In the meantime, Colonel Zas married off his daughter to the garrison officer Rantsev. He said that his surname was older and that Rantsev should, therefore, change his surname to Zas-Rantsev [an English equivalent of which would be Ord-Ure – LM]. Rantsev, who was from Mecklenburg and a real stickler for rank, pointed out that he had come to Russia with Peter III and that his surname was more distinguished. However, he agreed to this name Ord-Ure. The whole garrison laughed. But His Majesty, seeing no other way back, simply decreed that Rantsev be called Rantsev-Zas [Ure-Ord]. The father-in-law made a wry face, but had to submit to the wise will of his emperor.[3]

Anecdotes slipped also into Gogol's letters to friends:

> There was a dragoon. A fine fellow! With fierce and terrible side-whiskers, but of uncommon apathy. In order to show him everything of interest in the city, his chum took him the next day to a brothel; but the whole time the chum was labouring behind the screen, our dragoon coolly read a book. Then he left, without so much as laying a finger on anything.[4]

As for plots, Gogol did not only invent his own, but also reworked old ones, making them part of Russian life in the first half of the nineteenth century. Vladimir Sollogub noted down the following oral novella of Gogol, recounting in addition how it was narrated, what reaction it received (and Gogol was, moreover, clearly counting on such a reaction, close to shock):

> A woman sat at home with her children in deep mourning for her mother who had recently passed away. Gogol was announced and invited to enter. He comes in with a glum expression. As usually happens in such situations, a conversation begins about the transitory nature of all worldly things . . . Suddenly he starts on a long and lamentable story about a landed gentleman from Malorussia whose only son, whom he adored, was dying. The old man wore himself out, staying by the patient's bedside, day or night, for whole weeks on end. Finally, completely exhausted, he went to lie down in a neighbouring room, after giving instructions to be woken up if the patient got worse. He had hardly dropped off when someone came running in. 'Excuse me!' – 'What, is he worse?' – 'What do you mean, worse? He's quite dead.' At this twist everyone listened attentively to see how the story would turn out, they let out sighs, a general cry of exclamation and then the question: 'Oh, goodness! But what happened to the poor father?' – 'Well what was he to do?!', continued Gogol very coolly, with a dismissive

wave of the arm, a shrug of the shoulders, a shake of the head and even a whistle: 'Phoo, phoo'. This conclusion of the anecdote was greeted with loud laughter by the children, but the woman, quite rightly, was angered by this joke, which really was totally inappropriate at such a time of sorrow.[5]

This vivid Gogolian novella represents a variation of an anecdote about Khodzha Nasreddin:[6]

> One day Nasreddin went into his garden, lay down under a pear tree and dozed off. A friend then arrived with the news that Khodzha's mother had died. Nasreddin's son led him to the garden, shook his father out of slumber and said:
>
> 'Get up, father, Muzhkan Dzhekhaich has brought the news that your mother has died.'
>
> 'Oh,' said Nasreddin, 'how terrible! It will be even worse tomorrow when I wake up!' With these words he turned over and went back to sleep.[7]

This echo between Gogol and Khodzha Nasreddin may seem unexpected, but it is highly significant. It demonstrates that Gogol knew the international repertoire of anecdote plots and also that he, as a narrator, not only improvised with ease and inspiration, but also relied on well-established tradition.

II

Vassily Zhukovsky had his own repertoire of anecdotes, but his favourite among these was about Jean-Paul Richter. A. O. Smirnova-Rosset recalled:

> Zhukovsky came to me and narrated all the old anecdotes that I knew already. In particular he loved the incident when Jean-Paul Richter was visiting the Grand Duke of Koburg.[8]

This anecdote was one that provoked outrage in society and at the same time was one that Zhukovsky was particularly fond of telling:

> I recall the story of Jean-Paul Richter, which [Zhukovsky] would begin by saying: 'You see, it is an historic happening'. Here is the story. The Grand Duke invited Jean-Paul to spend a couple of days with him. He wrote him a very gracious letter with his own hand. After a hearty dinner, unable to find any chamber pot and having searched every corridor in vain for somewhere to relieve himself, [Jean-Paul] pulled out the letter from the Grand Duke, made use of it for his purpose, threw it out of the window and then slept extremely peacefully. The next day the Grand Duke invited him to an early morning breakfast on the terrace where he was supposed to admire the flower beds and statues: 'The most beautiful is the one of Venus, which I obtained in Rome,' and further: 'You will be in raptures.' But, how terrible! They approach the Venus: on its head is the Grand Duke's letter, and yellow tears flood the face of the goddess. The Grand Duke vents his anger on his servants, but the address 'Sir Jean-Paul Richter' calms him down. You can imagine the embarrassment of Jean-Paul![9]

After he had told this anecdote, Zhukovsky was sent out of the room like a naughty schoolboy, and indeed was lucky not to have to stand in a corner:

> Pletnev always told [Zhukovsky]: 'You know, you have told me this filth a thousand times over.' Mrs Karamzin forced him to leave the table after this anecdote. As he was born just before New Year, a dinner was always given in his honour on New Year's Day. . . . They simply sent Zhukovsky into the drawing-room and had food taken to him in there, but they did not give him any pie or champagne.[10]

It is interesting that Gogol censured Zhukovsky after the anecdote of Jean-Paul Richter, threatening to complain to Zhukovsky's wife:

> 'We know, we've heard that one before,' we said. Gogol wagged his finger at him, saying, 'What will Elizaveta Evgrafovna say when I tell her what filth you peddle?' It made Zhukovsky's wife angry when he told this nonsense.[11]

This was particularly wicked of Gogol since he himself, as a narrator, adored indecent stories, as the following examples illustrate:

> The witticisms of Gogol were unique, but sometimes not entirely in good taste.[12]
> For the most part Gogol's conversations consisted of anecdotes, almost always quite obscene.[13]
> Then Gogol spoke about Malorussia, about the character of the people, and brightened up so much that he began to tell anecdotes, one funnier and wittier than the other. Unfortunately, such anecdotes would never be fit to print.[14]

Gogol's reputation as a narrator throws a very curious light on the remark made to Zhukovsky. It would appear that, in threatening Zhukovsky with complaint, Gogol was taking into account his own reputation.

Furthermore, Gogol was not thrown out of the room nor deprived of pie and champagne. The whole thing is, he employed a more subtle and calculated strategy than Zhukovsky. Where Zhukovsky, as a rule, offered his listeners always the same repertoire of stories and they knew what to expect, Gogol always took his listeners unawares and this was, of course, done deliberately. Moreover, such a strategy of narrating anecdotes concurs exactly with Sigmund Freud's theory of wit, as interpreted by Marvin Minsky:

> The theory of Freud explains why witticisms are usually compressed, compact and have a double meaning. This is necessary in order to deceive the childishly simple-minded censors, who only see the superficial, completely innocent sense of jokes and cannot discern forbidden desires hidden in them.[15]

Gogol's love for the obscene was well known, but he always demonstrated his passion for narrating indecent stories in an extremely unexpected way, throwing society into such a state of shock that it was no longer able to censure him.

The strategy worked out by Gogol functioned faultlessly. Thanks to his ability to attack from ambush at just the right moment, he was excused for things for which someone else could not have been excused. Vladimir Sollogub illustrates this very well in his tale of how society reacted to the indecent stories that sometimes left the lips of Vladimir Odoevsky, and how it reacted to Gogol's oral novellas:

> [Odoevsky] was distinguished by the peculiarity that he told ladies the most indecent things in the most innocent way, completely sincerely and without any ulterior motive. In this sense, he was not at all like Gogol, who had the gift of narrating the most salacious anecdotes, without provoking anger from his female listeners, whereas poor Odoevsky was angrily cut short. Gogol, meanwhile, always transgressed deliberately.[16]

It was often the case that you simply could not interrupt Gogol, since the indecency of what was being narrated, because of the compositional effects specifically deployed, was only recognised by female listeners in the very last moment, as the novella was about to end.

When relating an anecdote, Gogol, as a rule, wore a very glum expression and adopted a completely trustworthy tone. This is seen particularly in the reminiscences of Vladimir Sollogub, who told of how Gogol related an anecdote about a brothel in the midst of the Vielgorsky family, in the company of the Vielgorsky ladies, mother and daughters. Even Emperor Nicholas I considered Louisa Karlovna Vielgorskaia, née Princess Biron, unnecessarily pedantic.[17] She was a stern, haughty lady, obsessed with the upbringing of her daughters. When a matter seemed to her to be a particularly delicate question, 'my mother-in-law,' wrote Sollogub, 'was dogged to the point of illness on account of morality.'[18] And then right in the presence of L. K. Vielgorskaia and her daughters, Gogol told an anecdote about a brothel.

At this point we ought to remember that Gogol was still the spiritual instructor of the Vielgorsky ladies. Furthermore the anecdote was told amidst a conversation, steeped in religious-mystical colouring, and Gogol began to relate it *as if in unison* with the conversation. It is also curious that all this happened in the late (mystical) period of Gogol's life (after 1847, when he settled in the house of A. P. Tolstoi).

His spiritual students started to console Gogol, who was plunged in black melancholy, and this is how he reacted. (I will include the complete text of this wonderful oral novella, starting with the very detailed version by Vladimir Sollogub, and then amplifying this with the short, but very expressive record by N. V. Kukolnik):

> Gogol was then living at Count Tolstoi's and was absorbed in the absolute mysticism that marked the last years of his life. He was sad, looked vacantly at everything around him, his words lost their ruthless precision, and his thin lips were gloomily compressed.

The Countess Vielgorskaia tried as much as she could to cheer him up, but did not succeed; suddenly the pale face of the writer livened up, the cunning smile we all knew so well appeared on his lips again, and the former light shone in the eyes that had grown dim.

'Yes, Countess,' he began with his sharp voice, 'you talk about rules, about convictions, about conscience,' – Countess Vielgorskaia had been talking about nothing of the sort at that moment, but, of course, none of us were going to start arguing with him – 'but let me inform you that in Russia you meet rules everywhere, nowhere excessive, of course. A few years ago,' continued Gogol, and his face somehow wrinkled from barely hidden pleasure, 'I sat the whole evening at my friend's where six of us who love a chat had gathered. When we got up, the clock struck three, the group dispersed and went home, but since on this particular evening I was not completely well, the host took it upon himself to walk me home. We went quietly along the street, talking; the night was wonderful, warm, moonless, dry, and in the east the dawn had already begun to break: this took place at the beginning of August. Suddenly my friend stopped in the middle of the street and started to look intently at quite a large, but plain and even, as far as one could judge with the dim light of the breaking dawn, quite dirty house. This place, although he was married, clearly seemed familiar to him because he muttered with surprise 'Why are the shutters closed and why is it so dark? Excuse me a moment, Nikolai Vasilievich,' he said, turning towards me, 'just wait for me, I want to find out.' And he quickly crossed the road and headed towards a low-set, brightly lit window, which looked out somewhat crookedly from near the gate of the house with the gloomy closed shutters. I was also interested and went up to the window (readers must remember that this is Gogol narrating). A strange spectacle presented itself to me: in quite a large and tidy room with a low ceiling and bright curtains, in the corner, in front of a large icon-case full of icons, stood a lectern, covered in shabby brocade; in front of the lectern a tall, portly and already quite old priest in a dark cassock was conducting the service, apparently a prayer; a thin, sleepy sexton joined in with him listlessly. Behind the priest, leaning on the back of a chair, stood a fat woman who looked in her fifties, dressed in a bright green silk dress and with a cap, decorated with multi-coloured ribbons; an imposing and formidable figure, she would occasionally glance around her; behind her were fifteen or twenty women, for the most part on their knees, in red, yellow and pink dresses with flowers and feathers in their curled hair; their cheeks glowed with such an unnatural blush, their appearance corresponded so little to the ceremony taking place in their presence that I involuntarily burst out laughing and looked at my friend; he just shrugged his shoulders and once again stared at the window with ever greater attention. Suddenly the wicket at the side of the gate opened with a noise and on the threshold appeared a fat woman, whose face looked very similar to that of the one in the room who was taking part so importantly in the service. 'Ah Praskovia Stepanovna, hello!' shouted my friend, rushing up to her and shaking her fat hand in a friendly manner. 'What is going at your place?' – 'Ah well,' said the fat lady in a deep voice, 'as my sister intends to go to the Nizhny Novogorod fair with the girls, she's praying for good business.' 'Then, Countess,' Gogol added, 'why talk about rules and

> customs here in Russia?' You can imagine what an outburst of laughter there was and at the same time with what amazement we listened to Gogol's tale; you had to be really ill to tell Countess Vielgorskaia such an anecdote in the presence of the whole of society.[19]

Kukolnik recorded a short, swift version of this same anecdote in his notebook:

> I happened to be going along a path on which there was a brothel. On the lower floor of the large house all the windows are wide open, the summer breeze plays with the pretty curtains. The brothel is as if made of glass, everything is visible. There are many women; all of them are dressed as if about to go on a journey: they run and bustle about; in the middle of the room there is a little table covered in a clean white tablecloth; there are icons on it and candles burning. . . . What could this mean? At the wing of the building I bump into a sexton who is going into the brothel. 'Goodness!' I ask. 'What are they having today?' 'A prayer service,' replies the sexton calmly. 'They are going to Nizhny Novogord to the fair; therefore, they must say a mass so that the Lord will bless them with success in their business.'[20]

I think that the shocked state into which the listeners found themselves plunged – above all the proud and haughty Princess Biron, Vielgorskaia through marriage – saved Gogol. But without a doubt, while narrating the anecdote, what he precisely counted on was the fact that he would be able to provoke such a state of stunned silence in his listeners. That is how the 'great melancholic' acted with those who dared to teach and console him.

III

Gogol's predilection for the anecdote can be related to the 'aesthetic of falsehood' and its underlying ethical significance, as exemplified by the role of Khlestiakov in *The Government Inspector*. The absurdity of Khlestiakov's fantasies is never concealed, a fact which, however, does not prevent Khlestiakov himself from believing in them absolutely. This aspect of the character is based on Gogol's own experience as a narrator. Gogol told nonsense tales, made people believe in them, and believed in them himself. He would for example, assure listeners that his stomach was in an unnatural position: 'He had allegedly been examined by renowned physicians in Paris, who had established that his stomach was upside-down.'[21] Weaving the absurdities that Khlestiakov peddles, Gogol was, I would suggest, trying to make sense of his own experience as mystificator, to look at it from the outside, and in doing so was trying to justify himself. After all, Khlestiakov, through his lies and fantasies, punishes the whole world of liars and scoundrels that surrounds him. Gogol may have been seeking an ethical justification for his own tricks and preposterous tales, seeing himself not as mocker and detractor but as an agent of punishment. This 'poetic of lies' is developed also in *Dead Souls*, where Nozdrev tells Chichikov his repertoire of fantastic tales, and extracts from Chichikov the explanation of why the latter wants to buy 'dead souls'. Nozdrev, from his lofty position as 'poet of lies', responds with a contemptuous, thrice repeated: 'You're fibbing!' Gogol knew how to construct the false tale precisely because he himself was such a masterly liar.

Gogol loved to tell stories about Spain, for example. His close friend A. O. Smirnova-Rosset did not believe in the slightest that he had ever been to Spain, and was convinced that all the stories he related were pure invention:

> Once we were talking about different comforts when travelling and [Gogol] told me that Portugal was the worst on this score and advised me not to travel there. 'How do you know, Nik [olai] Vas [ilievich]?' I asked him. 'I've been there, I went there from Spain, where it is also filthy in the inns,' he replied very calmly. I began asserting that he had never been to Spain, that it was just not possible that everything there was troubled, with fights at every crossroads; those who come back from there always have a lot to say, but that he never said anything whatsoever. To all this he replied very coolly: 'Why tell everything and take up the public's time? You are used to a person revealing to you, from the very first word, everything that he knows and does not know, even what he has in his heart.' I maintained my idea that he had never been to Spain and it became a joke between us: 'It was when I was in Spain.[22]

Be that as it may, Gogol turned his Spanish plots into lively, rich oral novellas, which compose a quite distinct cycle.

Gogol usually set up the beginning and (sometimes) the conclusion of the narrative with some observation that only a Jewish tavern is dirtier than Spain (the writer expressed himself precisely in this way and it is impossible to change anything here; the point is not even Gogol's anti-semitism: he had strained relations with the whole human race):

> In the 1830s, Spanish inns were much dirtier than Russian posting-stations; the only places I know that are dirtier than them are one Jewish tavern and a monastery in Jerusalem and also on Mount Athos where there is light and heavy artillery i.e. fleas, bedbugs, cockroaches and lice begin a mutiny at night and one day conducted a battle on my back![23]

This oral novella delineates the thematics and stylistics of the Spanish cycle as a whole, which is a chain of vivid depictions of Spanish filth:

> Another incident occurred in a hotel in Madrid. Everything in it was dirty as is customary in Spain; the linen was completely soiled. Gogol complained, but the owner replied: 'Señor, our unforgettable queen (Isabella) has been canonised, but during the siege she never took off her shirt for weeks and this shirt is, like a relic, preserved in the church, and you complain that your sheet is not clean when only two Frenchman have slept on it, one Englishman and a lady from a very good family: are you really cleaner than they are, sir?'

> When they served Gogol with a cutlet (cooked in olive oil and completely cold), Gogol expressed his displeasure again. The servant . . . very calmly touched it with his dirty hand and said: 'No, it's nice and warm: just feel!'[24]

Of course, it is impossible to reconstruct Gogol's Spanish cycle in full, but the general outline can be discerned. When talking about Gogol's oral legacy, a special place must always be kept for the Spanish tales.

IV

Strange, absurd, and often not entirely decent happenings provoked Gogol's intense interest. He collected them, recording some in his notebooks, but on the whole retaining them in his memory and masterfully relating them. The specific features of Gogol's favourite incidents were directly linked to his 'ability to note what seems to others neither amazing nor funny'.[25] Gogol brought out into the light of day stories that no-one else would have dared relate or have been able to communicate in such a lively and authentic manner.

The anecdote is wedged into a conversation, animating it, arousing and dumbfounding the listeners. The unexpectedness with which an anecdote appears is a necessary condition, the non-observance of which considerably weakens the resulting effect. However, an anecdote does not simply appear unexpectedly, it must also be opportune: the unexpectedness with which it appears should correspond to the accuracy of the hit, otherwise it does not count for anything. When Gogol told his anecdotes he observed these two conditions: the great master of attack from ambush considered the blow that he intended to deliver with the utmost precision. He knew, like no-one else, how to break listeners, literally how to throw them into disarray and send them into a state of shock.

Very telling in this sense is the example of the oral novella about the brothel, which Gogol told to his spiritual students: to L. K. Vielgorskaia and her daughters, moreover, telling it amid a conversation of spiritual-mystical content. It was the late Gogol: the period of the second volume of *Dead Souls*. However, he seems also to have related stories like that in his youth, when he was only beginning to consider a literary career, as indicated by the tale of the Malorussian landowner whose only son is dying, told to a well-known baroness in mourning for her recently-deceased mother.[26] The hostess was angry. The memoirist, who recorded the tale, found the joke inappropriate at such a moment of general sorrow. But Gogol had related the anecdote, fully aware of the unsuitability of what was being told. Hence, he masked the beginning of the story so that it would initially be in consonance with the mood prevailing at that moment in the drawing-room.

As a rule, Gogol introduced an anecdote into a conversation as a contrast, acting the same way in his youth as he did in the last years of his life. He constructed

Nevsky Prospect, the first of the Petersburg tales, in the same way. *Nevsky Prospect* combines the tragic story of the artist Piskarev, who passionately loved a maiden of easy virtue and ended up by committing suicide, with an anecdote about Major Pirogov, who started to chase after a pretty German girl and, because of this, was given a sound thrashing by the masters Schiller, Hoffman and Kunts. At first, Pirogov wanted to complain to the authorities, but then he ate two flaky pastries, went to a party, danced a splendid mazurka that aroused universal admiration and forgot the insult.

This anecdote about Pirogov is introduced into the tale as a counter-argument in a dispute, as a retort in a dialogue about romantic disappointments and great passions. Gogol formulated this principle of textual construction in an article written in 1831 *About Present-Day Architecture* (Ob arkhitekture nyneshnego vremeni), included with *Nevsky Prospect* in the *Arabesques*: 'A true effect consists in sharp opposition; beauty is never so bright and clear as when seen in contrast.'[27] The formulation of the principle preceded the creation of the tale *Nevsky Prospect,* but the experience of Gogol, the narrator preceded that very formulation.

CONCLUSION

As master of the oral novella Gogol largely worked on the law of contrast, whereby he calculated the astonishment of listeners, confounding their perception of stylistic hierarchies. Gogol also preferred relating anecdotes on 'foreign ground', as it were, and not in the situations appropriate to, and reserved for, this dangerous genre. As a result, the anecdote sprang into life: it became particularly effective and convincing, strikingly vivid and unforgettably graphic. While he was narrating, Gogol was honing this device of stylistic contrast, which subsequently became such an important principle in his artistic practice.

Translated by Hazel Grünewald

4

ANTONY POGORELSKY AND A. K. TOLSTOI: THE ORIGINS OF KOZMA PRUTKOV

MARIETTA TOURIAN

INTRODUCTION BY LESLEY MILNE

I well remember my first encounters with the nineteenth-century writer 'Kozma Prutkov', whose aphorisms were so liberally quoted by my Russian friends. 'No one can encompass the boundless' (Nikto ne obnimet neob'atnogo) was always a particular consolation to students, for example, before examinations.[1] *My attention was also drawn to Prutkov's sublimely solemn 'Project: Towards Creating Unanimity of Opinion in Russia'. In the Soviet era before glasnost', this 'project' read like an up-to-the-minute pamphlet satirising the mentality behind government thought-control. Prutkov stated the 'obvious harm of divergence in views and convictions' and affirmed that 'the opinion of the authorities' was 'the only material for opinion' among the populace. 'Otherwise there is no guarantee that the opinion is correct'. But how was the loyal citizen to guess the opinion of the authorities? Prutkov advocated the establishment of a governmental printing office that would give out guiding views on every topic, and modestly suggested himself as editor-in-chief.*[2] *Prutkov thus emerged as a parodic founder-figure of such organs of the Soviet press as* Pravda.

A further joke lay in the fact that this 'Prutkov' and all his 'Works', complete with a 'biography' of the writer, were an elaborate fiction, a piece of literary mystification. 'Prutkov' published regularly between 1853 and 1863, when his 'death' was announced (accompanied, of course, by an 'obituary'). It was only in 1884 that his inventors (or 'guardians', as they preferred to call themselves) publicly emerged as the writer A.K. Tolstoi and his cousins, the brothers Aleksei and Vladimir Zhemchuzhnikov.[3] *In Prutkov they created a hilarious combination of would-be romantic poet and actually most limited bureaucrat, who has risen to be Director of the Assay office in the Ministry of Finance. His every 'poetic' flight flops into bathos, and he is characterised through his 'writings' as a wonderful 'incarnation of self-centred and arrogantly naïve complacency.'* [4]

When discussing the genesis of Kozma Prutkov, we must examine the important role played by cultural traditions: that is to say we must study 'that sphere of relations and circle of ideas under whose influence Kozma Prutkov's "co-authors" formed their response both to the world and the word'.[5]

Viewed from this perspective, the figure of A. K. Tolstoi appears the most interesting. This is not only because, at the time of Prutkov's 'birth', he, the eldest among the director of the assay office's creators, had behind him both literary and epistolary experience, in which the satirical element is clearly marked. A further reason is that, because of his particular circumstances, Tolstoi was the only one of the 'Prutkovians' able to inherit the behavioural and literary traditions of the older generation. He imbibed this heritage directly through his uncle and guardian, Aleksei Alekseevich Perovsky, known in his writing profession under the name Antony Pogorelsky. Perovsky's considerable influence on the formation of his nephew's aesthetic tastes has long been recognised – but only in passing and in brief. It is time now to raise the question of whether he had direct influence on Tolstoi's worldview. The previous absence of this line of investigation can be explained both by the fact that there has been little research into Pogorelsky's artistic legacy and by the exceptional scarcity of materials available: the archives of both writers have vanished almost entirely into obscurity for reasons that remain unclear. However a consideration of Perovsky as figuring among Prutkov's 'origins' is interesting for two reasons: not only on a personal level, but also due to the fact that his literary position and artistic practice were formed directly through friendly and artistic links with those literary circles from which, researchers have shown, Prutkov's genealogy arises. These are the traditions of 'domestic' satirical poetry originating from the well-known Moscow poet-dilettante S. A. Neelov through to I. P. Miatlev and S. A. Sobolevsky and the comic poetics that formed among the Arzamas group.[6] The question of both the direct and the mediated influence of Perovsky-Pogorelsky on the satirical and humorous work of Tolstoi thus takes on particular significance.

After completing his studies at Moscow University, Aleksei Perovsky, the illegitimate son of the rich dignitary Aleksei Kirillovich Razumovsky, embarked upon an autonomous career. He had already shown a clear inclination towards writing. In 1810, in Moscow he naturally entered the circle of his idol Karamzin, around whom the new literary generation, relatively independent in aesthetic terms and unpuritanical in their life-style, were grouping. Among Perovsky's close friends at that time – and to the end of his days – were the future members of Arzamas, V. A. Zhukovsky and P. A. Viazemsky, both of them already well-known as epigram writers. Indeed, Zhukovsky was soon to become famous as a classic writer of parodic, Arzamas 'nonsense'. The parodic and epigrammatic works became an important part of the raging battle between the 'archaists' and 'innovators' for new aesthetic directions. They developed in a pre-Arzamas atmosphere, at the point of its formation, in the period of the 'pre-pubescent' Arzamas, as the congenial Moscow literary society of the first decade of the nineteenth century was christened by one of its members, Aleksandr Ivanovich Turgenev in a punning reference of their meeting place in A. F. Voeikov's house in Devich'e pole (Maiden's field).[7] For all their obvious respect for Karamzin, his self-willed 'fledglings' in their own literary practice formulated a poetics of 'absurdity' and 'nonsense' with its own innovations in the field of semantics and style, doing this on the periphery of strict Karamzinian aesthetics.[8] However, it was not just the product of 'pure' literary work, but also a reflection of a specific way of life, of a specific form of everyday behaviour among the young Moscow aristocracy. This was the time when Viazemsky – 'the madman and young squanderer' – 'blew' half a million on cards. Perovsky himself soon established a reputation as a striking wit and 'lovable mischiefmaker'. A not insignificant role was played here by the fact that both belonged to the circle of Sergei Alekseevich Neelov, Moscow's first wit and author of clumsy, but well-aimed epigrams and frivolous, satirical verses about any aspects of Moscow life and society events that were being spread by word of mouth around both capitals. Viazemsky valued in Neelov's 'idiotic amphigories' the ability to express 'communal living' and considered him 'the founder of a poetry school, whose followers were Miatlev and Sobolevsky'.[9] With discernable pleasure, Pushkin noted the exceptional qualities of Neelov: 'The poems of Neelov are charming', he wrote to Viazemsky, 'I was right when I once called him *le chantre de la merde!* (Let this be said between us and posterity).'[10]

Viazemsky and Pushkin's testimonials were not a chance thing: both clearly felt close to the traditions of domestic poetry and the verse of buffoonery in the 'nonsense' of Neelov and his friends. The principal expert on this question, P. N. Berkov, for example, ranked Viazemsky and Pushkin, who also cultivated the oral epigrammatic tradition, among Neelov's disciples.[11]

'Everyday mystification' flourished in this circle and Perovsky was a permanent participant in the funny and audacious practical jokes. The pages of his recollections inform us of such cases as the time when Perovsky appeared with one of his 'amphigories' before the then vice-chancellor of Moscow University and the chairman of the Society for Lovers of Russian Literature, A. A. Prokopovich-Antonsky, and in all seriousness insisted on being allowed to read them in one of the Society's public sittings. Further spice was added to the situation by the fact that Perovsky's father was the Minister of Education at that time, and poor Antonsky almost fell into a faint when he heard the following verses:

Abdul vizier
On his forehead a blister
    that he cares for and pampers.
Bayle, a geometrician.
Taking a thermometer,
    Sows wheat in the field.
But Bonaparte
With a pack of cards
    hurries to Russia
He gets in a balloon,
For a game of boston
And invites the Pope to join in
But the Pope's son
Taking an orange,
    hurls it in papa's face.
And a whale in the sea
Looks at them all
        And picks his nose.

One of Neelov's albums, in which Perovsky wrote these verses, fortunately, preserved for us this splendid 'nonsense', worthy of the absurdists of the twentieth century. Some time afterwards the host, Neelov, parodically transposed the lines into 'occasional verse': a characteristic device of 'domestic' poetry:[12]

Let the monk
In the monastery
Conduct mass,
Let the archbishop
Collect all the caviar
From the sturgeon for himself.

. . .

Let Bonaparte
With a pack of cards
Play patience alone.
Let Pope Pius the holy
With a simple soul
Wish him well.[13]

Incidentally, if you compare both amphigories, it can clearly be seen that Perovsky's original 'aesthetics of nonsense' and system of the absurd are much the more graphic, and it is these that later take shape in the works of Prutkov.

A most striking aspect is that both poems are distinguished by a free anti-clerical element, anticipating the widespread parodying of biblical texts in the works of the Arzamas members, in the spirit of the enlightenment tradition. Echoes of this parodying method manifest themselves in A.K. Tolstoi's satirical works, as will be discussed later.

Some letters by Perovsky, which have been preserved, are also notable for their spirit of light mystification and literary play. 'There is a lot that is new here', he wrote, for example, to Viazemsky from Saint Petersburg at the beginning of 1812. 'All the streets are covered in snow, the shores are covered in granite, some say that a monument to Peter the Great has been erected on St Isaac's square, depicting him sitting on a steed, but I cannot confirm any of this for sure.'[14]

Reappearing in the capital in 1816 after taking part in the 1812 war and following a stay in Germany, Perovsky became utterly absorbed in the sphere of the Arzamas, which by now was not only programmatically formed, but also flourishing – and for him, an Arzamas member in spirit and cast of mind, this environment was, doubtless, congenial and harmonious. In a letter dating from this time, A. I. Turgenev confirming to Viazemsky that Zhukovsky 'destroys' his 'drunken evenings', added: 'This notwithstanding, we sometimes got drunk on the merry atmosphere alone and on Perovsky's jokes, which are, incidentally, very decent and proper'.[15] Perovsky likewise clearly responded to the atmosphere of revelry and the reckless destruction of archaic canons. In 1820, he fiercely defended in print the innovative metaphoric style of Pushkin's 'Ruslan and Liudmila' against attacks from the classicists, not only giving voice to the position of the founder-members of Arzamas, but also widely deploying 'Arzamas language' with its playful and parodying elements, subtle puns and comically paradoxical oxymorons and periphrastic combinations.[16] Pushkin, in his southern exile, not yet knowing about Perovsky's authorship, remarked that these articles 'are the cleverest of all', and later called them 'witty and amusing'.[17] Not only the system of argumentation of his defender, but also Perovsky's parodying method, doubtless, attracted Pushkin. 'The imperturbably-serious and precise, but also point-by-point absurdly logical exposition of the basic ideas of another article' was a device used by Pushkin himself in his subsequent parodical social and political journalism.[18] When a year later Perovksy, writing under his pen-name of Pogorelsky, published the first fantastic tale in Russian literature, 'The Poppy-Seed Cake Seller from Lafertovo' (Lafertovskaia makovnitsa), he was subjected to attacks by the very same rationalist A. F. Voeikov from whom he had already recently defended 'Ruslan and Liudmila' – and attacked for the same riskily-ironic narrative style that lies at the base of Pushkin's poem. On the other hand, 'The Poppy-Seed Cake Seller from Lafertovo' aroused genuine pleasure in Pushkin, particularly for its portrayal of a cat turned civil servant, Mr Murlykin [Mr Purry]. 'My dear man, Grandma's tomcat, what a delight!', he wrote to his brother, 'I reread the tale twice at a stretch, and am now infatuated with Mr Murlykin. I step out smoothly, narrowing my eyes, turning my head and arching my back.'[19] Both writers retained a feeling of literary kinship, which later turned into friendly affection straightaway when they became personally acquainted.

And the 'pranks' and taste for mystification turned out to be very useful: both organically entered the literary method of Perovsky, which was developed to the full in his subsequent works, 'The Double or My Evenings in Malorussia' and the novel 'The Convent Girl', with their playful element and the ease with which they address the reading audience. E. N. Penskaia makes the just observation that the parodying manner of Kozma Prutkov's interaction with the reader and the 'playful reproduction of the contemporary literary world' was prompted specifically by Perovsky-Pogorelsky's 'The Double'.[20]

In the light of everything said, it is not difficult, at the very outset, to sense the obvious features of similarity between the satirical and humorous writing of Pogorelsky and A. K. Tolstoi.

Perovsky tirelessly occupied himself with his nephew's upbringing literally from the cradle, from the age of six weeks, when he took his sister Anna Alekseevna, who had separated from her husband, and her new-born child from St Petersburg to his estate, Pogorel'tsy. Among the epistles that have been preserved are letters from Perovsky to his small nephew, eloquently testifying, in particular, to the fact that he helped form the aesthetic taste of the future writer, in whose perceptions his uncle became a literary coefficient from the start. No less important is the fact that in those early years, during the time of Tolstoi's childhood, the quiet, sprawling estate with its wonderful library gave birth to the gently humorous first works of the writer Antony Pogorelsky, and it is reasonable to infer that his verbal exchanges with his nearest and dearest were characterised by the same unconstrained merriment of tone. In this sense it seems possible to generalise from a much later remark made by Viazemsky about 'The Convent Girl' in which, according to his authoritative opinion, 'the merriment is unforced and spontaneous'. Perovsky, in the words of Viazemsky, 'comes across very well in his style'.[21] The memory of those years was clearly stamped for the rest of his life upon the consciousness of the impressionable boy, Tolstoi. 'My childhood was very happy and left in me only very bright memories,' he stated in 1874 in an autobiographical letter to the Italian man of letters A. de Gubernatis.[22] The memories of a happy childhood permeate the most intimate of his letters as a leitmotif, together with the admission that he experienced 'great trust' in his uncle, despite forming early on a largely different system of opinions.[23]

In the letter to Gubernatis, Tolstoi iadmitted that 'he began to waste paper by writing poems' from the age of six and it is clear from Perovsky's letters to his nephew that these first literary experiences – among them, fables – were sent immediately and trustfully to his uncle for judgement. It is only from these letters that we know of an early plan of Tolstoi's first published work: the fantastic tale 'The Vampire'. Incdentally, we must also mention Tolstoi's attraction to the genre of the fantastic as being a direct artistic 'legacy' from the writer Pogorelsky.

In 1831 the Perovskys travelled to Italy, an experience that left a profound aesthetic imprint on the boy's soul and which is recorded in his diary. This fact in Tolstoi's biography is very well-known and has been commented upon often enough. However, outside the usual bounds of consideration, there remains one fact that is of real importance to our discussion: the meeting in Rome with Sergei Aleksandrovich Sobolevsky, another sharp-tongued acquaintance of Aleksei Perovsky and a friend of Pushkin, a brilliant follower of Miatlev's 'non-normative' poetry and the 'unknown writer of all well-known epigrams'. 'This morning we arrived in Rome . . .' notes the fourteen-year-old Tolstoi on 30 April in his diary. 'Having hired a house belonging to an innkeeper, Uncle sent someone for Mr S[obolevsky], who immediately came to see us'.[24] On 2 May the Perovskys, together with Sobolevsky, looked around the Vatican and on 5 May Tolstoi and Sobolevsky both went to Caesar's Palace 'in order to look for antiquities. We went around there a long time,' wrote the boy ingenuouslyly, 'but we did not find anything.' Sobolevsky joined the Perovskys in a subsequent trip to Naples and Pompei. In other words, the youth, who avidly took in all the diverse impressions, spent enough time in the company of Sobolevsky. The direct emotional legacy of this society was not reflected on the pages of the diary, which, in general, is notable for its factual laconism. Given the scarcity of information at our disposal, this well-known meeting, which was most certainly not the only one, should undoubtedly rank among those impressions that later resonated in Tolstoi's artistic conscious. The important thing here is that we are fortunate enough to hear the 'living voice' of Sobolevsky at that time: in letters from Rome to St. Petersburg to his old friend Odoevsky, he set forth a chronicle of his Italian trip. 'Although I arrived at the wrong time, although I am not one to get carried away,' he wrote in one of his 'joking' messages, 'I will tell you that he who has not seen Rome is living in darkness. When I climbed to the top of S[aint] Peter's, I understood those Indian philosophers whose hearts almost stopped beating from delight when they looked at the sun; had my nerves been weaker, I would have soiled my pants. What I did here was stupid: I began by rushing to the Vatican; my feelings have become numbed by this, and I am no longer able to get a proper impression of the other churches and artistic collections. Looking at them, you want to say, in the words of the late lamented Durasov: this is nothing special, sir; this is shit, sir.'[25]

Several years later, in this very same 'joking' style, unmistakably assimilated from his uncle and his milieu, Tolstoi would begin to write letters himself. His messages to N. V. Adlerberg 1837–1838, similar to those of the Arzamas circle, interspersed with humorous and parodying verses and intermedias,[26] are rightly considered as obvious precursors of Kozma Prutkov who was 'born' just over ten years later.

The following episode is revealing: one day Perovsky published one of the early poems of Tolstoi, who was clearly longing for public recognition, and he accompanied it with his own highly critical review – for the young poet's edification.[27] This dates, apparently, to the 1830s: a time marking the complete formation of Tolstoi's aesthetic views and literary tastes. Perovsky introduced him to his literary circle, giving the works of the young writer to friends for judgement. 'And I saw Zhukovsky,' wrote Perovsky to his nephew on 27 March 1835. 'He approves of your last play and he told me to tell you that he never said to Vania that the "Summit of the Alps" is not good: on the contrary, he likes it. He only told him that he prefers your Greek plays because they prove that you deal with antiquity.'[28] These early dealings with 'antiquity' were also, without a doubt, stimulated by Perovsky, who was something of a connoisseur. One thinks here of the reply of the narrator – the writer's alter ego – in 'The Double': 'I admit that I am quite attracted to antiquity.' This bears an openly autobiographical character, as, indeed, does much else in the work.[29] This enthusiasm of the young Tolstoi for antiquity was to manifest itself brilliantly in the 'works' of Kozma Prutkov, where parody of the 'false-majestic' 'anthologists' of the 1840 and 1850s occupies a prominent place. It was Tolstoi who penned the best examples of this 'anthological' genre in Prutkov's oeuvre, such as the well-known 'Ancient Sculpted Greek':

> I love you, maiden, when you hold a lemon
> Golden and sunlight-bathed,
> And I see the downy chin of a youth
> Among the acanthus leaves and the columns white.
> The heavy folds of the beautiful chlamys
> Fall one after another...

Or the no less famous 'Letter from Corinth':

> I have recently arrived in Corinth.
> Here are the steps and the colonnade.
> I love the local marble nymphs
> And the sound of the isthmian waterfall.
> The whole day I sit in the sun.
> Rubbing balm around my loins.
> Among the Parian marble chips
> I follow the writhings of the blind slow-worm.[30]

As testimony of conscious literary continuity between uncle and nephew one could cite an incidental but none the less eloquent fact. After Perovsky's death in 1840,

Tolstoi signed one of his joke letters, addressed to P. A. Pletnev, using his uncle's pseudonym, changing only the first name: Afanasy Pogorelsky.[31]

Pushkin too gave his seal of approval to Tolstoi's first modest poetic undertakings: they met in person in 1836, also in Perovsky's house. The legacy of the great poet was preserved in Tolstoi's artistic conscious throughout his life and this interest left its mark upon his work, including his attempt, unique in its own way, to write a humorous commentary on Pushkin's poetry. According to several scholars, Tolstoi's 'Prutkovian' poem 'My Portrait', which opens the poetic 'legacy' of the director of the assay office,[32] is also linked to Pushkin and is a parody of his poem 'Poet' ('Poet, set no store by the love of the people').[33]

However, of particular interest to our discussion is 'Revolt in the Vatican', one of Tolstoi's best poetic satires. It is not in the Kozma Prutkov collection, but was written just a year after his 'death'. It is interesting not only in so far as it is a subtle adaptation of 'another's text', but also because it is a unique synthesis of intersecting traditions. 'Revolt in the Vatican' is distinguished by its erotic motifs, which are uncharacteristic for Tolstoi's serious lyrics, and appears partly inspired by Pushkin, that is, by the denouement of his poem 'The Tale of the Golden Cockerel', when the astrologer-eunuch, blinded by hopeless passion, demands the Tsarina of Shemakha from the Tsar Dadon as a reward. To this demand Dadon responds with the resounding question, brilliant in its laconism and powerfully grotesque effect: 'And why would you want a maiden?' The 'Revolt...' is built on this erotic theme:

The eunuchs were in rebellion...
They enter the Pope's chambers:
'Why aren't we married?
What are we guilty of?'
The Pope tells them sternly:
'Aren't you afraid of God?
What kind of Synagogue is this?
Off with you! Don't darken my door any longer.'
They say to him: 'It's all right for you,
You have it easy,
But we are so forlorn
It's really very annoying!'...
To them the Pope said: 'Children!
You should have looked ahead:
Once you've lost these things,
You just have to endure it...
'This thing,' pronounced the Pope,
'Even if it were Priapus who lost it,
Can't be put back on ...
It's a thing ... not a hat ...[34]

According to V. V. Vatsuro, a researcher into the semantics of the plot of 'The Tale of the Golden Cockerel', the 'battle' for the 'maiden' takes on the character of the absurd, the phantasmogorical; the plot's motive power is blinding, uncontrollable passion, which gives birth to a crime.' The parodic character of this scene has been registered in critical literature.[35] It is probable that Tolstoi was drawn precisely to the 'character of the absurd', refracted by him in the plot of the eunuchs' revolt, which also leads to a crime: an attempt to emasculate the Pope himself:

'Do you not want to surprise us
By yourself singing "Casta diva",
Not in a rumble but a squeak,
In a subtle, special way?'

On the other hand, one cannot help recalling the anti-clerical motifs of Perovsky's aforementioned amphigory, and the attack by both Perovsky and Tolstoi directed against the Roman Catholic Church, which in Tolstoi's works is by no means an isolated instance. There are adequate grounds, therefore, for research into Perovsky's literary experience as a possible "genetic" ideological and literary first inspiration, onto which was then mapped an impulse generated by Pushkin.

Since the principles of Tolstoian satirical poetry generally remained unchanging in the post-Prutkovian period, this observation might subsequently help to explain new "roots" in the works of Prutkov himself.

And, finally, when talking about the continuity of traditions, we cannot pass over the well-known fact that the figure of Kozma Prutkov was conceived in the same atmosphere of unity between life and literary practice as had once been the case with Arzamas. Arzamas was programmatically directed at travestying the conservatively inclined 'Colloquy of Lovers of the Russian Word',[36] and had its beginnings in its Moscow prelude and the venturesome artistic pieces of the Neelov circle, of which Perovsky was a member.

The analogous tricks of the 'Prutkovian circle' – the Zhemchuznikov brothers and A. K. Tolstoi – have been repeatedly described in literature and there is no real need to dwell on them here. However, the factors governing their 'group behaviour' – the violation of generally accepted laws – were already different in their essential features and were dictated both by different socio-historic prejudices and different ideological, ethical and aesthetic norms. But this is a separate issue altogether.

This essay has analysed the evolution of A.K. Tolstoi's satire in pursuit of a narrow and defined aim. There are on-going arguments about the "specific weight" of the Zhemchuznikov brothers and A.K. Tolstoi in the formation of Kozma Prutkov's image, style and ideology.[37] The facts listed here should provide another argument in favour of those who suggest that, despite being relatively unproductive in comparison to the Zhemchuznikovs, it was actually Tolstoi who was the more authoritative, and possibly the main, generator of the ideas that coalesced into the immortal character of Kozma Prutkov, splendidly stupid and self-satisfied director of the assay office in the ministry of finance.

Translated by Hazel Grünewald

5

COMEDY BETWEEN THE POLES OF HUMOUR AND TRAGEDY, BEAUTY AND UGLINESS

Prince Myshkin as a comic character

NATALIA ASHIMBAEVA

MANY facets of the comic play a huge role in the works of Dostoevsky. Dostoevsky is a tragic genius, a 'cruel talent', but there are just as solid foundations for discussing him as a genius of humour and the comic. Many outstanding Dostoevsky scholars have already focused on this unique feature of his artistic world: Iu. N. Tynianov, M. M. Bakhtin, P. M. Bitsilli, I. I. Lapshin, R. G. Nazirov, V. A. Tunimanov, A. E. Kunilsky and others.

Dostoevsky's novel-tragedy, according to Bitsilli's observation, can also be categorised as a tragi-comic novel.[1] I. I. Lapshin wrote that Dostoevsky was acutely sensitive to 'the tragic as the basis of the comic' in the works of the great humorous geniuses – Cervantes, Gogol and Griboedov.[2]

All aspects of the comic are present in Dostoevsky's *oeuvre*, from gentle humour to boulevard buffoonery. In almost all of his works, starting from the very earliest, we find various types of parody. Research has turned more than once to different forms of satire, presented by Dostoevsky in diverse ways and with various nuances, from satirical journalism to philosopho-satirical images, scenes and dialogues.

Also relating to the sphere of the comic are joke images and buffoonish escapades, the unexpected and inappropriate appearance of absurd characters into dramatic situations, striking discordant notes in fundamental events (General Ivolgin in the scene of Nastasia Filippovna's visit to the Ivolgins in *The Idiot*; the tenants' shouts of idle curiousity which accompany the death of Marmeladov in *Crime and Punishment*).[3] 'Comic ugliness and cynical buffoonery', notes N. M. Chirkov, 'are essential conditions for the creation of dramatic tension.'[4]

Scenes of this type, with a large number of participants between whom tension arises, leading to scandals and excesses (and there are numerous examples in

Dostoevsky's novels), have been termed 'conclaves' by L. P. Grossman. In Bakhtin's definition, they relate to the sphere of the 'seriously funny'.[5] The inextricability of the humorous and the tragic, of life and death, the liberating element of *carnival laughter*, breaking down social hierarchies – we find all this in Dostoevsky's world.

A particular layer of his artistic world, demanding completely separate research, is the comic on the level of discourse and intonation.

Critical literature on comedy is Dostoevsky is very extensive, from specialist works on one variety of the comic or another to individual observations and judgements in general research.[6] However, there is no full description of all the examples of comedy in Dostoevsky's *oeuvre*, and the problems of such a description would be enormous, as the comic element underpins his entire artistic world.

Comedy in Dostoevsky's work is based on and caused by disharmony, chaos, disorder, unattractive beings, and every type of dissonance and misunderstanding existing in relations between people; that is to say, the tragic and the comic in his artistic world have the same source. In Bakhtin's diary there is an important entry on the nature of the comic: 'Laughter is a corrective measure; comedy is the improper. The difficulty of analysing the authentically comic (the laugh-able) lies in the fact that the negative and the positive in comic scenes are inseparably fused, and a boundary between the two cannot be drawn.'[7]

In order to understand Dostoevsky's poetics as a whole, and the place of the comic in his works, Bakhtin's principle, formulated in *Problems of Dostoevsky's Poetics*, is particularly important: 'The fundamental category in Dostoevsky's mode of artistic visualising was not evolution, but *co-existence and interaction* . . . For him, to get one's bearings on the world meant to conceive all its contents as simultaneous, and *to guess at their interrelationships in the cross-section of a single moment*' [Italics in original].[8] This idea of Bakhtin's is exceptionally fruitful. Bakhtin's idea of a link with the traditions of Menippean literature and folk carnival reveals its deep genetic roots ('genre-memory'). They elucidate how the general laws of literary creation in Dostoevsky's world work. However, these same laws, which are realised outside the author's conscious plan, are like the laws of nature. But 'co-existence and interaction' is a principle linked to the foundations of Dostoevsky's artistic and philosophical world-view, which is consequently incarnated in the poetics of his works. This seems to be an extremely productive way of studying the poetics of comedy in his works.

We will attempt in the light of Bakhtin's position on this to examine the place of comedy in *The Idiot* and to analyse those moments of '*co-existence and interaction*' of various kinds of elements in some of the principal themes and scenes in the novel, which relate primarily to the image of the main hero, Prince Myshkin.

I GOSPEL REMINISCENCES AND COMEDY

In *The Idiot*, gospel stories, reminiscences and allusions are clearly expressed, and researchers and commentators have revealed a large number of such associations and direct references to the Gospels. But this lofty, sacred plan for the novel and the image of its main hero, Prince Myshkin, who is directly called 'Prince Christ' (9: 246, 249) in the notebooks, is in the text of the novel presented in a somewhat 'effaced', camouflaged way, and is most often of all 'underlit' by comedy. The theme of the donkey, and the 'sermons' which characterise the Prince's conversations in the Epanchins' drawing room in Chapter 5 of Part I are examples of such moments. A mass of literature dedicated to interpreting this aspect of the novel has already accumulated. Some treatments tend to stray away from the context, striving towards a particular metaphysical idea, which does not always tie in with the novel. These types of interpretations do not take into account the comic components of certain scenes, while the interpretations themselves take on from time to time some comic nuances that have astonishingly not been noticed by the investigator. One such interesting article is by T. A. Kasatkina, which is saturated with original judgements. From listening intently to the donkey's bray, 'ia, ia' (which is not reproduced in the novel), she heard the sound as relating to the Russian first personal pronoun, I (*ia*), and defined this moment as the beginning of the 'personal incarnation' of Myshkin.[9]

From the point of view of polite conversation, the theme of the donkey, whose cry Myshkin heard on his arrival in Basel and somehow particularly remembered, looks rather ridiculous. The absurdity is reinforced by Lizaveta Prokofievna's lightly whimsical incomprehension: 'An ass? That's odd,' remarked the General's wife. 'But then there's nothing odd about it, any one of us could fall in love with a donkey', she remarked, looking angrily at the giggling girls. 'It happened in mythology.' The literary and mythological associations (of Appulius's 'Golden Ass') camouflage the reference to the Gospels. Amidst the laughter of the sisters, the theme of the donkey is developed for another page and a half. Jokey hints link the donkey to the Prince, who in the eyes of his new acquaintances is either an idiot or a rogue, although they already sense that everything is much more complex than this. The Prince recognises this word game perfectly, but laughs very sincerely, accepting the comedy of the situation. The deeper level, referring to the Gospel episode of Christ's entrance into Jerusalem on a donkey, remains hidden from the participants in the conversation, and is not immediately heeded by the reader.

Furthermore, the conversation featuring the donkey is about Basel, where Hans Holbein the Younger's painting 'Christ in the Tomb', which is so significant to the novel, was and is to this day to be found. The Prince attempts to share his impressions: 'not long ago I saw a picture like that in Basel. I'd really like to tell you about it. . .,' but Adelaida interrupts him and the story is not told. But Basel is not Jerusalem, and the Christ in Basel is a dead Christ, 'in the Tomb'. Myshkin is here dreaming of something quite different.

After the theme of the donkey, the theme of sermons arises. The Prince tells of his life in solitude, his dreams: 'I kept dreaming of a big city, like Naples, full of palaces, thunderous noise, life... What didn't I dream about! And then it seemed to me that even in prison one might discover immense life.' The reflections and dreams of the Prince are 'anamnesis', recollection. The 'big city' is the heavenly Jerusalem, which he sees at the point 'where earth and sky meet' where the 'whole puzzle' is resolved, and where 'you will see a new life.' In this way, the motif of the entrance into Jerusalem is developed, but as an unconscious reverie.

However, these reflections arouse a sarcastic response from the sisters:

> 'I read that last laudable sentiment in my school book when I was twelve', said Aglaia. 'It's all philosophy,' observed Adelaida. 'You're a philosopher and you've come to teach us.' 'Maybe you're right,' smiled the Prince. 'I am in fact a philosopher and who knows, perhaps I really do intend to teach people. . . That's possible; indeed it is.'

The whole conversation in the drawing room, and the entire encounter of the Epanchins and the Prince proceeds on two levels. Images, slips of the tongue and individual words which echo gospel episodes point to the sacred level. The Prince, sincerely although not intentionally, *unconsciously* introduces a kind of 'second' story of a providential premonition of his purpose and fate. This premonition is concealed in the Prince's recollections about death sentences, his life in Switzerland, and Marie. The *realistic* level is the living picture of the General's family. The mocking tone of the sisters as they ridicule the Prince, their jokes and hints to one another, and their affectionate irony towards their mother – all this creates a situation lit up by comedy, which 'cancels out' or draws a veil over the higher level.[10] And the secret of Dostoevsky's artistry lies precisely in the coupling of these two levels of artistic expression, the practical and the sacred, in their 'co-existence and interaction'; neither the individual 'cataloguing' of gospel references and their 'deciphering', nor the strictly psychological description of relations between the Prince and the Epanchin family leads to an adequate understanding of the hero. Here we should recall Bakhtin's idea made in relation to comic expression in Gogol: 'The *zone of laughter* in Gogol becomes the *zone of contact*. Here the contradictory and incompatible are united, coming to life as a linkage.' Idle chatter 'sounds in this context like a problem of speech, like something significant, appearing, as it were, through verbal rubbish that seems to have no meaning.'[11]

The association of the 'contradictory and incompatible', the comic and the serious, is conveyed quite consistently through the image of Prince Myshkin. Of course, those around him see in him some sort of *other essence*, but in the 'heady atmosphere' of earthly relations and social hierarchies, the Prince, with his anti-social behaviour and existential profundity instead of the short-term values laid down by society's criteria, stands out as a crank and a comic character. This tendency of Myshkin's character can also be traced in the final stages of Dostoevsky's creative work in the preparatory notes for the novel: 'The Prince agrees. He becomes betrothed. He is ridiculous. How he turns laughter aside'; and, '? Wouldn't it be better to present the Prince as a perpetual sphinx? ? Several blunders and comical traits in the Prince.' (9: 242)[12]

All the important encounters, which have fatal significance for the hero of the novel, also take place so to speak simultaneously 'on two levels' and are inevitably accompanied by comic elements. One example is the Prince's first meeting with Nastasia Filippovna at the Ivolgins' flat in Chapter 8 of Part I, when she takes him for a servant. But in the following chapter there is a moment of recognition: 'I've certainly seen your eyes somewhere... but that can't be! I'm just... I've never even been here before. Perhaps it was in a dream...' A profound, so to speak 'premature' layer when Myshkin and Nastasia Filippovna 'recognise' each other (another variation on the theme of 'recollection') comes to light through the comic absurdity of the first moment of their encounter.

In the relationship between the Prince and Aglaia, the comic and the serious are intricately interwoven, as if reflecting all their complexity and instability. In order to understand the Prince, Aglaia in Chapter 6 of Part II compares him to the 'poor knight' and Don Quixote. All Aglaia's vacillations in her evaluations of the personality and conduct of the Prince are encapsulated in this comparison: 'it's clear the 'poor knight' didn't care what his lady was or did. It was enough that he had chosen her and believed in her 'pure beauty' ...; that was the merit of it, that even *were she to become, say, a thief* later on [N. A.'s italics], he would still be bound to believe in her and break a lance for the sake of her pure beauty'. But alongside these venomous words there is quite a different idea:

> 'The "poor knight" is Don Quixote, but serious, not comic. At first I didn't realise it and I laughed, but now I love the 'poor knight', but more than that, I applaud his heroic feats.' Thus Aglaia concluded, and looking at her it was hard to tell whether she was being serious or laughing.

Comedy and the comic most frequently arise in *The Idiot* in contexts where they emphasise far from comic circumstances.

2 COMEDY IN THE SOCIAL EXISTENCE OF THE HERO

Prince Myshkin is never comic or funny when he is alone with his thoughts, premonitions and doubts. The complex structure of his tragic, divided inner life has been shown by Malcolm Jones.[13] The comic arises precisely in intercourse between people, where various types of disparity, non-coincidence, dissonance, and misunderstanding create the grounds for its manifestation. In society, even at the most dramatic moments, there is always somebody present who can see and understand the situation 'from the sidelines', or does not understand it at all, and reacts in an inadequate manner.

Such is the scene at the Epanchins' dacha in Chapter 6 of Part IV when the Prince appears in the role of Aglaia's fiancé. Society, assembled at the Epanchins' house in expectation of an announcement of betrothal, is depicted satirically and moreover through a dual perspective. The narrator sarcastically notes their vanity, arrogance and inner ill-will – in general, the very characteristics of society already described by Griboedov in his comedy *Woe from Wit* of which this scene from *The Idiot* is indisputably an echo. But Prince Myshkin sees society through different eyes (in contrast to Griboedov's clever Chatsky, Myshkin is 'an idiot'): 'all this society,' the narrator comments, 'the Prince took for the genuine article, the purest, unalloyed gold.' From this misperception arises his fervour and sincerity in the ensuing conversation, when he 'gets too carried away'. Myshkin speaks his mind about Pavlishchev, the Jesuits and Catholicism with a seriousness and passion (to the point of trembling) which is out of place in 'polite society'.

The culmination of the ill-founded engagement arrives at the moment when Myshkin breaks the Chinese vase, which is followed by his epileptic fit. The story of the broken vase also serves as a '*zone of contact*'. It comically demonstrates the Prince's awkwardness, his lack of skill and inability to conduct himself freely and spontaneously in society, and at the same time it reflects Myshkin's fate; it is no accident that he is afraid of standing too close to the vase and has a sort of premonition that it could happen. This feeling is heightened by Aglaia's provoking, mocking words the night before the party: 'at least smash the vase in the drawing room! It's valuable; please, smash it.'

However, the breaking of the vase and Myshkin's subsequent fit acquire a cathartic significance; the suspicious, hostile, wary attitude of others towards the Prince vanishes, and is replaced by fellow feeling, sympathy and compassion. At the cost of a seizure, which frightens the guests, Myshkin humanises the masks.

> In a letter to Sofia Ivanovna, Dostoevsky wrote,
> Of the beautiful characters in Christian literature, Don Quixote is the most complete. But he is beautiful only because he is at the same time also comic . . . compassion for the one who is mocked, who doesn't himself know the value of his own beauty, arises, and this should arouse sympathy in the reader as well.
>
> (28.2: 251)

This is a mechanism of the human psyche which Dostoevsky shows in the novel: from ridicule to compassion and purification. If people were unaware what laughter was, it is terrifying to think what would constitute society. A ridiculous man 'agreeing' to be comic is in Dostoevsky's world a man not yet dead, even if he is laid low and will not recover in social terms.

But the ideal in the real world is the humorous, the comic, and / or the tragic.

3 MOCKERY IN THE CROWD

There are also scenes in the novel involving many characters where laughter at the Prince takes on the form of mockery, taunting and profanity. One such scene occurs in chapters 15 and 16 of Part I, at the conclusion of Nastasia Filippovna's birthday party, when the Prince proposes marriage to her. This turn of events arouses 'sniggers' from Ferdyshchenko and Lebedev, and hypocritical smiles and chuckles from others present. The situation seems funny to vulgar worthless characters and buffoons, who represent the opinion of the crowd. The possible union of Myshkin and Nastasia Filippovna is a constant source of rumours, ridicule, obsessions and tittle-tattle. The crowd's laughter acquires a sinister edge in the period of the wedding preparations and at the moment when the wedding is abandoned.

The Idiot has a certain characteristic 'rhythm' in its plot development. Scenes which are full of drama, tension, fraught with incandescent passion and scandals ('conclaves') alternate with 'cursory surveys' when the main participants in events do not act actively, but are depicted as objects of interest to society; some knowledge about them is communicated with primary support from rumours, which occupy an essential place in the novel.

Events are profaned by gossip, tittle-tattle and rumours. Thus in the opening chapter of Part II, after Nastasia Filippovna's party, Myshkin is 'spoken of' as 'a simple-minded princeling (nobody could be sure exactly what his name was) who had suddenly come into an enormous fortune and married a visiting French lady, a famous can-can dancer from the Château des Fleurs in Paris.'

It is noteworthy that the more populous the society making judgements on the Prince and the further he seems from the specific people who judge him, the more the perception of his personality acquires a ridiculous, absurd and abstract character. The two poles of such 'remote' treatment of the Prince are on the one hand rumours and gossip, and on the other the article 'Proletarians and Scions...', written by a band of nihilists and presented as a progressive and radical idea, directed against a retrograde millionaire prince.

Lies about the man appear in the form of both unprincipled scandal-mongering and an unscrupulous article with an ideological subtext.

4 PRINCE LEV NIKOLAEVICH MYSHKIN

The 'Prince Christ' of the notebooks for the novel is converted in the final text into Prince Myshkin. Why precisely is he called Myshkin, Lev Nikolaevich? There are several answers to this question in critical literature on *The Idiot*, all of them in their own way correct. The fact that Myshkin belongs to an ancient but impoverished family, mentioned in Karamzin's *History*, is important; the oxymoronic combination of his first name and surname, in which the unity of strength (the lion) and weakness (the mouse) is simultaneously indicated, is also important. Undoubtedly the combination 'Prince Myshkin' also contains kenotic motifs.[14] But it seems we would not be mistaken in saying that there is also something comic in the hero's name. This assertion does not contradict all these other interpretations, but in a sense colours them, giving all the other meanings a special warmth, and does not cancel out any of them. Thus even in the hero's name we find the image of the principle of 'co-existence and interaction', which pervades the poetics of the novel and gives the possibility of sensing all the depth and capaciousness of life, where nothing exists in isolation, but everything is connected and interacts.

Translated by Sarah Young

6

THE YOUNG LEV TOLSTOI AND LAURENCE STERNE'S *A SENTIMENTAL JOURNEY*

The test of irony

GALINA GALAGAN

The disparity between people's moral ideals and their behaviour in practice is a problem that unites the artistic consciousness of different eras and nations. Addressing the problem by means of philosophical and artistic thinking is commonly associated with reliance on comic techniques such as those of irony, humour and satire. With respect to this last area, it would seem that Lev Tolstoi and Laurence Sterne, at least at first glance, are very different artists. The diary of the young Tolstoi, however, shows this to be not quite the case.

The beginning of 1847 clearly shows that in Tolstoi's aspirations the idea of moral self-perfection is key. His tables of precepts for the development of will ('intellectual' and 'sensual'), his affirmation of doubt as the first principle of knowledge in his philosophical sketches, his reflections upon the reasons for his early 'spiritual depravity'[1] are all things that predetermine the diary's purpose, the first entry in which was made in April 1847. It was used for setting down future plans, schedules for the following day and strict controls over their implementation, as well as for an intense, self-critical analysis of all divergences between intentions and deeds.

The diary was started by a man who had very recently said to himself: 'Have a goal for the whole of your life, a goal for a certain period . . ., a goal for a particular time, a goal for the year, for the month, for the week and for the hour and for the minute, sacrificing the lower goals for the higher' (46: 269). But every passing day showed with unrelenting clarity that 'lower goals' do not want to yield their position and be sacrificed to 'higher goals'. They stubbornly uphold their rights, giving rise at times to a feeling of spiritual bankruptcy in Tolstoi.

Discrepancies between what exists and what should be, as Tolstoi perceives them, are all the more acute because the reason for them is clear to him: the contradictions in his desire simultaneously to be established in society, and to resist it.

After a three-year break, Tolstoi returns to the diary with the experience of the past. His never-ceasing self-analysis has made knowledge about himself (and man in general) the major discovery of these years, even though Tolstoi refers to them as spent 'dissolutely' (46: 38). The unceasing voices of vanity, sensuality, pride, conceit, indecision, haste, laziness etc. motivate Tolstoi to ask himself the question: 'How could I set my intellect in train without any verification, without any application?' (46: 38).

It is precisely at this time that he first reads *A Sentimental Journey*, an encounter that must have taken place no later than early March 1851, since the fragment *A Story of Yesterday* (*Istoriia vcherashnego dnia*) (which, according to the diary, dates back to the second half of this month) bears witness to Tolstoi's very careful reading of Sterne's book. He soon sets about translating it, jotting down extracts of it in his diary, leaving there the acknowledgement: 'Have been reading Sterne. Delightful' (46: 110).

The theme of two worlds – the world that exists and the one that should be – internally motivates the test of irony, to which Sterne's sentimental traveller, many of those who meet him along the way and, of course, the reader are subjected. Nuances, shades of feelings, their opposition and mobility, the interweaving in a single impulse of motifs of sympathy and hypocrisy, of modesty and the desire to surrender oneself, of spiritual breadth and shallowness and so on: this is the knowledge about humankind that Sterne bestows upon his reader. Likewise imparted to the reader is an awareness of the historical tradition's reliance upon the comic when depicting the movement from evil to good.

At first glance, this last piece of knowledge cannot inspire great optimism in the reader. The story about the dissolute inhabitants of the town of Abdera, which bears no relation to the geographical route of Yorick's journey, would appear to imply the artistic impotence of irony: 'The town of Abdera, notwithstanding Democritus lived there trying all the powers of irony and laughter to reclaim it, was the vilest and most profligate town in all Thrace'.[2] This text occurs in the chapter 'A Fragment', which Tolstoi translated (1: 263–4). Sterne's self-irony prompts this mention of the activities of Democritus in Abdera: Sterne himself is continuing the age-long tradition of reliance on the comic. And this in itself is already a testimony to the creative possibilities of irony, humour and satire.

Reflecting upon Sterne's book, Tolstoi returns repeatedly to one and the same thought about himself: '. . .there is never any firm improvement, in many things, no progress' (1: 290). And at the same time the concepts of 'weakness' and 'the ridiculous' start to be perceived by him as being of the same order, as being qualitatively similar concepts. Here is the diary entry from spring 1851: '... they describe human weaknesses and the ridiculous tendency of people, transposing them to fictional characters, sometimes successfully, depending on how talented the writer is ... We know about human weaknesses from ourselves and in order to illustrate them in a believable way, it is necessary to express them in oneself, because a particular weakness only goes with a particular character. If everyone were to reveal themselves as they really are, then what was previously ridiculous and a weakness would stop being so. It is surely a great blessing to rid oneself, even just a little, of the terrible yoke we carry: the fear of the ridiculous' (46: 76).

Tolstoi encounters such a uniting of weakness and the ridiculous on the first few pages of *A Sentimental Journey*, in the Sternian analysis of what takes place between intention and deed in the spirit of the hero:

> Now where would be the harm, [thought Yorick], if I was to beg of this distressed lady to accept half of my chaise? – and what mighty mischief could ensue?
>
> Every dirty passion, and bad propensity in my nature, took the alarm. ... – It will oblige you to have a third horse, said AVARICE, which will put twenty livres out of your pocket – You know not what she is, said CAUTION – or what scrapes the affair may draw you into, whispered COWARDICE –
>
> Depend upon it, Yorick! said DISCRETION, 'twill be said you went off with a mistress, and came by assignation to Calais for that purpose –
>
> You can never after, cried HYPOCRISY aloud, shew your face in the world – or rise, quoth MEANNESS, in the church – or be any thing in it, said PRIDE, but a lousy prebendary.[3]

Sterne concentrates the reader's attention on the weaknesses and passions that are all trying together to make the hero change his intention by emphasising them through the type-setting. The similarly emphasised indications of his own weaknesses and lapses from intention which appear in Tolstoi's diary (during the period when he was reading Sterne) are, of course, linked to *A Sentimental Journey*. It should be noted that, in his translation of the book, Tolstoi reproduces all of Sterne's typographic emphases in the most attentive way. Tolstoi's concentration in his diary on weaknesses (with the aim of ridding himself of them) is usually explained by reference to Benjamin Franklin's 'method'[4] and the influence of Rousseau's *Confessions*. These explanations, however, are not enough. The 'Franklin Journal' kept by the young Tolstoi is a task, above all, of a 'technical' order. As far as Rousseau is concerned, it should be pointed out that Tolstoi's acquaintance, as a youth, with the *Confessions* did not yet make the theme of weaknesses the central concern of his diary. The renewed attention to Rousseau, in the summer of 1852, serves only to reinforce the firmness of this theme in Tolstoi's artistic consciousness.

Furthermore, in the translation of the chapter 'Montriul' (the fourth of the same name) Tolstoi makes a mistake: a subconscious and very significant mistake. Yorick concludes the dialogue with the landlord (about the weaknesses of La Fleur's heart) thus:

> [I am] firmly persuaded, that if I ever do a mean action, it must be in some interval betwixt one passion and another: whilst this interregnum lasts, I always perceive my heart locked up – I can scarce find in it to give Misery a six-pence; . . . the moment I am rekindled, I am all generosity and good-will again . . .. – But in saying this – surely I am commending the passion – not myself.[5]

The Tolstoyan translation of Yorick's confessions is almost literal, except for the concluding part of the hero's opinions. Instead of: '. . .I am commending the passion')[6] Tolstoi writes: '. . . I blame passion'.

The subconscious mistake is a consequence of Tolstoi's long and stubborn battle with sensuality which, time and again, led to chance liaisons and immediate repentance for them. The mistake in the translation resulted from the view of 'passion' (not only in connection with sensuality) which Tolstoi had formed towards this time: namely, that passions were responsible for the overwhelming majority of his departures from the path of perfection.

Tolstoi's self-irony thrives on the psychological ground of self-analysis. The everyday self-accounts of the diary record how he overcomes the fear of the ridiculous: 'In the morning I did not get up for a long time, pulled a face over this, let myself down. Read novels when I should have been doing something else, . . . Threw myself from the grand piano to a book, from the book to my pipe and then to something to eat . . . I don't remember whether I lied. Probably. . . I looked at myself often in the mirror. It is a stupid, physical self-love from which nothing can come except more of the stupid and ridiculous' (46: 47–8).

Self-irony, revealing the multi-layered nature of consciousness, conveys on the pages of the diary every manifestation of laziness, indecision, haste, self-deception, inconsistency, inconstancy, arrogance, absent-mindedness etc. etc. Weaknesses and passions are place in the same negative rank.

Self-irony intrudes upon the immediate act of contemplation and feeling, fixing attention upon the externally unmotivated transmutability of feelings, testimony to their multi-layered nature: 'Yesterday I didn't sleep almost the whole night. Having written a bit in my diary, I began to pray to God. The sweetness of feelings which I experienced in prayer is impossible to communicate. . . . How terrible it was for me to see the whole petty-depraved side of life. I could not understand how it could so seduce me. . . . I did not feel myself as flesh, I was all spirit. But no! The carnal-petty side took over again: not even an hour had passed, before I almost consciously heard the voice of vice . . ., knew where this voice came from, knew that it would destroy my felicity, struggled and yielded to it. I fell asleep, dreaming about glory, about women; but I was not to blame, I could not help it' (46: 61–2).

Self-irony reveals the combination in one psychic act of directly opposing tendencies: 'And why am I so sad? Not so much sad as painfully conscious that I am sad and I don't know what about. . . . But now I think with relish about the saddle I ordered on which I'm going to ride in my Circassian costume, and how I'm going to chase after Cossack women: and how I will despair because my left whiskers are worse than my right and I take two hours correcting them in front of the mirror' (46: 76, 78).

The self-irony gives no quarter to indulgence, conceit, nor arrogance, but the most careful attention is fixed upon vanity, its manifestation not only in the present, but also in the past:

> I don't know by what paths there drifted into my wandering imagination those memories of gypsy nights . . . I sang . . ., sang with great spirit, shyness did not constrain my voice . . . I listened to myself with great pleasure. Vanity, as always, stole into my soul, and I thought: 'It's really nice to hear myself, but even nicer perhaps for strangers to hear me.' I was even envious of their pleasure, of which I was deprived.
>
> (46: 81–3)

Removing from vanity the covers masking it, self-irony in the Tolstoyan diary gives way to a sharply satirical lampoon (for all Tolstoi's repeated declarations in the same diary about his alienation from all things satirical). 'Vanity,' writes Tolstoi, '. . . is one of those evils by means of which, like mass epidemics – hunger, locusts, war – Providence punishes people . . . This is a sort of moral illness, like leprosy – it does not destroy one part, but disfigures everything – it creeps in little by little, unnoticed and then develops in the whole organism; there is not a single manifestation, which it would not infect – it is like venereal disease; if it is banished from one part of the body, it appears with greater force in another . . . Vanity is a kind of immature love of glory, a kind of self-love, transferred into the opinion of others . . . I suffered a lot from this passion: it ruined the best years of my life' (46: 94–5).

An increase in Tolstoi's sceptical attitude towards his own spiritual possibilities (although here we must remember the extreme demands he placed upon himself) accompanied the overcoming of his fear of the ridiculous. 'Scepticism led me to a problematic moral position' (46: 143), he confessed to his diary in the summer of 1852. It must be noted, however, that the entry was made several days after the completion of his novel *Childhood.* The need to relate the 'remarkable' events in life, i.e. those where 'one needs . . . to justify oneself' stood at the source of its intention.

The self-irony of the young Tolstoi is healing and curative. It leads to disturbance in the soul, exposing its neglect of creative work: the guarantee of moral rebirth. The very first pages of the diary declare this understanding of its purpose: 'A change in the way of life must take place'. This change 'should be a product of the soul' (46: 30).

Cicero it was who linked the movement from what exists to what should be with a 'disturbance in the soul'. For Cicero, the only medicine that could return the soul to its state of vigilance was complete reliance upon reason (*Tusculan Disputations.* The treatise 'On Passions').[7] At the beginning of the 1850s, Tolstoi was not yet familiar with this treatise. But the ground for self-irony, retaining all its fertility, reinforced his doubt every day in the indisputable authority of 'intellectual will'. Anticipating his later reflections about the 'trickery of the mind', 'chess game of the mind' (48: 53), he admitted to his diary: 'Believe reason only when you are convinced that no passion speaks in you . . ., when passions possess (a person - G. G.), . . . they dominate . . . his reason' (46: 181). Later 'the path of the mind' will be artistically discredited in three Tolstoyan novels.[8]

The possibilities of reason are debunked in Sterne too, in *The Life and Opinions of Tristam Shandy, Gentleman.* And on this front, Sterne, like Tolstoi, enters into polemics with Cicero. As far as feelings are concerned, Sterne's all-encompassing irony in *A Sentimental Journey* reveals weaknesses in the bearer of feelings, the weakness of humankind in general, in different times and nations. The discrepancy between what exists and what should be presented itself to him as far more insurmountable than it did to the young Tolstoi, striving to make a perfect personality out of himself.

Tolstoi's self-irony transformed the creative energy of his scepticism into the driving principle along this path to self-perfection and thus had direct bearing upon the formulation of key ideas in his philosophical and historical thinking.[9] These ideas are the recognition of the constant movement of the individual personality in time and its freedom in an infinitely small moment of the present.

The young Tolstoi's reliance on the resources of irony links him to Sterne. If we bear in mind that in 1891 Tolstoi, recalling the books which had the greatest impact on him in his youth (see: 66, 67), names *A Sentimental Journey* immediately after Matthew's Gospel, we can perceive the general course of development within which his reception of Sterne's book is also located. This course may be defined as follows: the striving to renew the moral vision of humankind and of the world.

Translated by Hazel Grünewald

7

FASHIONING LIFE

Teffi and women's humour

EDYTHE C. HABER

If I were writing at the beginning of the twentieth century instead of the twenty-first, my title would no doubt raise the question: '*What* women's humour?' For it was a commonplace well into the last century that women *have* no sense of humour. According to one American researcher, such influential thinkers as Schopenhauer, Bergson and Freud held this view.[1] Even as recently as 1976 J. B. Priestley, when talking about such an obvious exception to this generalisation as Jane Austen, dismissed her humour as 'feminine small potatoes'.[2]

At the present time one need hardly argue as to the existence of a sense of humour in the female sex, yet it must be acknowledged that in the established canon of a century ago, one finds no tradition of women's humour. Even in England and America, where much energy in recent years has been expended into putting together anthologies of women's comic writings, scholars note their absence, or at best their invisibility, in earlier periods.[3] Various reasons are given for the uncommonness of women's humour, of which I will mention a couple of the main ones. It is said, first of all, that humour implies the superiority of the story-teller to the butt of his or her jokes. It is an instrument of power and authority, and therefore has been largely reserved for men. As the psychologist Paul McGhee asserts: 'Because of the power associated with the successful use of humour, humour initiation has become associated with other traditionally masculine characteristics, such as aggression, dominance, and assertiveness. For a female to develop into a clown or joker, then, she must violate the behavioural pattern normally reserved for women.'[4] A related reason for the dearth of feminine humour is that women are trained to be lady-like and to remain in the private realm. Women could not be physical comics, could not be bawdy, obscene.[5] Therefore, even when feminine humour exists, it tends to be mild, gentle, having to do with little domestic mishaps rather than the large social and political matters, reserved for authoritative male humorists.

These reasons, especially the authoritative voice of the humorist, are hardly unassailable. They do not, after all, apply to a major subdivision of humour: that of the underdog or the outsider, which includes the humour of ethnic and racial minorities. Nancy Walker explains such 'minority humour' as 'a common device for creating solidarity among members of minority groups: laughing at the oppressors minimises their authority, and the ability to make fun of one's own oppression provides a psychic distance from it.'[6] The question then is why women, as traditional underdogs, did not develop an analogous tradition. One possible answer (as Walker in part suggests) is that women were not outsiders, but excessively insiders, enclosed within the family, dependent on men, limited by strict rules of comportment.[7] It has been proposed, in fact, that it is precisely when women achieve the status of outsiders – when the traditional relations of the sexes are changing and women are gaining independence and standing outside the home – that feminine humour with some bite in it emerges.[8] Such periods would include turn-of-the-century Russia, a time when an active women's rights movement arose; when more and more women were foregoing marriage for higher education and paid employment; when divorce laws were liberalised. It was a time, moreover, when the amoral aestheticism and decadence so widespread both in elite culture and in such popular literary works as Artsybashev's *Sanin* and Verbitskaia's *Keys to Happiness* much changed the traditional image of pure and demure womanhood.[9]

It was precisely within this period that Nadezhda Aleksandrovna Teffi became both an independent woman and a professional writer. Teffi, whose real name was Nadezhda Lokhvitskaia, was born in 1872 into a distinguished St. Petersburg family. Her father was the well-known jurist, professor, and raconteur, Aleksandr Lokhvitsky, while her older sister, Mirra Lokhvitskaia, was a celebrated poet at the turn of the century. In around 1890 Teffi married a Polish lawyer, Wladyslaw Buczynski, with whom she lived in the provinces for about a decade. Apparently unable to endure her morose husband, she left him around 1900 to pursue a literary career in St. Petersburg. As Teffi explained in a letter to her daughter almost fifty years later, 'circumstances drove me from home, where, had I remained, I would have perished.'[10]

Teffi wrote a few short comic works early in her career centering upon women's issues, most notably the one-act plays, 'The Woman Question' (1907) and 'The Male Congress' (1909). The humour of 'The Woman Question,' apparently Teffi's first staged play and the best known of her works on feminist issues, is based upon a reversal of roles. At first the eighteen-year-old heroine, Katia, speaks out not merely for the equality, but for the dominance of women over men. She declares that she will not marry her fiancé until she's ready to take control: 'I'll finish my studies, become a doctor, then I myself will take him for my bride [*na nem zhenius*]. Only he mustn't dare to do anything. Only housework.'[11] She then falls asleep and dreams that roles are indeed reversed. It turns out, however, that once women have power they behave exactly like men. When she wakes up, Katia cries out to her father: 'I'm overjoyed! Papa dear, you know, we're also good-for-nothings [*driani*]!' Since this is the case, she concludes, she can now in good conscience marry her fiancé.[12] Thus 'The Woman Question,' while showing Teffi's awareness of women's issues, indicates the limitation of her feminism.

'The Male Congress', produced in 1909 is, judging by the date, a response to the First All-Russian Women's Congress of 1908.[13] The participants in the men's gathering are against women's equality and for the usual reasons: woman's proper role as male adornment ('I love woman, *une charmeuse*, and you know, *frou-frou*'); her mental inferiority ('Her brain has absolutely no convolutions'). At the end of the congress, however, they decide upon a compromise. While the women demand the same rights and responsibilities as men, they decide to go halfway: 'Let them take our responsibilities, but as for our rights, they can wait a little longer.'

These early examples notwithstanding, it is hard to characterise Teffi as a feminist writer. One reason, I think, is that to her sceptical eye any abstract ideology adhered to unbendingly leads to the ridiculous. Moreover, Katia's conclusion in 'The Woman Question' – that we are all 'good-for-nothing' – leads Teffi to explore the foibles both of men and women, although on the whole the latter are treated with greater sympathy. For these reasons it is more productive to examine not simply the feminist, but the feminine in Teffi's humour. I will concentrate on the two aspects of humour mentioned earlier, one generally associated with men – the authoritative voice – and the other with women – the domestic and what might in Teffi's work be called the post-domestic. I will be dealing only with her early, pre-émigré work, since I am interested here more in the genesis than the total body of her humour.

I AUTHORITY

In her analysis of Jane Austen's comedy, Rachel M. Brownstein asserts that Austen achieves the requisite authority by utilising her class position. By adopting 'the enthroned image of The Proper Lady,' she exercises 'ladylike authority in ladylike language.'[14] Teffi too very much enjoys such authority over her comic world. From her Olympian heights as educated and witty Petersburg lady she regards with condescending amusement – albeit not without self-irony – the foibles of both sexes at various levels of society. This is apparent in her lexicon, where she often plays upon the disparity between her lower-class or less-cultivated subjects and the ladylike style of her narrator. Thus, in 'The Merry Party,' one of Teffi's earliest stories, she describes the attire of a servant boy dressed up for a party: 'His blond hair glistened with oil; a bright pink moiré bow shone in beauty [*krasuetsia*] from under the collar of his sky-blue satin shirt, and this combination of colours in the taste of Madame de Pompadour imparted an incredibly stupid look to his fat, whiskerless, and browless face.'[15]

Here the incongruous appearance of Mme de Pompadour in a description of a peasant lad – as well as the ironical 'shone in beauty' and the categorical, dismissive judgment at the end – create a sharp distinction between narrator and subject and establishes the former's disdainful sense of superiority. A ladylike condescension is characteristic of many of Teffi's stories set in a lower or middle class milieu. In 'The Resort,' for example, she juxtaposes the conventionally beautiful (flowers) and the banal (fish), thus undercutting the desire of the hero, a druggist's assistant, for a more exalted life: 'The local fishermen brought the flowers right on their boats, together with the fish, and along the way these gifts of nature cordially exchanged aromas. Therefore the restaurant of the hotel [*kurgauz*] frequently served pike that smelled of gillyflower, while the pink carnation on the druggist's breast was redolent of herring [*salakoi*].'[16] (Note here also the ladylike lexicon: 'cordially exchanged aromas' [*liubezno obmenivalis' aromatami*]; 'was redolent of' [*blagoukhala*].)

Teffi's authoritative tone allows her to put down not only her class inferiors, but also those on her own level. A genre she practices often, which raises this authoritativeness to the highest level, is what can be called the pseudo-scientific essay. She here adopts a traditionally masculine form, but puts it to subversive use. And this is where the category of *feminine* humour comes in, for the verities she expounds generally overturn those established by the masculine world.

A good illustration is the sketch, 'Fools'. There the narrator rejects the accepted idea that a fool is simply a stupid or senseless person. On the contrary, she asserts, fools are characterised by their logicality and consistency: 'A real total fool [*kruglyi durak*] can be identified, first of all, by his extreme and absolutely unshakable seriousness. The most intelligent person can be frivolous and act thoughtlessly – a fool constantly discusses everything and, having discussed it, acts accordingly and, having acted, knows why he did precisely this thing and not another.'[17] Such fools usually have a respected position in life: 'The fool's entire behaviour, just like his appearance, is so staid, serious, and imposing that he is received everywhere with respect. People gladly choose him as chairman of various societies, as representative of certain interests. Because the fool is proper.'[18]

Thus, serious and logical men, entrusted with authority, are in Teffi's world not the crown of human development, but are utter fools. By implication the supposed female weaknesses – frivolity, illogicality, emotionality – become strengths. A justification of sorts for rejecting the path of reason and logic appears in another sketch, 'Causes and Effects.' Here Teffi expresses her disagreement with the assertion that people should be taught to think logically, since nowadays there is absolutely no relation between cause and effect. Therefore she advises her readers to act contrary to all the truisms advising caution and prudence:

> ... I sternly instruct you:
> Always cut [the cloth] without measuring a single time, instead of the usual seven.
> Always answer without thinking.
> Never look where you're going.
> Well, Godspeed! Let's begin![19]

Thus Teffi does not overthrow female stereotypes; rather she suggests – a view characteristic of the Silver Age of which she was a part – that women's putatively irrational nature is more in touch with the reality of the world than man's reasonableness.

2 THE DOMESTIC AND POST-DOMESTIC

Teffi is not a domestic humorist in the Anglo-American sense of the term; the minutiae of housework and child-rearing are rarely the object of her laughter. Indeed, early in her career – during and following the 1905 Revolution – she entered the comic world traditionally reserved for men, writing a good deal of political satire.[20] Nevertheless in a sense she does remain a domestic writer, since most of her stories, especially in her earlier collections, take place in the home, their subject family (usually conjugal) relations. In contrast to most women's domestic comedy, however, Teffi's adopts the point of view of the outsider, who looks sardonically upon spousal relations. Typically in her works relations between husband and wife are marked by mutual hostility or indifference and, as a corollary, by sexual deception. Many are the husbands who claim to have an evening business meeting, but are betrayed by a box of candies or a pink ribbon falling out of their briefcases. And no fewer are the wives talking endlessly and foolishly about how irresistible they are to some Pavel Andreich or Andrei Pavlych. To be sure, such themes as adultery, cuckoldry, flirtations are common fare in comic literature, but in Teffi such stories taken in the aggregate are more than the usual naughty fun; rather, they produce an impression of the fragility of the very institution of marriage.

One good example is the story, 'The Brooch,' where a cheap pin breaks up four relationships: between husband and wife, husband and lover, wife and lover, and maid and fiancé. As the wife concludes: 'We lived so well, everything was comfy-cosy [*shito-kryto*] and life was full. And then this damned brooch descended on us from out of nowhere and just like a key it opened everything. Now I don't have either my husband or Chibisov. And Fenka's fiancé has left her. And what's the reason for it all? How can it all be made cosy again? What can be done [*kak byt*]?'[21]

In search of an answer to this question – 'What can be done' when life has been drained of meaning and happiness – many of Teffi's characters turn to fashion. Yury Lotman describes fashion as 'the continuous process of transforming the insignificant into the significant.'[22] This very much defines its function in Teffi. Although the comedy of fashion was certainly not new at the beginning of the twentieth century, style came to the fore at that time for reasons both artistic and commercial. On the one hand, the aesthetic movement, which championed turning one's life into a work of art, led to highly individualised, eccentric modes of dress. On the other, the commercialisation of Russian life, the rise of the department store, the mass production of clothes, made fashion a broad preoccupation in society.[23]

Both of these are reflected in Teffi's stories. Thus, the sketch 'In Stores' relates how all eventualities in a woman's life require a special fashion statement to give them meaning:

> The kinds of things that can happen! For example, an outing in a boat with your husband and children requires a grayish dress and high-button shoes.
>
> The same outing, but without your husband and children, requires instead a low-cut white dress and fishnet stockings.
>
> One must weigh everything, consider everything, find and buy everything.[24]

Cosmetics also promise to transform a middle-aged matron into a seductive and fascinating creature, to make her look not only younger and more beautiful, but also more interesting. There is, for example, the Krasotin Powder of 'The Beauty Factory', 'which will impart instant intellectuality to your features', and the 'cornflower water, which lends expression to your eyes'.[25] Men too are caught up in this need for aesthetic transformation. An extreme example is the landowner hero of 'Without Style', who in his search for style puts on his wife's green housecoat, rings on his toes, a watch on his forehead, and loftily addresses the astounded servant boy: 'Swain! . . . Bring me an assuaging potion!' ('*Otrok! . . . Prinesi utoliaushchee pitie!*')[26]

Sometimes in the hierarchy of values style is placed even higher than the traditional foundation of feminine life, marriage. As the narrator of 'Gaiety' declares: 'Well, my dear, a husband isn't a hat. Once you've bought a hat you have to drag around in it for the entire season. But if you're no longer fond of your husband, who can stop you from getting a divorce?'[27] In 'Life and a Collar' an article of apparel actually destroys a marriage. Olechka, the heroine, a shy woman totally devoted to her husband, purchases a lady's collar at the St. Petersburg shopping arcade, Gostinyi dvor, and it completely transforms her: 'She began to lead a strange life. Not her own. A collarly [*vorotnichkovuiu*] life.'[28] She bobs her hair, begins to smoke, flirts with another man. Things come to such a pass that her husband leaves her. A little later the collar is lost in the laundry and Olechka, who now has to work in a bank, returns to her former meek self. Indeed she is so modest that she blushes even at the word *omnibus* because it sounds like *obnimus'* (I will embrace).[29]

The plight of Olechka at the end of 'Life and a Collar' brings us to the question of how the ever-increasing number of single women in early twentieth-century Russia fare in Teffi's works. If fashion is an essential corrective for the married, one would think it all the more indispensable for women who have to make their own way in the world. Teffi herself made full use of the 'fashion defence' by creating and maintaining an image – or various images – to survive and prosper in the treacherous wilds of the St. Petersburg literary and journalistic life. She could appear as an elegant, if somewhat extravagant, Petersburg lady, performing her songs at the famous artistic cabaret, The Stray Dog, dressed in a black velvet dress with a red fox boa.[30] Or she could indulge, like the hero of 'Without Style', in the passion for outrageous costume, as she recollects in her memoir of Zinaida Gippius: 'And in my day I wore a watch on my leg and instead of a lorgnette a flat amethyst.'[31]

The Teffi character who succeeds best in manipulating those around her by creating a striking persona is the title character of 'The Demonic Woman.' As the opening of the story asserts, she is distinguished primarily by 'her manner of dress': her 'black velvet cassock, the chain on her forehead, the bracelet on her leg, . . . and the portrait of Oscar Wilde on her left garter.'[32] She is an excellent example of how style changes the insignificant into the significant. This is how she asks for herring and onion:

> 'Herring? Yes, yes, give me herring. I want to eat herring, I want to, I want to. Is that onion? Yes, yes, give me some onion . . . I want to eat, I want banality, quickly . . . more . . . more, look everyone. . . I am eating herring!'
>
> In essence, what happened?
>
> Her appetite was simply acting up, and she felt like having a little something salty. But what an effect!
>
> 'Did you hear? Did you hear?'
>
> 'She mustn't be left alone tonight.'
>
> '?'[33]

If Teffi herself and her demonic woman are masters at the fashion defence, however, most of her single women fail at the game. Her portrayals of vulnerable solitary women, indeed, form one category where the comic tone falters or is absent altogether. The plight of poor office girls provides the theme for two of Teffi's earliest serious stories, 'The Princess's Ruby' and 'Duck-Billed Platypus,' published in the magazine *Niva* in 1905.[34] In the former, an article of adornment –

the ruby of the title – plays a pivotal role. It is the only beautiful thing that the poor heroine has left from her happy upper-class childhood, when she was called Princess. When the ruby disappears she perishes.

A later story where the vulnerability of the poor office girl is tied to the failure of the fashion defence is 'Whitsunday'. The heroine, Lizaveta Nikolaevna, 'who bears the magnificent title of junior subclerk [*mladshei podbaryshni*] to the assistant to the junior secretary',[35] is expecting a gentleman caller for the holiday. She puts on a new white muslin dress with a bunch of forget-me-nots at the waist and, since she doesn't own a mirror large enough to see how she looks, is very pleased with her appearance. But then she catches sight of her reflection in a window: 'Her figure turned out to be fat, while the little bouquet was a small, dirty lump, not even blue, since the forget-me-nots had crumpled. In a word, there was nothing to hope for.'[36] And indeed the male guest does not appear and, to add to the injury, sends a letter asking to borrow five rubles.

The few professional women who appear in Teffi's stories hardly fare better than the pathetic office girls. One example is the middle-aged doctor and lecturer Migulina in 'The Rosy Student'. Despite her accomplishments and status, Migulina is vulnerable to the mockery of the student of the title. This is in part because of certain verbal idiosyncrasies (such as addressing even a single interlocutor as 'ladies and gentlemen' [*gospoda*]),[37] but primarily due to her unprepossessing appearance, unenhanced by cosmetic camouflage. The rosy student begins to flirt with her, explaining to his aesthete friends: '. . . perhaps I am too refined, but I am attracted by this woman's unhatched [*neotshelushennyi*] Eros' (105). As he continues to court Migulina, she pays more and more attention to her appearance, with predictably ridiculous results. The story reaches its dénouement when she 'coloured her lips with something, probably wishing to redden them, but for some reason they came out lilac' (107). At this point the student ends the flirtation, declaring that he has fulfilled his mission: 'I have awakened the eternal feminine in her . . . I have hatched her Eros' (107). At the story's end he judges his prank immensely funny: 'How I am to blame if life is such a funny thing [*takaia smeshnaia shtuka*] ?!' (108).

The student's merriment raises important questions about Teffi's humour and, perhaps, about women's humour in general. For while in many of her pseudo-scientific sketches she uses the authoritative voice to subvert male authority, in the portrayal of such butts of traditional male humour as Migulina (a variant of the stock comic type, the ridiculous old maid), her laughter is typically muted by pathos. The narrator in 'The Rosy Student' is, to be sure, complicit to some degree in her hero's laughter, yet as the story progresses their perspectives diverge. The narrator does not simply continue to join in the student's laughter; she also records Migulina's reactions to it, utilising such adjectives and adverbs as 'amazed and bewildered,' 'frightened' (*udivlennaia i rasteriannaia*, 106; *ispuganno*, 107), and such verbs as 'was embarrassed,' 'was disconcerted,' 'felt shy' (*smutilas', skonfuziias'*, 106; *stesnialas'*, 107). And most significantly Teffi gives Migulina the last word – a repetition of the student's comment, but with the meaning reversed when repeated by her lilac lips: '"Yes . . . yes . . . a funny thing, ladies and gentlemen . . ." her lilac lips replied in a trembling smile' (108).

Concluding her comic stories in a minor key is characteristic of Teffi. As Zoshchenko wrote in an essay on her: 'And try to retell any, even her funniest story, and, truly, it will turn out not at all funny. It will be absurd and, perhaps, tragic as well.'[38] It has been said that in general 'women write comedies without "happy endings".'[39] This is certainly true of Teffi, although it is questionable whether this is an exclusive trait of women's humour. There is much Russian male comedy, after all – that of Gogol and Chekhov, for instance – without happy endings (hence the old cliché 'laughter through tears'). What might be relevant here is Virginia Woolf's observation (following Coleridge) that 'a great mind is androgynous'. For a writer, she adds: 'It is fatal to be a man or woman pure and simple; one must be woman-manly or man-womanly.'[40] In this sense one might conclude that the best Russian humorists – and perhaps all outstanding humorists – partake of women's humour.

8

TWO FACETS OF COMEDIC SPACE IN RUSSIAN LITERATURE OF THE MODERN PERIOD

Holy foolishness and buffoonery

IVAN ESAULOV

In recent Russian literature there is a name that, as it were, symbolises comedic deviancy: 'V. Erofeev'. At the same time this name also offers a perfect illustration of the theme of this article. In fact it embodies two comedic poles of Russian literature both in its unity, and at the same time also by its splitting into two: the late Venechka Erofeev, noted author of the cult text *Moskva-Petushki*, was drawn towards holy foolishness in his work, while another writer, Viktor Erofeev, still alive, is fully enrolled in the ranks of the buffoons.

A particular interest in these two facets of comedic space in Russian literature can be seen in recent works by Western scholars: the German researcher Hans Günther raises the question of the place of holy foolishness in the works of Andrei Platonov,[1] while the British academic Lesley Milne writes about the tradition of buffoonery in the fiction of Mikhail Bulgakov.[2] In the framework of the current article I will attempt to compare these two types of cultural deviancy which appear in Russian literature. My work makes no claim to be an exhaustive examination of the literary (not to speak of the cultural) material involved; however, I will try to navigate some of the problems of comedic space in Russian culture.

Holy foolishness and buffoonery are close but in no way coinciding spheres of deviant behaviour. It is precisely by virtue of their deviancy that they can be seen as parodies of the dominant norms of one cultural system or another. Moreover, it is incorrect to think of holy foolishness and buffoonery as phenomena that are not systemic. It is rather the case that they are necessary subdominant forms of various types of cultures.

Buffoonery, as is well known, is not only an indispensable attribute of Carnival, but can also be seen as its quintessence (however carnival culture is interpreted – in the spirit of Mikhail Bakhtin, Aron Gurevich or D.-R. Moser).[3] Comedic culture is the element for buffoonery, whether it is understood broadly in the Bakhtinian sense or narrowly as with Moser.

Holy foolishness is similarly part of comedic culture, although it is only 'comic' from the external point of view. People of course laugh at the holy fool, but only those who are dull-witted and do not understand the innermost meaning of holy foolishness.[4]

Dmitry Likhachev and Aleksandr Panchenko rightly note the distinctive functions of laughter. If the jester-buffoon can cure a vice through laughter, then the main task of the holy fool is the opposite – to provoke weeping for the laughably absurd. The semantics of holy foolishness, as Panchenko shows, consist of ascetic self-annihilation, and faked madness.[5] It is a voluntarily assumed act of Christian heroism.[6] This originates in a literal interpretation of the words of the Apostle Paul, 'We are all fools for Christ's sake' (I Corinthians 4.10). Moreover, it is precisely the life full of voluntary suffering which also gives the holy fool the right to violate hierarchies and parody all the fixed norms of earthly life as untruths. Boris Uspensky characterises the holy fool's way of life as 'anti-behaviour'. We should also note that this research, correctly identifying the didactic nature of the holy fool's 'anti-behaviour', even suggests that the meaning of parody itself is in principle not applicable to the characteristics of the holy fool.[7] It seems to us nevertheless that it is quite correct to look at holy foolishness as an aspect of parody – although, it is true, of a very specific type.

Mikhail Bakhtin, of course, wrote of the carnivalistic character of parody. 'Parodisation is the creation of a dethroning double, it is a 'world turned inside out'.'[8] Within its limits parody is the profanation of *everything* sacred and everything serious; 'everything has its own parody, that is, its comedic aspect'.[9] In the abolition of hierarchies, the assumption of free and familiar contact (risqué gesticulations and indecent language), holy foolishness and buffoonery are allied by their eccentricity.

However, there is a clear difference between the two. The holy fool in no way repudiates and profanes everything, but only earthly hierarchies and the earthly world order in general. Hereby he can attain honour in the heavenly kingdom. He often does not make merriment, but is subjected to beatings and deprivations – and secretly prays for his persecutors.

In psychoanalytic terms, to all appearances, the buffoon can be understood through the prism of *sadism*. The *malicious*, often physically inferior fool is a typical figure, and it is no accident that by municipal law the fool was on the same footing as the executioner. This, of course, in no way excludes also the figure at the opposite end of the spectrum, the wise and noble buffoon.[10] The model of cultural behaviour of holy fool meanwhile gravitates more towards *masochism*, although the holy fool suffers not for himself, but 'for the sake of Christ'. In other words, he relates his model of behaviour to another model, to another, sacred text, which he imitates, for all his *external insanity.* Again this does not exclude another type of holy fool, who in Russia has been given the name the 'pseudo-holy fool'. In both cases, looking at holy foolishness and buffoonery, we will see henceforth speak of *invariant* types and moreover how they in this way appear specifically in *Russian* comedic space and mass consciousness.[11] So if in relation to the earthly, sinful world we may speak of parodisation on the part of the holy fool, then in relation to the behaviour of Christ we may speak of a kind of sacred plagiarism, or mimesis.

It should also be noted that there are elements of *mystification* in the social conduct of the holy fool. As is well known, they often went about naked. For the majority of spectators this nakedness was a sign of sinful folly, base carnality and in general temptation.[12] This is the reason why holy fools were so often beaten and mocked. Demons are, for example, often depicted unclothed on icons. But behind this 'disguising', so to speak, as the devil, lies the very mystification. For the holy fool nakedness is not a mask (as it is in carnival activity for the buffoon), but a disdain for the flesh and for adornments; nakedness is a symbol of an open soul.[13] The holy fool and the buffoon's relations to the body are diametrically opposed.

However, the main difference consists in the *functionality* of the figure of the buffoon and the *substantiality* of the holy fool. If carnival, according to Bakhtin, 'celebrates the change itself, the very process of change, and not what is being changed',[14] and the buffoon therefore easily plays with different masks, then the holy fool in all his conduct confirms a higher substantiality – God's will. One could say that the buffoon plays (or is forced to play) according to quite regular *rules* fixed by one cultural paradigm or another. Therefore he is to a much greater extent dependent on the cultural systems he parodies than the holy fool, and is more specifically a participant in the system.[15] But the holy fool, being privy to the substantiality of a 'higher law' has the opportunity just to ignore the rules of the earthly world order; his is a life 'without rules'. To put it another way, the buffoon in all events is determined by the sphere of the *Law* – even when he parodies it – and cannot exceed the degree of deviancy defined by the Law. The holy fool on the other hand strives towards another value – *Grace.* In Russian culture the correlation between holy foolishness and buffoonery is inscribed in the invariant opposition of the Law and Grace.[16]

In Russia holy foolishness and buffoonery correspond to different periods in different ways. The emergence of holy foolishness took place from the fifteenth century to the first half of the seventeenth century. The Orthodox East had little experience of holy fools before this stage. In general it should be emphasised that in Byzantium the spread of holy foolishness was limited. The phenomenon was likewise alien to the Roman Catholic world. It has been noted that Western travellers would write with great astonishment about the institution of holy foolishness in Russia.[17] Some of these holy fools, such as Mikhail Klopsko, Nikolai Kochanov, Vasily Blazhennyi and others, were subsequently canonised and accepted into the sainthood.

However, when all the holy fools allied themselves to the Old Believers at the time of the Russian Schism, the reforming patriarch Nikon attempted to eradicate holy foolishness as such, as a social institution, anticipating in this way future persecution by Peter the Great. Meanwhile buffoonery, as is well known, actively took root in the Russian cultural milieu in the Petrine period.

As a result of this process that began in Russian culture in the seventeenth century of encouraging one type of deviancy and restricting the other, two poles which differ in their cultural origins coexist: holy foolishness and buffoonery. We may thus speak of two types of parody and two variants of unofficial cultural behaviour, permeating every layer of Russian culture of the modern period. Of course, we have in mind not buffoonery and holy foolishness in their original sense, but precisely the different cultural traditions that actualise the 'memory' of these archetypes.

Examination of literary texts of the modern period from this angle can sometimes lead to unexpected results. For example, in Dostoevsky's *Brothers Karamazov*, we can note the concealed authorial linkages between the most repellent and most sublime characters, between Smerdiakov and the spiritual adviser Zosima, if only through the common thread of *stinking*. The corpse of Zosima unexpectedly begins to stink after his death, as Smerdiakov's soul does in his life. However, the fact that Smerdiakov was born to a holy fool is also significant. The image of the almost saintly Zosima and the stinking holy fool correspond within the limits of the same cultural system. Meanwhile Fedor Pavlovich Karamazov as a buffoon, but not a holy fool, intrudes into the system and becomes a cause of its fluctuation. Another, very interesting interpretation of this interrelation is suggested in the work of Lena Szilard.[18] Some of Dostoevsky's works (for example, *The Idiot*, *The Devils*) present a field of *battle* for holy fools and buffoons, and what is more, holy foolishness *always* has positive authorial connotations, while buffoonery has negative ones. We can say that, in *The Devils*, devilry simultaneously turns out also to be buffoonery, while in *The Idiot* in the very opening chapter the central character is defined as a holy fool.

The features of holy foolishness are revealed in Gogol's repudiation of his own literary activity and by his move to 'spiritual prose'. The limited receptivity to this prose is also significant: Gogol's book *Selected Passages from Correspondence with Friends* was accepted neither by the orthodox clergy nor by worldly critics. Characteristic *rejection* in print of Gogol's ideas was accompanied by equally characteristic rumours of his *madness*. Precisely these features are frequently connected to holy fools.

We should also recall the similar repudiation of his artistic texts as 'lies' on the part of Lev Tolstoi. His reproaches to the evil into which the world had plunged, his appeals to non-resistance, his attempts to escape property and refusal of all royalties, his violation of church hierarchies (as he stated, 'for the sake of Christ'), and, finally, his flight from home: this is practically the canonical path of the holy fool.

In Soviet culture two variants of cultural tradition can also be traced. So-called 'Soviet satire' (for example the works of Ilia Ilf and Evgeny Petrov) is located almost entirely within the bounds of the buffoonish side of this tradition. *The Twelve Chairs* is constructed around the adventure-buffoonish 'disguising' of the hero, while each of his 'masks' has a purely functional purpose.

When Viktor Shklovsky at the end of the story 'Zoo, or Not-love Letters' wrote an 'application to the All-Russian Central Executive Committee of the USSR' with a request to allow him to return from Berlin to Soviet Russia, this appeal had a purely buffoonish character. The letter concluded with the following request: 'Allow me into Russia with all my artless baggage: six shirts (three on me, three in the laundry), a pair of brown boots that have been cleaned with black polish by mistake, and old blue trousers which I have tried in vain to press into a crease'.[19] The 'artless' baggage, as the author called it, is the baggage of the clown-buffoon, whose 'art' lies precisely in the fact that in this letter the buffoonish enumeration of his luggage negotiates the terms of the agreement between the victorious government power and the defeated individual ('I raise my hands in surrender').[20] The main point is to establish a free and familiar contact with the lord and master. This is exactly the freedom of the buffoon.

At the same time, by no means all writers can comply in full, or to any extent, with buffoonish liberty of this sort. In my view, Mikhail Bulgakov is one such example. I consider Lesley Milne's analysis of the work of Mikhail Bulgakov in the context of the European tradition of buffoonery to be very competent and interesting. However, I would like, at the same time, to draw attention to the fact that the supreme 'jester' in *The Master and Margarita* is, of course, not Behemoth the cat, but precisely the 'great mocker' Woland, the devil, that is. In the enigmatic denouement of Bulgakov's novel the Master is not granted 'light', for the further possible reason that this denouement may derive from the Orthodox apocrypha 'The Descent of the Virgin Mary into Hell', where God the Son does not grant forgiveness to sinners – even after the tears and prayers of the Virgin herself, but grants them peace (*pokoi*) from Maundy Thursday to Pentecost.[21] It is characteristic that this is precisely an apocryphal text, that is to say a deviant work in relation to the fundamental corpus of Christian texts; but this is precisely the kind of deviancy that, like holy foolishness, is indissolubly linked to the vector of Orthodox culture and – for all its deviancy – is defined by it.

What does it mean, staying within the boundaries of the Orthodox binary opposition of heaven and hell, to *forgive* sinners? To lead them out of hell into heaven, avoiding the Purgatory that does not exist in Orthodox theology. Woland's question, 'Why don't you take him [the Master – I.E.] with you into the light?'[22] bears witness precisely to the hypothetical possibility of full forgiveness, analogous to the light, which also in Bulgakov has ontological status. 'With you into the light' has the same meaning, of course, as heavenly bliss, if we recall the final return of Woland to the diametrically opposite spiritual space: 'the black Woland dived into the abyss'.[23] In general it is worth mentioning that the conception of the correlation of light and darkness not only for the author, but for Woland too, reveals a kinship with the Orthodox tradition: the dark does not have ontological status; it appears only as an absence of light; it is, in the literal sense, shadow.[24] Of course, 'the spirit of evil and sovereign of shadows' defends the shadows in his dispute with Matthew Levi ('What would the earth look like, if shadows disappeared from it?'),[25] but the main point is that he too appears to agree with his 'shadow' status.

The peace that Bulgakov's Master receives can of course be interpreted as the result of Western influence, as a kind of variety of Catholic Purgatory. But another interpretation is also possible, originating in the ancient Russian apocryphal tradition, to which I drew attention above. At least, the phrase that Bulgakov's Matthew Levi uses about the Master – 'He does not deserve light. He deserves peace' – can be interpreted not in a ternary system (as something halfway between light and dark), but as an artistic assimilation and working out in detail of that *peace* granted to the sinners in the Orthodox apocryphal tradition. The sinners who find themselves not in a 'halfway' position between Heaven and Hell, but still continuing to remain in Hell, outside the light, are granted peace as a deliverance from unbearable torment.

Therefore the request 'to take the Master with you and reward him with peace' is carried out precisely by the 'evil spirit' Woland. Deliverance from torment is something quite different from heavenly bliss. It would seem that in this projection the Master's lack of memory (as freedom from torment, but not as an ideal condition) becomes a little more understandable than in any other cultural tradition: 'The Master's anxious, needled memory began to fade.'[26] It differs from the Apocyrpha in that it is not the Virgin Mary who intercedes for the sinners, but Matthew Levi, acting as a messenger of God. And he addresses his request to the 'evil spirit' precisely because the 'eternal home' of the Master and Margarita is completely within the confines of hell, in Woland's jurisdiction, so to speak. I do not wish to cast doubt on the connection of Bulgakov's work to the Western tradition of buffoonery; on the contrary, Lesley Milne has already convincingly proved this. I merely wish to emphasise that by using this tradition, Bulgakov at the same time transforms it most powerfully. In any case, the way that buffoonery is so firmly attached to the infernal forces, the powers of evil, in Bulgakov's novel is very significant (whatever sympathies many readers may feel for 'Woland's retinue'). The buffoon Koroviev-Fagot is compelled to wear a buffoonish mask because 'he once made an unfortunate joke' about light and darkness.[27] Buffoonery thus enters the sphere of unfreedom, and the comic behaviour of the former knight 'with the gloomy and never smiling face' is prescribed by his infernal master and is in no way chosen by himself: 'And after that the knight *had to* go on joking a bit longer and more than he supposed.' [My italics. – I.E]. Woland's other jester, Behemoth, once outside the bounds of the earth, turns out to be 'a slim youth, a demon-page, the best jester the world has ever seen.' But this 'best jester' is none the less a demon. Furthermore in the narrative structure of the text he stands alongside the other demon, Azazello, who is directly defined as 'a killer-demon'. Thus the leitmotif of buffoonery in Bulgakov's novel becomes increasingly complex.

The line of holy foolishness in the comedic space of Soviet literature can be traced, for example, in Nikolai Kliuev's lyric poetry or in Andrei Platonov's work (a theme investigated in the article by Hans Günther mentioned above).

Lena Szilard in her work focuses the analysis on Dostoevsky's *The Devils* and Andrei Belyi's *Petersburg.* At the same time she also points to more general cultural idea-clusters. In particular she emphasises that 'the problem of retreat into holy foolishness as a problem of life appears again in new and acute forms at the very beginning of the twentieth century.'[28] Thus, for Andrei Bely, according to Szilard, 'the true path lay not in the enactment of holy foolishness in the space of real life, and not in its deployment as an artistic theme; the natural and necessary realisation of this form of behaviour lay in the area of *grammatical space*'.[29] [Lena Szilard's italics – I.E.] In my view, however, the question of holy foolishness (and not buffoonery) as the 'mental foundation of the narrative'[30] as concerns the prose of Andrei Belyi is not fully proven by Szilard. None the less, the attempt itself to delimit holy foolishness and buffoonery as cultural codes in concrete examples of artistic texts (sketched out only briefly in Szilard's work) does deserve every attention.

Even scholarly discourse can sometimes yield to this sort of systematisation. Thus not only Aleksei Losev's artistic prose but also some passages of his academic writings are distinctly 'holy foolish' in character. Let us take, for example, *The Dialectic of Myth* (*Dialektika mifa*, 1930).

> Not only schoolchildren but all the respected scholars do not notice that their world of physics and astronomy is a pretty boring, sometimes repulsive and sometimes simply mad mirage, that same hole at the back of beyond that we can still find love and respect for all the same. But I, for my sins, can never get my mind round the idea that the earth rotates and orbits. How can that be happening? I've read the textbooks, at one point I

> wanted to be an astronomer, I even married one. But I still can't convince myself that the earth is in motion and there is no sky. You read about pendulums of some sort or another and displacements from something to somewhere, parallaxes or whatever... I'm not convinced. It's downright thin as an explanation. We're talking here about the whole earth, and you're rocking some pendulums or other at me. But the main thing is, it's all so uncomfortable, so alien, nasty, cruel. There I was on the earth, under my native sky, hearing about a world 'that also is stablished, that it cannot be moved'[31] And suddenly none of it exists: not the earth, or the sky, or the 'cannot be moved'. You've been thrown out on your ear into some empty abyss, and sent on your way with a curse. 'That's your native land – spit on it and smear it out!' Reading astronomy textbooks I feel that someone has taken a stick to drive me out of my own home and is spitting in my face. And what have I done to deserve it?[32]

For the full picture, let it be noted that in this same passage of Losev's text, with its talk of holes, sticks, marrying astronomers, being spat at and, of course, the immobile and definitely not rotating planet Earth, there is a completely neutral academic statement: 'Newton's mechanics are built on the hypothesis of a homogeneous and infinite space.' I shall cite three other examples of Losev's holy foolishness, which have a particularly shocking ring against the background of his argument, which otherwise on the whole observes the academic conventions:

> As tobacco is incense to Satan, so kerosene is sauce for the demons. Eau-de-cologne in general exists only for hairdressers and salesmen, and maybe for fashionable archdeacons. Only someone who has abandoned the true faith can pray with a stearin candle in his hands and smelling of eau-de-cologne. This is heresy in the full sense of the word, and such impostors should be anathematised.[33]

> You will probably also say that the heart cannot sink into the boots. As far as I am concerned, then – alas – I have to say that my heart has sunk into my boots too many times for me to be able to treat this as a metaphor or a lie. I really do sometimes feel my heart in my boots. I even know what paths through the organism it takes to get there. If you don't understand this, there's nothing I can do about it. Not everyone is equally able to understand everything. [34]

> That's enough of your lecherous language. You go on and on about 'subjectivism'... Such a refutation carries no weight at all. ... So what in nature is *objective* [Losev's italics. – I.E.]? Matter, movement, force, atoms and so forth? But why? Concepts of matter, movement, force and atoms change too, like all our subjective constructs. In different epochs they are completely different. So why do you not talk of subjectivism here, but when I start saying that nature is merry, mournful, sad, majestic etc., you suddenly accuse me of subjectivism? What happens here is that under all such 'objectivism' there lies your own doctrine, more precisely your metaphysical whims and all sorts of sympathies and antipathies. When someone is in love, they exalt the objectivity of the corresponding loved one. You are in love with an empty black hole, calling it 'the

> universe', studying it in your universities and worshipping it in your heathen temples. You live off the cold lechery of an ossified universal space and maim yourselves in your self-built black prison of nihilistic natural sciences. But I love the sky, its blue blueness, deep deepness, my very own native sky. And wisdom itself, Sophia, the Divine Wisdom has the same blue blueness, deep deepness, very own nativeness. But what's the point of my talking to you?[35]

It is particularly interesting that immediately after this holy-foolish tirade against the 'cold lechery' of university 'objectivists' who are in love with the 'black empty hole', Losev argues his case by referring to the (in this case similar) position of Vasily Rosanov. Thus it would appear that we can talk of a purely scholarly 'support by reference to predecessors in the field'. However, from the very first words of this citation it becomes clear that the support is primarily by reference to the tradition of holy foolishness in Russian literature. For what lines from Rozanov does Losev find so congenial? They are these:

> Does the sun care about the earth? Not from anything that we can see: it 'attracts it in direct proportion to the mass and in inverse proportion to the square of the distance'. Thus Copernicus's first answer about the sun and the earth was stupid. Simply stupid. He 'calculated'. But the 'count' when applied to a moral phenomenon is in my view simply stupid. It was this stupid answer by Copernicus to the moral question of the sun and the earth that began the vulgarisation of the planet and the voiding of the Heavens. 'Of course the earth does not have the sun's concern for it, but is only attracted according to the cube of the distance.' Makes you want to spit.[36]

It is significant that this purely holy-foolish 'Makes you want to spit' of Rozanov's is likewise quoted by Losev, and further more as a kind of last and decisive argument, in so far as what follows the 'spit' is a fully rational and logical philosophical disquisition beginning as a numbered section 2, and couched in completely neutral academic language: 'Secondly, in so far as history is a coming-into-being of facts that *are understood* [Losev's italics. – I.E.]...'[37]

It has to be emphasised that Aleksei Losev in all his works (especially those of the 1920s) was trying to lay the basis of a completely new and deeply serious model of the world, built on a Christian foundation and with links of inheritance to the Russian religious-philosophical thought of the twentieth century. However the form in which Losev's model of the world is affirmed, like the form of his polemic with the imposed 'materialist' ideology, follows precisely the holy-foolish tradition in Russian culture – if only because (although not only because!) another variant of opposition was not available to Losev. An open and 'serious', not comic, that is a purely academic form of polemic with Marxist-Leninist materialism was impossible in the USSR; the line of buffoonery was, however, unacceptable to Losev, who secretly became a monk in 1928. Losev's attitude to the carnival culture of the Renaissance (and likewise to Bakhtin's book on Rabelais) was unequivocally negative. In order to appreciate this one only has to leaf through his monograph, *Renaissance Aesthetics* (*Estetika Vozrozhdeniia*).

It is possible to single out a special 'third' line, in which one can see the combination (contamination) of holy foolishness and buffoonery. An interesting example of such a combination is Maksimilian Voloshin's collection of poems *The Deaf-mute Demons*, published in 1919.[38]

Three parts of the collection ('The Angel of Retribution', 'The Torches of Paris' and 'The Paths of Russia') are deliberately arranged by the author in that precise sequence. The author's position can be discerned in this construction: by moving away from the contemporary Russian catastrophe back to the time of the French Revolution, Voloshin demonstrates typological features of revolutionary violence that have clear demonic attributes, and the 'return' to Russia in the third part, creating the effect of an artistic cycle, is accompanied by a clear historical retrospection.

The 'voices' of the rebellious False Dmitri ('Dmitri the Emperor'), Stepan Razin ('Stenka's Judgement'), and the archpriest Avvakum (in the poem of the same name in the third part) do not appear and disappear episodically, but are the compositional elements of the whole cycle's lyric plot. These are the 'voices' of the executed sufferers, each of whom has his own *truth*, and their fates, according to Voloshin, are mysteriously linked with the fate of Russia.

Therefore the significance of the heroes' 'voices' cannot be reduced simply to one or other compositional function isolated within the framework of each separate poem. Thus the words of the archpriest Avvakum 'Satan asked God to give him bright Russia'(52) sound not only in the 'Avvakum' text of the collection's third part but also appear as an epigraph to the first part of *The Deaf-mute Demons*. One should note also the final identification by Voloshin's Avvakum of his true native land as the heavenly Jerusalem and not the earthly Russia. The hero experiences execution as return: 'I am to return home... Oh my dearest Christ! Back to you in heavenly Jerusalem!' (54)

All three parts are united by a bloody carnival ambivalence, very consonant with Aleksandr Blok's image of the universal conflagration in blood, demanding in addition God's blessing on this. The artistic world of the collection is saturated with phantasmagorical proximities of the demonic and divine, the profane and the sacral. Here not only are the demons the servants of God, without knowing it, and Satan in his turn can ask God to give him 'bright Russia', but also the martyr archpriest Avvakum, wishing to 'cast off' in his fiery boat for the heavenly Jerusalem, does not wait for the execution. He himself uses a candle to light the wattle of the hut in which he has been placed by his persecutors and thus, strictly speaking, commits suicide.

The severed head of Madame de Lamballe ? whose perspective sets the dominant point of view in the text that opens the middle part of the collection, calls herself 'the people's herald' when it is impaled by that same 'people' on a pike. Raised above the crowd on the pike, her head seems to dance 'at a ball in Versailles', while the 'bacchanalia' of the mob has a defiant sacral subtext: the bloody 'madness' of the people is called 'holy' (20) – and by their victim herself, as if satisfied with this, her last, 'dance'.

However the artistic logic of this particular type of ambivalence is explained also by another, holy-foolish, subtext which is immanent in Russian culture. According to this, sinful Russia, in order to be resurrected in the status of Holy Rus', has necessarily to pass through sufferings and – in the extreme case – through complete destruction, which is understood by no means metaphorically. Resurrection is, alas, impossible without previous death. This is perhaps the source of Voloshin's typically holy-foolish desire for sufferings and humiliations: 'I love you [Russia – *I.E.*] defeated,/ Desecrated and in the dust' (10); 'Send down fire, plague and scourge upon us, / From the Germans of the west and the Mongols of the east'; 'You will become a barren and trampled cornfield' (36). There is also the thirst for martyrdom, which for Voloshin has not only an ambivalent but also a clearly Christ-centric character. Avvakum is grateful to the Devil for 'martyr's blood' – 'You have thought well, Devil,/ And we gladly consent:/ To suffer sufferings for the sake of Christ' (53). Here of course it is possible to see only a formulaic and abstract mythopoetic ambivalence of Good and Evil. However I would like to stress that this desire for 'sufferings for the sake of Christ' and this at first sight insane gratitude to the Devil for humiliation and spilt blood reflects Voloshin's own holy-foolish vision of the world.

Resurrection is by no means a second Birth; it is not being born again. It is, on the contrary, salvation through passage into another (spiritual) dimension, into a qualitatively different realm. Therefore in Orthodox Russia the festival of Christ's Resurrection, Easter, was always experienced as the main church festival, not only in religious but also in cultural terms. Christmas, by contrast, was always celebrated much more modestly, in comparison with the West. Different concepts of humankind show through here. In one case the main event of human life is Birth. In the other, it is its future Resurrection. [39] In the example from Voloshin cited above, the move into another dimension (carrying with it an extremity of tension) is presented in holy-foolish terms: 'we are, you see, monsters for the sake of Christ' (51). It is precisely holy foolishness that Voloshin's Avvakum can use to justify the suicidal (self-willed) accelerated departure of his fiery 'boat', in the hope of a swift Resurrection.

In the poem that opens the third part of the collection and bears the characteristic title 'Holy Rus'', holy foolishness is, in the first place, directly equated to sainthood and, secondly, as represented by Voloshin, determines not just individual representatives (the holy fools themselves), but also the whole country in its entirety:

> Who am I to dare to cast a stone at you?
> Shall I cool the tempestuous flame of Holy Week?
> Shall I not bow my face down to you in the mud,
> Blessing the track of your bare foot,
> You, homeless, carousing, inebriated
> Rus', holy-foolish in Christ! (26)

The other side of the moral 'rebellion' of Voloshin's Avvakum and the artistic 'mutiny' of the author is the awareness of the metaphysical gap between the given features of the earthly here-and-now (changing 'masks' so easily that it is almost impossible to discern the true 'face') and the Divine providence that guides it. For Voloshin, in brief, the relationship between Holy Rus' and the real Russia is conceived not as a relationship of the ideal and its imperfect embodiment, but as something of a binary opposition.[40] For ideal, or Holy, Rus', to triumph and *reveal herself* (be resurrected), the logic of this position necessitates the destruction of the real Russia. But not only is there is no Resurrection without death, there is also no Resurrection without firm faith in the real possibility of this miracle. Faith in its turn is inconceivable without a strict and ontologically serious division between the saintly and the sinful. In the opposite case, the 'will to death' – 'Russia is finished' (13), 'Smoulder to ashes, Russia' (29) – becomes a carnival-buffoonish delusion, as Voloshin seems to understand when he writes 'the devilish round dance holds sway' (12).

Of course in the period when totalitarianism was coming into being, the deviancy of buffoonery and holy foolishness took on particular connotations. Both carnival buffoonery and serious-comic holy foolishness parodied the nature of the official Soviet world-order. (Of course, as is 'customary' for buffoons and holy fools, they often employed the clichés and stereotypes of the dominant culture, for example the use of Marxist terminology not only by writers but also by the Formalist critics, and by Losev, and Bakhtin.) But in the present chapter I wanted to emphasise that in some cases the parody has buffoonish attributes in its relationship to the authorities, in others it bears characteristics of holy-foolishness, and in yet others we are dealing with contamination of these two categories.

The present article only outlines the theoretical possibilities of such a demarcation, which are illustrated by almost arbitrarily chosen literary material. A systematic description of the interrelationships between holy foolishness and buffoonery in Russian literature of the last three centuries is the task of a separate large study.

Translated by Sarah Young and Lesley Milne

9

JOKERS, ROGUES AND INNOCENTS

Types of comic hero and author from Bulgakov to Pelevin

LESLEY MILNE

THE three lead words in the title of this essay are not so easy to translate directly into words of Russian origin. They present a variant on Bakhtin's triad of 'the worldwide images of the rogue, the clown and fool' (*plut, shut, durak* in the Russian original).[1] The variant of joker, rogue and innocent is, however, filtered through the medium of English language and culture. In his contribution to the present volume Ivan Esaulov, while accepting a general European context within which Russian literature can be analysed, stresses that there are also concepts that are specifically Russian, such as the tradition of the 'holy fool'. In turn, while fully accepting the need for sensitivity to what is 'native', we could argue that it is often illuminating to approach the literature of another culture 'from outside', which raises the whole question of the role of the 'foreign specialist' in literary scholarship. As foreigners we must concede that we do inevitably import experience from our own native cultural traditions into our examination of the literatures of other countries. Furthermore, our own native languages act as a kind of grid through which we perceive the world and categorise and conceptualise different phenomena. Often, however, this conceptual grid can successfully be translated into the foreign culture that is the object of study.[2]

In the triad of 'joker', 'rogue' and 'innocent', only 'the rogue' has a full equivalent in native Russian: *plut.* The rogue is indeed a universal character in both Eastern and Western European culture, with a literary genealogy that reaches back to antiquity and marked its first modern European flowering in the sixteenth century with the Spanish picaresque novel. In subsequent centuries the picaresque genre, based on the adventures of the rogue (*picaro*) was disseminated throughout European literatures, establishing itself firmly in each tradition. In Russian there is a native word for 'joker': *shutnik*, one who makes jokes. The word *shut* (Bakhtin's 'clown') incorporates the idea of court jester. My meaning here, however, is specifically that of the joker in the deck of cards, an English word imported (like much of sporting terminology) into many languages and in Russian rendered in transliteration as *dzhoker*. Although in many card-packs the joker is depicted in the jester's cap, he far outclasses the jester in the power hierarchy of the court, for he can out-trump all the kings, and the aces too. To hold the joker is thus to hold the lucky card, the highest trump, which for the course of that round alters the previously determined power structure of play. The idea of 'the innocent' is most difficult of the three title words to translate directly into Russian. It signifies one who is ingenuous and unsuspecting and thus combines elements of the fool (*durak*) and simpleton (*prostak*) with that of the *blazhennyi*, the person blessed with blissful ignorance (*blazhennoe nevedenie*). The concept of 'the innocent' will here be used in a sense generated specifically from English, with the three English words of joker, rogue and innocent denoting three models of behaviour which provide a framework for an analytical survey of classic works and writers in post-revolutionary Russian comic literature.

After the Russian Revolution, with its attempt to establish a new, unprecedented political and social order, writers had no choice but to position themselves in relation to its ideals and its reality. In this context, the innocent, the rogue and the joker offer three different standpoints for a humorous and satirical perspective on contemporary events. The three words represent, initially, three different types of comic hero, exemplifying three different modes of response to the given situation. These three modes of operation are as follows. The innocent *accepts the situation as given and tries to make things work*. The rogue *accepts the situation as it is and tries to turn it to his own advantage*. The joker, however, *does not accept the given situation*. Instead he *creates an alternative world* where he has *control*, however temporarily, and where he sets his own agenda. From this alternative world the joker observes that other, historically given, situation, with something approaching *disdain*. In the second stage of analysis these modes of response can then be transferred from the comic heroes to the authors themselves, as means by which the writers operate within the given historical constraints of their place and time.

Woland in Mikhail Bulgakov's *The Master and Margarita* is my first example of the joker. (As metaphors from card-games figure in several of Bulgakov's works and letters, the concept is in the spirit of his own writings.)[3] The whole complex plot of *The Master and Margarita* is based on the idea of a world alternative to the time and place in which the novel is set, Bulgakov's contemporary Moscow of the 1930s. As professor of Black Magic, and devil incarnate, Woland is at home in this other world, enjoying the freedom and power it gives him to stage havoc among the citizenry of the new Soviet society, all the assumptions of which he challenges and rejects. The inset story of the encounter between Pontius Pilate and a figure representing Jesus in first-century Jerusalem, of which Woland is the initial narrator, disproves the official dogmas of militant atheism. His retinue then act as agents who systematically create chaos, exposing the existing order of Soviet society in the 1930s as corrupt and false. The love story of the Master and Margarita intersects with Woland's alternative world, allowing the two to escape into the fantastic realm of Woland's protective domain. Woland's farewells to the city of Moscow towards the end of the novel express his relationship of superiority over it: he surveys the city from the top of a high building (Chapter 29), or from a hilltop (Chapter 31). His stance here mirrors that of Bulgakov as author, surveying his contemporary society from a position of lofty non-acceptance. In the last ten years of his life Bulgakov found himself dependent on the favour of Stalin.[4] However humiliating this situation of dependence may have been for him, by writing this novel at that time he maintained a hauteur of literary demeanour that Anna Akhmatova in her obituary poem for him characterised as 'magnificent disdain' (*velikolepnoe prezrenie*).[5] These two words also express the essence of Woland. In the novel's fictional world Woland assumes control over the Master's manuscript, demonstrating in Chapter 24 that 'Manuscripts do not burn'. This credo that true art is imperishable mirrors Bulgakov's faith in his own novel, which did indeed prove unpublishable in its time but was preserved for posterity. Through Woland, Bulgakov projected a control over his own literary fate, and by writing *The Master and Margarita* he played a joker card that trumped the hands holding the aces of power, overturned the official literary hierarchy of his day and won him his posthumous place in world literature.

When *The Master and Margarita* was finally published in Russia in the 1960s, Bulgakov's intellectual rejection of Soviet society and his imaginative recreation of the Easter story facilitated his immediate and lasting acceptance into Western culture. Less well known in the West are writers of that same period who did not reject socialism or disdain the given historical situation in which they were working. Among them are lodestars of Russian twentieth-century comic literature, namely Mikhail Zoshchenko, and the writing partnership of Ilia Ilf and Evgeny Petrov. These writers all believed in the justice of the social revolution in Russia in 1917. Their books, however, have not lost popularity in their native land with the collapse of the great Soviet 'experiment' at the end of the twentieth century. On the contrary, their works have fresh resonance as people once again find themselves in the midst of a mighty social, economic and political upheaval, once more having to adjust to a new, imperfectly understood ideology with its own new, strange and often misused vocabulary. It is a situation of changing values which offers huge opportunities for the rogue, who wants to exploit the confusion for his own advantage.

The prototypical rogue in Soviet literature was created by Ilf and Petrov in *The Twelve Chairs* (1928) and its sequel, *The Golden Calf* (1931). The humorous tone of these novels is accepting and celebratory, while also being subversive. To Ilf and Petrov it was the simplest common sense that the security of employment and free health service offered by the new socialist regime in Russia were desirable.[6] They were responsive to the heroism of the gigantic construction projects of the Five-Year Plan, for example the accelerated completion in 1930 of the Turksib railway line that ran for over 850 miles between Turkestan and Siberia.[7] There is no doubt that they believed instinctively in socialism, but they were young and merry, and their joint irreverence kept their eye clear and their tongue sharp. Together they created a comic hero of mythic proportions who became the perfect vehicle for this irreverence, the splendid Ostap Bender. Grand Schemer, Contriver and Wheeler-Dealer, golden tongued con-man, Ostap Bender is part of every Russian's literary baggage and his turns of phrase are part of everyone's stock of quotations. He is a rogue in the picaresque tradition, and the plots of the novels follow the traditional pattern of the picaro's journeys. In his quests, Ostap roams over vast geographical spaces of Soviet Russia, financing his travels by deploying what in chapter 2 of *The Golden Calf* he calls his 'four hundred comparatively honest ways' of relieving other people of money. The very scale of his journeys confers a certain grandeur on him and his enterprises. Towards the end of the first novel he has already acquired such stature that it takes an earthquake to stop him in his tracks, and then not for long. Even being murdered in the denouement of *The Twelve Chairs* interrupts his career only briefly. The authors' youth and literary-commercial inexperience showed in the blithe way they killed their hero off at the end of their first novel, then regretted this and decided to resurrect him for a sequel. In commercial terms he was a veritable 'golden calf', a chance of fame and fortune. But he is also a literary achievement of a very high order, and thus by no means a false idol.

True, he is an opportunist, but not a cynical one. What drives him is not so much desire for wealth, as the enjoyment of living off his wits, that, and the thrill of the chase. His scepticism is combined with verve and boundless optimism. He is, in his own way, a poet, a philosopher and even something of an aesthete. (In Chapter 11 of *The Twelve Chairs* he refuses to rent a room where the walls are hung with 'landscapes'.) His creators gave him their own tastes, their own wit, and an ironic freedom of perspective that would almost turn him into a joker, except that, in the end, they force him to accept his given historical situation. In the denouement of *The Golden Calf* he attempts to escape over the border, but is caught, beaten up and stripped of all his possessions by a Romanian border guard, and sent back to live in the Soviet Union of the Five Year Plan.

Now, as an ending, this carries exactly as much conviction as the Epilogue to *Crime and Punishment*, and exactly the same methods could be used to construct arguments for and against it as a close to the narrative. In order not to offend the religious sensibilities of his readers, at the very end of the Epilogue Dostoevsky offers a promise that Raskolnikov will truly repent of his crime, a conclusion that Mochulsky calls a 'pious lie'.[8] But Dostoevsky was a fervently believing Orthodox Christian, and thus the 'lie' does not create an artistic falsehood. By the same token, Ilf and Petrov wanted their novel to be accepted for publication within the closed borders of the Soviet socialist state, and therefore could not let their unregenerate hero escape to live elsewhere. But this ending accords with their own faith in socialism. The conclusion therefore establishes an artistically truthful balance between the vitality of the egregious Ostap Bender and the authors' genuine Soviet patriotism.

And thus Ilf and Petrov achieved what should have been an impossibility. In that self-same Soviet Union of the Five Year Plan they created two enormously popular, endlessly republished books around a character who, in Chapter 2 of *The Golden Calf* comes right out and declares that he is 'bored with building socialism'. Such a character is obviously not an appropriate positive hero for a Soviet novel: to be bored with building socialism is heresy, but the heretic himself is depicted in the novels as seductive and authoritative. Although the denouement of *The Golden Calf* contrives his defeat, Ostap Bender is never an object of satire, but its agent. He functions as the 'eternal outsider' in the world of the novel, the targets of his satire being not the socialism with which he is 'bored', but gullibility, affectation, social conformism, and mechanical or expedient behaviour. The exploitation of predictable behaviour patterns is, after all, the whole secret of his success as rogue and con-man. His defeat in the end by the forces of socialism is the necessary condition for the novels about him to be published in the socialist state, and here the authors were, in their own way, acting as rogues by accepting the given situation and turning it to their advantage.

For the third type of comic response, that of the innocent, I turn to Mikhail Zoshchenko. Zoshchenko's short stories of the 1920s typically display a narrator-hero telling the tale from his own limited perspective, in his own idiom, and with a deformed vocabulary. In many of these heroes we can see the model of the innocent, muddling along, accepting the given situation, and trying to make things work. In this, the hero is almost always frustrated as he grapples with institutions, bureaucracies, concepts or vocabulary that are beyond his control or comprehension. Typically the plot-line describes a comic failure, as in the classic tale of 'The Bathhouse' ('Bania'). Here the narrator displays endless resourcefulness in the face of frustration as he encounters one problem after another. These build up, with escalating comic effect, until he finally gives up and goes home, unwashed and having lost his bar of soap to boot. He has set out with a modest desire: to have a bath. When this aim is thwarted, however, he never wonders why.

He simply plods on, accepting things as they are and making the best of them. He can see no further than his own nose. Sometimes he does not even realise that he has in fact experienced failure, as in the story 'The Overshoe' ('Galosha'), where he sets out to reclaim a lost galosh. At the end of his account he still only has one overshoe, but he treats this single item of what should be a pair as a trophy, proof positive that things are working for him as they should.

Sometimes the hero is a would-be rogue, but even here he retains an essential innocence, because of his limited perspective and lack of grasp of the situation. The Zoshchenko hero enjoys being in step with the new post-revolutionary ideals and has absolute faith in them. The only problem is that he does not always know quite what the new codes of behaviour are. Assuming that in a 'worker-peasant state', everything must now be designed for the working man's advantage, the hero of 'Working Clothes' tries to travel on a tram carrying open buckets of paint.[9] In 'Bourgeois Deviations', he tries to enter a restaurant while drunk and disorderly.[10] But the heroes of these tales discover that although they may belong to the newly ascendant social classes, this does not give them the right to breach the social rules of consideration for others. The heroes' naïve attempts to 'play the system' bring them up against the law, which imposes boundaries on their behaviour. Many of Zoshchenko's tales of the 1920s follow this pattern in which a quarrel or fight erupts, and the denouement takes place in the police station or court-room. In this sense they are 'moral tales' for the new society.

Zoshchenko wrote his stories for 'the masses', and published them in comic magazines, as an attempt to give the newly literate readers in post-revolutionary Russia something entertaining that was accessible to their own language and experience. The plots of the stories parody real life, and parody the perspective of the 'little man' as he tries to find his place in the new society, or work out its rules of behaviour, or grasp its language. The hero's state of naïve ignorance, his function as 'innocent', is a comic exaggeration that is a secret of the stories' appeal, since the reader, however lowly his own social or educational status, can always feel 'wiser' than the hero.

Zoshchenko's stories were enormously popular not only in the new Soviet Russia but also in Russian émigré circles, where they were read, however, as a realistic critique of the 'absurd' Soviet experiment. Fastidious émigrés observed with horrified fascination the hero-narrators' cheerful faith in Soviet ideology.[11] This was a faith shared, although less cheerfully, by Zoshchenko himself. Like many famous comedians, he was a hypochondriac and melancholic, with a degree of psycho-neurosis that could on occasion be life threatening.[12] A new, transformed, socialist society seemed to him to offer the possibility of escape from his own crippling depressions. Zoshchenko himself therefore had a willed faith in Russia's 'great experiment' in creating a new society. He chose his themes according to his own personal agenda, which concurred with the vision of socialism as a new, healthy society. All through the 1920s and 1930s, well into the era of high Stalinism, the Great Terror and the purges, Zoshchenko stuck to this personal agenda. He was not blind. He could see that things were going badly wrong. But this man racked by the demons of psycho-neurosis behaved with impeccable decency throughout that dangerous period.[13] In this given historical situation, he accepted it and did his best to do what he could, did his best to make it work. He openly and publicly extended help to families of imprisoned and exiled acquaintances, despite the risk that this entailed of himself becoming implicated in the accusations being made against them.[14] And all the time he continued, desperately, patriotically, to believe in the Soviet socialist experiment. As the USSR entered the war against fascist Germany, Zoshchenko made his own literary contribution to the war effort, but again entirely according to his own personal agenda. Fascism he saw as a philosophy of the irrational. In order to master his own irrational fears he had turned to psychotherapy and auto-therapy. Thus, in 1943, he offered *Before Sunrise (Pered voskhodom solntsa)*, a literary account of his auto-therapy as demonstration of a victory achieved over irrational forces. Astonishingly, this introspective autobiography was accepted for publication during the war and the first part appeared, but the second part was suppressed. What was wanted of war literature was heroics, not introspection. Proffering such a book at such a time had been the act of an 'innocent', as Zoshchenko himself became aware during a nasty press campaign against him in 1944. The onslaught, however, was brief, and it must have appeared that he had been forgiven for his wayward choice of themes.[15] When the attack on him finally came, in 1946, in the shape of the Communist Party Resolution on the journals *Zvezda* and *Leningrad*, it was devastating in its suddenness, the flimsiness of its immediate pretext, its viciousness and its length.[16] Zoshchenko never recovered from this attack on his good name. He died twelve years later, in 1958, ill and destitute, sustained by the unobtrusive support and, indeed, charity from the few friends with courage to stand by him. In my three categories, Zoshchenko himself as author represents 'the innocent'. He accepted the given historical situation and loyally attempted to work within it, but fell victim in the end to forces beyond the scope of his comprehension and to agendas that betrayed him for their own political ends.

Zoshchenko, Ilf and Petrov, Bulgakov – these are the great comic writers of the first post-revolutionary period, with their comic heroes and their own modes of response as authors categorised as that of the innocent, the rogue and the joker. These categories are also productive for comic writers of later periods, and the comic heroes of their works.

Not surprisingly given the fate of Zoshchenko, during the last years of Stalinism writers with a gift for the comic tended to keep this talent to themselves.

Towards the end of the 1960s however, with the post-Stalin 'Thaw' apparently well under way, Russian literature was invaded by a group of young writers with fresh, irreverent voices but also idealistic beliefs in the ability of the Soviet system to transform and renew itself. One of them was the young Vladimir Voinovich. He began his career happily enough in terms of success and acceptance, but then he invented a hero, Ivan Chonkin, who wrought complete havoc all around him, as much havoc in the real life of his author as he did in the fictional life of the book that bears his name: *The Life and Extraordinary Adventures of Private Ivan Chonkin.*

One of Chonkin's literary ancestors is the good soldier Sveik, but whereas Sveik has a pronounced element of roguery, Chonkin is purest innocent. His acceptance of any given situation is stolidly practical. When a plane crash-lands in a remote corner of the Soviet Union, Private Chonkin is sent to guard it against the depredations of the locals. He soon shacks up with Niura, the local postmistress, moving the plane into a corner of her garden to that he can still fulfil his duty as guard while also helping Niura cultivate her vegetable patch. His domestic and patriotic roles are thus in complete harmony with each other and with the natural world. But the year is 1941, Germany attacks the Soviet Union and, in the chaos of the first weeks of the war, the little soldier and his plane are forgotten. Yet he remains at his post, unswervingly loyal to his duty, improvising practical solutions to the predicaments in which the plot places him and doing the best he can. His efficient resourcefulness, however, is not matched by the political and military institutions of the Stalinist state, which are in a state of delusion, confusion and panic. A classic comic situation ensues where Chonkin finds himself heroically defending his plane not against attack from the Nazi invader but against a regiment of his own Red Army.

The thrust of Voinovich's humour is satirical, directed against falsehood, hierarchies and incompetence, and Chonkin is the honest innocent in an absurd world of pretence, conditioned by fear of Stalin and the secret police. In a Soviet Union committed to de-Stalinisation, such a novel would have become part of that patriotic project. But by the end of the 1960s de-Stalinisation had been abandoned. Publication of the novel proved impossible and events took their course: the novel circulated in *samizdat*, found its way abroad and was published in the West in 1975.[17] Its sequel, *Pretender to the Throne*, appeared four years later, likewise in Western publication.[18] By 1980 its author had been forced into exile and shortly afterwards he was stripped of his Soviet citizenship. The narrative of Voinovich's life thus followed a line that paralleled the plot of his own novel, where the honest and loyal hero finds himself unwittingly on the 'wrong' side. As with Zoshchenko, the innocent, as author, became a casualty. The historical situation was, however, kinder to Voinovich that it had been to Zoshchenko. With *glasnost* and *pere-*

stroika Voinovich's good name was rehabilitated, his Soviet citizenship was restored and publishing houses in Russia made his works widely available to the Russian public.

For the model of the rogue's response in the same period, 1960s to 1980s, we can turn to Fazil Iskander. Abkhazian by nationality, Iskander writes in Russian but sets the majority of his tale in his native Abkhazia. This is the setting for the three-volume epic *Sandro from Chegem*, composed of a series of short stories set in and around the fictional mountain village of Chegem, and intended by its author initially as a parody of the picaresque novel.[19] Sandro of Chegem is an ambiguous figure, simultaneously both rogue and exemplar of the traditional Abzhazian virtues. He is a fine horseman, as we see in the story 'The Gamblers' ('Igroki') and a leading dancer in the Abzkhazian song-and dance ensemble. The importance of dance in the warrior cultures of the Caucasus is indicated in the story 'Belshazzar's Feast' ('Piry Valtasara') where the dance is an ostentatious display, symbolising warrior spirit and physical prowess. Sandro's dancing is also sublimated horsemanship in that both require the same physical attribute of 'iron knees'.[20] Sandro is a repository of his nation's culture in another way too, in that he is a renowned master of ceremonies, a 'toastmaster' or *tamada*. The traditions of Caucasian hospitality are enshrined in the rules of the Caucasian feast, and the *tamada* it is who maintains them. As master of ceremonies, Sandro's role shadows that of Stalin. While Stalin was hailed in his time, as 'the greatest leader of all times and peoples', Sandro is, we are told, 'the greatest *tamada* of all times and peoples'.[21] But Stalin acts as a mighty master of ceremonies on the historical arena, instigating and controlling a bloody carnival. The sphere of Sandro's influence extends only to the festive table and the protection of his native Abkhazian culture. He may be armed to the teeth, but his weapon is a hunting rifle and his dagger is ceremonial. Sandro's exploits are those of the mock epic. Historically, the fate of his small Black Sea country depends on events in the vast neighbouring empire, first tsarist and then Soviet, and this is a historical situation that Sandro accepts and exploits for his own advantage. When the Russian Revolution comes to Abkhazia, he makes the transition quite easily, ending up with a cushy job in the headquarters of the Abkhaz Communist Party, but without altering the traditional Abkhazian principles of his behaviour one jot. He remains an ideology-free zone. Russian literature has traditionally been concerned with the fate of the 'little man' overwhelmed by the mighty forces of the state. In his preface to the American edition of his novel Iskander declared that he was depicting the inner life of a 'little country'.[22] Sandro, in his function as rogue, represents a 'little country', retaining its own heritage through nimble-footed negotiation with the political culture of a dominant neighbouring state.

Sandro's creator, Iskander, managed an equally skilful negotiation with the Soviet literary establishment. The novel *Sandro from Chegem* is composed of separate short stories, most of which were published in Soviet journals but some of which, like 'Belshazzar's Feast', could be published only in the West before the freedoms introduced by Gorbachev and *glasnost.* Iskander did not escape scot-free, for there were periods when his name was barred from Soviet publications.[23] He was not, however, forced into exile and deprived of his Soviet citizenship. Thus he was able to combine the qualities of Soviet writer and sharply dissident wit, and can therefore, as author, be classified as a successful 'rogue' in the same category as Ilf and Petrov.

Veniamin Erofeev and the first-person narrator-hero of his novel *Moscow-Petushki* might have been candidates for 'joker' status, the alternative world here being that of the dedicated drunkard. But the drunkard lacks both disdain and control, while his alcoholic tears are those of the wilful innocent, trying in vain to make things work – in this case trying but failing to reach the desired destination of Petushki. To find a pure example of the joker in the second half of the twentieth century, we had to wait until its very last year, 1999, and the publication of *Generation П* by Viktor Pelevin.[24] This is the Russian title, and its mixture of Latin and Cyrillic script reflects the current state of confusion in Russian culture as it absorbs Western capitalist ideas, vocabulary and consumer goods. Pelevin is an *enfant terrible* in today's Russian literature, offering playful but devastating perceptions of his contemporary society. Vavilen Tatarsky, the hero of *Generation П,* is very like his creator: a poet who has to find a means of earning a living in the hustle of the post-Soviet market-place. Tatarsky finds his niche in the new profession of advertising, which gives Pelevin wonderful scope for imagining comic hybrids: for example, a cosy TV advertisement, featuring a grandfather and his grandson, advertising Kalashnikov rifles (two characters being needed because two models are to be displayed). Another of Tatarsky's commissions is to define the 'brand essence' of that most volatile of cocktails, the messianic 'Russian Idea'. As this last example indicates, the novel's frame of reference is the whole centuries-long culture of the Russian intellectual elite, forcibly transplanted into today's market-driven economy and having to find a place in it that is no longer there. This is the context of the novel's ironic dedication: 'To the memory of the middle class'.

Pelevin has the fury, bile, pain and brilliant comic invention of the true satirist. He is a contemporary reincarnation of Bulgakov, with the spiritual element in Pelevin provided not by Christianity but by the adoption of a Zen Buddhism that then collapses into a hallucinatory alternative world of drugs and alcohol. This brings illumination to the hero Tatarsky and restores control to him, however, because he emerges with the discovery that, for the individual, the only control possible is through a philosophy of purest solipsism, where the self is the only object of real knowledge. This tendency towards solipsism was marked in Pelevin's earlier works.[25] In *Generation П* it has become supreme and triumphant. By the end of the novel Tatarsky has imposed himself as controller of the entire political and commercial power structure of his country, the supreme oligarch. It is from this elevated standpoint that Pelevin projects his pain and contempt upon the historical moment of transition at which he is writing.

Generation II is a jigsaw of cultural references without any apparent pattern of moral coherence. We could call it the acme of post-modernism, except that what we have in Pelevin is not just an artistic construct. He gives us a satirical take on a lived-in historical moment of non-optional reality for Russians, who have to orientate themselves in a plethora of competing value systems, none of which exercise moral authority. All the old certainties are gone. This situation is easier for the younger generation, which is one reason why in its native culture *Generation II* was so readily received by the young. Pelevin in Russia today enjoys almost film-star status, and articles about him appear in the Russian *Playboy.*[26] The novel, however, aroused antipathy among the older generation of intellectuals, who cling to the Russian and Soviet tradition of literature as a source of moral education.[27] It could, however, be pointed out that *Generation II* is so full of references to the Russian cultural heritage that any reader who systematically followed them up would be undertaking a crash course in Russian culture, which thus emerges as an object of intrinsic worth. In an anti-intellectual environment dominated by a vicious interplay of political and commercial interests Pelevin's novel establishes a virtual alternative world in which a literary tradition has value. Pelevin's immense popularity is, furthermore, evidence that this world of literature exists. The author as joker has trumped the aces held by the oligarchs. Significantly, the image of the card game is one that Pelevin himself has used, likening the current power-plays in Russia to card games played by cheating crooks: 'They're trying to make you play. You'll never win.'[28] Pelevin 'wins' by refusing to play anyone's game but his own.

Thus we have the jokers, rogues and innocents of Russian Soviet, and now post-Soviet, literature. As characters, the innocents wreak their havoc by accepting the given situation and trying to make it work. Round-eyed and literal in their understanding, they take things at face value, and the comic frustration, failure or chaos caused by their efforts exposes the gap between appearance and reality. When the author is forced by his historical situation into enactment of the role of innocent, however, the narrative line of his biography can take a tragic twist. As characters, the sharp-eyed rogues accept the situation, understand how it works, and adapt to it for their own benefit. Their adjustments reveal the underlying values of the social group in which they are operating. The author as rogue successfully manages to pursue his own agenda while negotiating a path that still remains in contact with the dominant ideological highway of his time. The jokers, as characters, look down on the situation they inhabit, see it for what it is, and refuse to play by its rules. As authors, the jokers create a parallel fantasy universe that imposes a fictional order upon a disordered society.

These categories of innocent, rogue and joker in no way imply a literary hierarchy. One is not 'better' than the other; they are simply different modes of organising the comic and satirical response. The popularity of all these books in the marketplace of Russia today is testament that the authors have all played their cards and 'won'.

10

ESCAPING THE PAST?

Re-reading Soviet satire from the twenty-first century: The case of Zoshchenko

GREGORY CARLETON

ONE of the rarely admitted pleasures of being a teacher is the opportunity to play tricks on your students – which I did recently in a course on Stalinist culture. The point of discussion was a story by Ilia Ilf and Evgeny Petrov written in 1934, 'Conversations Over Tea' which, it will be recalled, is a devastating indictment of the indoctrination of children via rote memory of ideological slogans. The twelve-year-old at the centre cannot answer his impatient father's most simple questions at the kitchen table. On the judgement of Gogol as a writer, the son can only produce 'a degenerate, petty mystic of reactionary inclinations'. In his tortured mind Catherine the Great is likewise reduced to a 'product of the epoch of the growing influence of mercantile capitalism'. And the definition of a peninsula, since geography rarely displays its ideological colours, is perforce passed in over in silence.

My students, understandably, assumed that this had to be a brazenly anti-Soviet work which was obviously banned, and upon learning that Ilf died three years later in 1937, one ventured that of course he had been shot for writing like this. I frankly had no problem with their conclusions – a natural death for a writer certainly seemed like an unnatural occurrence then. Moreover, if we look to certain canons in the West, it would appear that their speculation was not entirely off-target. One could turn to the 1983 two-volume anthology, *Humour and Satire of Post-Revolutionary Russia*, which served at least for my generation in graduate school as a worthy introduction to the genre. Here one could find an estimable selection of such banned writers as Mikhail Bulgakov, Evgeny Zamiatin, Vladimir Voinovich and Andrei Siniavsky. Introductory material was brief because the anthology's purpose was presumably apparent to all. As one of the editors reminded us, 'the dogma of marxism-leninism-communism intrinsically excludes laughter', and he illustrated the point by reciting the tribulations that these and other writers had experienced under the Soviet government.[1]

Here we find as well the same story by Ilf and Petrov, printed in full, followed as with all other contributions to the anthology by a date: 1934. Year of publication or, more ominously, only of composition? The question, by appearances mundane, is of critical importance in this context. Since 'Conversations' is accompanied by Bulgakov's *Heart of a Dog*, which was banned until glasnost, might we not assume that it too suffered a similar fate? Anthologies, by intention or not, gravitate towards canon formation, and here, as is obvious in the editors' eyes, the principle that links these works is not just generic as the title claims but explicitly political: all the satires are presumed to be anti-Soviet. No wonder, then, that the original place of publication of 'Conversations' was not included. The pages of *Pravda* for 21, May 1934, would hardly seem the most 'anti-Soviet' of places.

In truth far more was absent with this exclusion. Gone was the possibility of considering how Soviet literature could accommodate what, at first sight, would appear a most egregious taboo. What cultural mechanisms were in place to absorb and appropriate such provocative texts? How could official culture clarify the story's target so as to deflect criticism too close to home? Why was it published on the most hallowed of party pages?

With hindsight (which was available to the editors as well) we recognise that official Soviet culture could embrace certain criticisms if directed to specific (and limited) targets. And, in fact, that is what we face here. The impetus for writing 'Conversations' was nothing less than a party resolution of April 1934 that condemned the 'overloading' of schoolchildren with 'questions of marxist-leninist theory' when they were too young to make sense of it all. While this, of course, is not to say that Ilf and Petrov believed that their feuilleton was thus limited in scope, the editors of *Humour and Satire* a priori allowed no room to evaluate the story within its home environment. Ilf and Petrov's anti-Soviet intentions were taken as an article of faith, and all information necessary for the reader to understand the story correctly was expressed by the very company of anthologised authors. In other words, the case was made by the posthumous juxtaposition with other 'known' anti-Soviet writers and, more importantly, by the absence of any concrete material or information regarding the conditions – or even the fact – of its publication.

There ultimately was no trick to play on my students. How they received 'Conversations Over Tea' replicated methodological procedures that have underwritten most interpretations seeking to paint popular Soviet writers, particularly those of humour and satire, as covert dissidents instead of social critics operating within the bounds of acceptable criticism. In 1995, when the passing of the Cold War would seem to have lifted ideological pressures on western perspectives, M. Keith Booker and Dubravka Juraga again advanced Ilf and Petrov as explicitly anti-Stalinist writers – this time moving the calendar even further forward.[2] Their opposition to the state was explicitly clear, according to Booker and Juraga, in the Bakthinian 'openness, change, and multiplicity' that marked their work. That it should be 'obvious' such features run 'directly counter to the ideology of Stalinism' needed no qualification; Stalinist culture is such a known entity that we can presumably dispense with explication or definition. 'Monologic' and 'oppressive,' we are obliged to accept, cover all its bases.

The economy with which one whole side of the problem – the historical context – is treated quickly leads us into a few tight spots. Matters of chronology become secondary. Thus Father Fyodor, a get-rich-quick schemer from Ilf and Petrov's tremendously popular novel published at the beginning of 1928, *Twelve Chairs*, 'can potentially be interpreted as an indirect criticism of Stalin and his techniques of ruling.' How the connection is made is another case of guilt by association. If Fyodor represents the church, an institution with a vested interest in monologism, then any attack against it via a lampooning of Fyodor's character can properly be seen as evidence of hostility towards Stalin's monologic tendencies. To be sure, Booker and Juraga hedge themselves ('potentially', 'indirect'), but a more useful hedge would be to recognise that Fyodor is, above all, a stock motif from a centuries-long tradition of ridiculing religious hypocrisy and, more importantly, in 1927, when the novel was being written, few of Stalin's 'techniques of ruling' were evident. Historical chronology comes even less into play with a subsequent charge that *Twelve Chairs*, along with its sequel, is a parody of socialism realism though the novel made its debut a half decade before the infamous doctrine appeared. While we can fairly attribute to Ilf and Petrov a healthy dose of wit and daring irreverence before authority, such foresight is more problematic.

Dogmatic presumptions about Soviet culture, unsupported by a substantive vetting of empirical conditions then, have a tendency to boomerang back. How Ilf and Petrov have been enlisted into the anti-Soviet camp is not an isolated phenomenon for it illustrates in microcosm what has shaped as well the interpretive canon in the West regarding their more famous contemporary, Mikhail Zoshchenko, whose work is also prominent in *Humour and Satire.* For most, Zoshchenko's legacy has been defined by Zhdanov's attack in 1946 and its tragic aftermath. The persecution and veritable ostracism he suffered until his death in 1958 became the bedrock, admitted or not, in the near-unanimous view of him as an anti-Soviet satirist – an image projected backwards to his literary debut in the early 1920s in order to confirm his life-long hostility to the Soviet system. In truth, however, just as with Ilf and Petrov, Zoshchenko's critical reception was one of tremendous vicissitudes. In the 1920s he was generally suspected of giving voice to all the philistine cretins and enemies of the state. Yet a decade later critics learned to distinguish narrator from author and praised him for attacking these same enemies. By exposing negative elements of society, his short comic vignettes of contemporary life were seen as necessary and therefore welcome additions to the didactic principles that defined approved Soviet literature. On the twenty-first anniversary of the revolution he was showered with ritualistic praise by readers' letters published in the press and in 1939 awarded the Order of the Red Banner of Labour. The Zhdanov-inspired period of persecution, devastating as it was to him both in his professional and personal life, was a relatively brief part of his critical legacy. By the 1960s and in the following decade up through to the 1980s, he was rehabilitated in the Soviet Union in much the same guise as in the 1930s, that is, as an optimistic, pro-Soviet writer.

In the West, conversely, Zoshchenko's reputation has displayed remarkable continuity. During the Cold War he was acclaimed as a documentary realist who, according to Marc Slonim, 'reveals the ruts and rots of daily existence with its vulgarity and stupidity behind the façade of magnificent slogans.'[3] From the preponderance of scholarly studies and editor's introductions to his collections, it seemed that there was no question that Zoshchenko's intention was to 'demonstrate the harmful effect of the Revolution and communism on mankind.'[4] During the early stages of perestroika, this impression grew even more as post-Soviet critics advanced him as a martyr, one who was broken by the state for telling the people the truth of their tragic lives under the Soviet system. Tellingly, even in our ostensibly post-ideological age, the enduring impression of Zoshchenko as an unrelenting opponent of the Soviet system has received a new lease in western criticism through deconstructionist and post-structuralist readings of his work.[5]

The common denominator in these Western and post-Soviet interpretations of Zoshchenko is a binary perception of the Soviet literary environment. Writing is inherently of two types: oppositional to or supportive of the Soviet Union. This division is upheld by situating him against a fixed background of something called 'the state,' 'the party,' or 'the system' – always employed in the singular so as to enforce the impression of an omniscient, omnipresent controlling voice or doctrine against which one can only agree or disagree. So too do these 'something' entities generally remain in the abstract, the unwritten principle being that the reader, long-weaned on knowledge of the state's persecution of writers, already knows what they stand for and thus there is no need for further explication. If 1946 put Zoshchenko on the map in the West and fixed his value for us, our subsequent reading of Soviet totalitarianism has made his intentions as a writer unequivocally clear.

As a result, Zoshchenko has often been read through a limited palette and I understand why this has taken hold. No one would want to side with Zhdanov (even if, ironically, the canon of western opinion essentially proves the thrust of his accusation, and it makes the most sense, given our tradition of tagging Soviet writers in political either-or terms). To be honest, however, it is an interpretive canon that generates problems precisely because of its streamlined, clarifying benefits.

Its fundament is that Zoshchenko, particularly in his heyday of the 1920s and the early 1930s, was daringly revealing all the dirt hidden by propaganda. He was doing, in effect, that which was officially proscribed. To be sure, if we compare his works to a Kremlin tract or *How the Steel Was Tempered*, then they certainly seem heretical. But this is where we are perhaps mistaken. We recognise that this was a time of experimentation and diversity, but in interpreting Zoshchenko we too often read him against a limited background of party declaration or platform on one hand and, on the other, the high literary intelligentsia made up of such figures as Pasternak, Akhmatova and Chukovsky. Yet it behooves us, particularly if we are to be free of the ideological blinders that underwrote Cold War interpretations, to move beyond these two poles when discussing the literary-discursive environment then. Contrary to traditional assumptions, the Soviet press liberally covered cases of deficiency, crime and corruption in contemporary life – indeed, we seem to forget that this is where Zoshchenko often found source material for his stories. Much of what one could read in the press offered far worse pictures than anything Zoshchenko ever produced, such as the1926 study, 'Society's Detritus Before the Soviet Courts,' with its detailed accounts of rape and battery, gang rapes, a drunk father raping his one-year-old daughter, an uncle raping his niece and so forth. This was the 'bitter truth,' as the author Ilia Ilinsky admitted and salted the wound by adding in bold print that these cases were 'not so much exceptions, rather the most repellent reflections of that reality which is sufficiently repellent in and of itself.'[6] This position, declared openly by a marxist in a leading marxist journal, gives a good sense of how the press then was far less enamoured of glossy propaganda, both in a quantitative and qualitative sense, than we assume dominated the print environment. Ilinsky's sharp conclusion was not unusual for its time since it dovetailed precisely with Trotsky's memorable reminder to Soviet citizens in one of his broadsides that no effort was required to find evidence of social ills in the new society: 'you don't have to search at all; just look around.'[7]

Situating Zoshchenko within this broader context is vital so as to recognise that what we hold as the canon now often bears little resemblance to what was being read then, what generated queues in libraries, and what spurred debate, controversy and dialogue both within the party and, for want of a better word, among 'mass' readers. Of dozens that could be cited – Panteleimon Romanov's 'Without a Cherry Blossom,' Sergei Malashkin's 'Moon on the Right;' Gleb Alekseev's 'The

Case of the Corpse,' Nikolai Bogdanov's *First Girl*, Boris Gorbatov's *The Cell* – all give us devastating pictures of contemporary conditions. The primary themes revolve around youth disenchantment, apathy, sexual promiscuity, suicide, hooliganism and the like. These portraits, frankly, are far more uncompromising, shocking and often more incisive than much of what Zoshchenko or Ilf and Petrov did. Emblematic would be Aleksandr Arosev's novella, *The Notes of Terenty Zabyty*, published in 1923 when Zoshchenko's popularity was rapidly ascending.[8] Its theme, setting and characters are all, in a word, grey. The city, unlike the expected industrial ideal, is now a 'god-forsaken hell,' full of 'darkness, hunger and the groan of metal, like in a slum.' One character, the former carpenter Derevtsov, is unsure of the future of both his country and party, which is now awash with petty intrigue, bureaucracy and 'false' (that is, recent vintage) communists. He finds temporary relief by snorting cocaine, and a more permanent one by shooting himself in the mouth, an act graced with the simple, but all-telling note: 'I'm tired and everything's just a waste.' He is complemented by Kleiner, a 'chekist from head to toe,' which is shorthand for an insane automaton whose obsession is to broadcast executions on a giant film-screen for edification purposes: the more people fear being shot, the fewer crimes they will commit and, in the end, the less capital punishment there will be. Terenty's neighbour, Sheptunovskaia, is willing to self herself for food; she later joins the party and marries Derevstov. With the exception of Sheptunovskaia, Arosev's communists are members of the old guard and, what is more, proletarians in origin. The title character, whose name means 'the forgotten one,' goes to the country to confiscate grain, which affords us a portrait of less than loyal peasants. His notes end abruptly when he dies of typhus. In the last lines, where we first get a glimpse of optimism, this is undercut by a final, despair-ridden question:

> 'The sun will come out. . . there will be bread.' And we have to march to it, to the sun, to the source of heat and energy.
>
> No, this is not a dream, but true life.
>
> But when? . . .

Like Ilinsky, Arosev was a member of the party, having joined in 1907 and experienced pre-revolutionary arrest and exile. *The Notes of Terenty Zabyty* was published not, as one might expect given its content, in a period of personal doubt and contrition, but when the writer was working at the Institute of the History of the Party and Revolution and would soon become assistant director at the Lenin Institute. While Arosev was shot in 1938, this in no way means that he was anti-Soviet (just as one would not assume with Bukharin); in fact, his next substantive work after this surprising novella comprised three biographical-analytical pieces on Lenin.

Perhaps more important than just the existence of such literature is that it was published and circulated with the express consent and encouragement of other party members who made up the rank and file behind the decade's journals. This crucial facet of the environment is generally overlooked – that there was a significant contingent of marxists operating in the literary culture who favoured and actively supported the kind of literature that might later be condemned as anti-Soviet. The clearest example would be those centred around the journal *The Young Guard* which truly stood out as a cutting-edge publication. Under the direction of Averbakh, Ermilov, Libedinsky and others, *The Young Guard* took on a leading role in embracing texts that upset stock pictures of a perfect Soviet Union and thus awakened audiences and made them think – not with the objective of undermining the party's authority but of improving its relevance and thereby safeguarding its primacy. Of course this group, later during the dominance of RAPP, earned the reputation of being so vulgar and unprincipled that they have remained a favorite target for scholars to this day. Yet a different impression emerges if we move beyond theoretical proclamations and infighting and actually read what circulated then and what, particularly for younger readers, constituted the reality of Soviet literature.

Put simply, many of the works that appeared in *The Young Guard* (and not there alone) refused to present life as free from contemporary problems and deficiencies. As letters to its editors (and to Zoshchenko as well) substantiate, this was precisely what many readers wanted and felt they needed in order to resolve the hardships, difficulties and contradictions of life during NEP. Assuming a central role in this campaign, *The Young Guard* published some of the most provocative (and literally speaking) 'dirty' works of the 1920s including Malashkin, Romanov, and Bogdanov as well as Kollontai, Tarasov-Rodionov's *Chocolate*, and Gerasimova's 'The False Ones.' This last, while now forgotten, appeared the same year as Arosev's novella and presented a similar picture of a despondent, ideologically barren Komsomol. In the eyes of the protagonist, whose name is, symbolically, Eve, its members are 'rude, primitive and uneducated'. Ridden with lice, they gather to drink in a filthy building, where casual sex is the norm. Eve is sucked into their mindlessness after admitting to herself that 'there's no reason to live.' She leaves a suicide note with a friend, but as the story ends it has not yet been acted upon. By her very title, Gerasimova made clear that these were not the true revolutionaries, yet again the last lines eliminated any sense of hope: 'Dawn's grey eye looked into their forgotten windows.'[9]

By opening its pages to such writers, as archives now reveal, the editors of *The Young Guard* were roundly attacked by those higher up in the party. But reproach, when it came, was notably after the fact. Behind-the-scenes correspondence demonstrates that the editors enjoyed much leeway in bringing to readers decidedly non-traditional portraits of the early Soviet Union.[10] What should not be forgotten, however, is that none of these members of the party saw themselves as disloyal. In fact, the opposite was true. Their intent, ironically much like that of Zoshchenko himself, was to call attention to domestic imperfections – not in order to replace the system but to improve it.

This internal dissension suggests that no matter how the party may have appeared on paper, no matter how it may figure in our minds as omniscient and omnipotent, it is problematic to automatically assume that there existed in the 1920s a single, coherent, consistent political ideology to be enacted, enforced and imposed on all writers. Our tendency to speak of state, party or power in the singular can unfortunately seduce us into believing that there was a unified strategy in the marxist literary establishment. While, it should be noted, all predicted a triumphant future, some nevertheless were genuinely concerned about a problematic present – one that could not and, as the Young Guardists believed, should not be resolved by recourse to optimistic sloganeering and propaganda.

Evidence of internal confusion in the party comes from no less a source than the chief censor, Lebedev-Poliansky, in a 1927 report. While one should question the deleterious impact of censorship as operated by Glavlit, one should also not assume that its abilities, power, and reach operated in consistent or predictable fashion. Called to account before the Orgburo of the Central Committee because of the less than encouraging state of Soviet literature, Poliansky confessed that:

> Regarding the quality of the product [literature] it must be said that despite individual merits of books there is a conspicuous dominance by books of poor quality. Russian belle-lettres suffer more often than not from the following deficiencies: a boulevard character, worthless eroticism and pornography, idealistic tendencies, the absence of a class orientation, groundless emotionalism, empty fantasy, the unconvincing portrayal of positive heroes, psychologism not of the best sort, ideological confusion, mystical attitudes, the distortion of Soviet reality, the idealisation of old *byt*, political mistakes (but still tolerable in terms of censorship), affirmation of moral feelings, overattention to unhealthy criminality, an overflow of eroticism, a maudlin, sentimental portrayal of the revolution and Soviet *byt* and confusing, deliberate ambiguity.[11]

The reason for the censor's inability to shape literature at this time into a single voice was, as is clear in his lengthy report, bureaucratic misdirection, overwork and incompetence. Yet, demonstrably, it was due as well to the mixed messages he himself was receiving regarding what he was supposed to be doing. Surely not alone, he hinted that the Kremlin had abdicated its leadership role by offering guidance only in the form of platitude or, worse, equivocation as with the 1926 resolution that commanded literature for the Komsomol 'to reflect life in all its contradictions, avoiding painting everything in positive red and, at the same time, depiction of only the dark sides.'[12]

Poliansky's admission, combined with the active efforts of the Young Guardists to strip sheen and gloss from representations of Soviet life, should give us cause to re-evaluate the context of Zoshchenko's writing in the 1920s. Not only was it inherently ambiguous, it was published in an atmosphere of wide latitude which was not only a product of inconsistent functioning of state-party apparatuses but of the deliberate actions of some of the most vocal marxists on the literary scene. While Zoshchenko did not associate with the Young Guardists and he did not publish in their journals (his Serapion pedigree assured that they would never be allies), the examples presented above, however brief, suggest that perhaps we should reconsider our understanding of state control. Whatever its power then, it was also beset with internal contradictions and sometimes conflicting purposes – all of which contributed to a chaotic, open and thus unpredictable environment which does not yield to the standard, traditional binarism used to describe the position of the writer in the 1920s. Put bluntly, as foolish as this might sound, I would be hard-pressed to define what exactly constitutes 'anti-Soviet' writing for this decade when in 1929 we can still find a positive portrait of Trotsky as in Platoshkin's *On the Road* or, alternately, in Chetverikov's *Aftergrowth* where the Cheka headquarters is portrayed as Lucifer's den. There are, of course, clear-cut examples of writing openly directed against the state or the system, and I would leave aside the obvious cases of a Zamiatin or Bulgakov. But if the subject is mainstream literature then how are we to catalogue the marxist journals in which one can find almost any topic including depictions of party members as sexual predators, despondent suicides or drug abusers, and which avoid the expected *deus ex machina* ending or leaden didacticism? Indeed, what label does someone with impeccable party credentials like Gladkov deserve when he followed the success of *Cement* with 'Drunken Sun,' a novella set at a rest home where party members are recuperating from sexually indulgent lives that have left them nerve-shattered and exhausted?

Ironically, the question as to what constituted 'anti-Soviet' was not clear-cut to Poliansky himself, as he admitted that the very directives issued to him by the Politburo were too ambivalent, allowing for the 'dark sides' of Soviet life to be portrayed if the work overall was not 'inimical to the Soviet state.' Such indirection dramatises the clouded atmosphere where clarity of political affiliation becomes problematic – not only for critics then, as evidenced by the vicissitudes of Zoshchenko's reception and the contradictory claims made on him, but also now for us as well. If he is to be an anti-Soviet satirist for attacking the precepts of the state in the 1920s, then the question arises: what precisely were these precepts? There was, as of yet, no single canon, ideologically or aesthetically, but rather a plurality of differing and often contradictory canonettes nurtured by this or that marxist group or faction.

The result was an amorphous, ambiguous literary environment where much more was circulating than we commonly assume, and many writers in the 1920s therefore rightfully considered they had a licence to explore negative sides of *byt* whether for comic, satiric or documentary purposes. Many, like Zoshchenko and Ilf and Petrov, were not marxists but this in no way means that their writing was intended as attacks against the system or the ideals of the state. By looking at the full context of their work – which cannot be fully addressed in the scope of this paper – we can see that the substance of what they were doing was not out of the ordinary, was not unprecedented and not outrageous. At least in the 1920s, as the experiences of *The Young Guard* show, one could see oneself as loyal and yet still criticise elements of the system.

I am all the more convinced that it is necessary to read Zoshchenko across the whole spectrum of early Soviet literature with all its contradictions, given recent studies – not only that of Booker and Juraga – which resurrect him again as a strict anti-Soviet writer while claiming to avoid the straitjacket of early ideological blinders.[13] The end of the Cold War, combined with the theoretical premises of post-structuralism, has certainly made us suspicious of a binary definition of culture, yet for individual writers this does not mean that in our critical activity we have necessarily forsworn its benefit. The dominance of 'transgression' and 'subversion' in contemporary theory has given new impetus to read Zoshchenko through a one-way ideological frame. Revealingly, in these cases proof of Zoshchenko's intent lies almost solely at a theoretical level that once again allows little provision to register a writer outside of a zero-sum, anti/pro stance and is bolstered by an unwillingness to grapple with the cultural context of his work outside of traditional schemata. The canon, in effect, is upheld by its very absences.

If we are to learn from satire – after all, its primary role is supposedly pedagogic – it would be worthwhile to see its lessons directed at us. Regarding that of the early Soviet Union, its value today may be more metacritical, that is, forcing us to confront our own interpretive demons born of prejudices and ideological assumptions that have not necessarily passed with the end of the Cold War. If Zoshchenko is to be a satirist, then we should allow for more latitude in our understanding of him. We should avoid, I believe, coming to him with preformed assumptions that because it is Zoshchenko and because of his persecution we must, therefore, assume anti-Soviet intentions. This would not make sense given the literary environment in which he wrote but would also be an injustice to him. Many Soviet critics in the 1920s did admirable jobs in reducing him to a monochromatic palette, flatting his complex writing into pancake political tracts. We should avoid doing the same. There is no one word to qualify his stories; no one political label to define his intentions.

Today we have more of an opportunity and, arguably, responsibility to graduate from a binary moulding of Soviet culture, whether born of old ideology or resurrected in certain applications of contemporary theory. Our field has witnessed a veritable revolution due to the opening of archives and increased opportunity for academic-intellectual exchanges, which have vitalised our ability to penetrate behind the walls thrown up by official Soviet culture and the consequent ones we have reflexively built. This profound change makes the past, whether seen in artistic, political or social terms, infinitely more complex and confusing. This, however, should be employed to our benefit and give us cause to re-evaluate how we read the icons of literature from decades ago – no matter what our ingrained notions of Stalin, Socialist Realism or the Soviet Union itself.

11

EVGENY ZAMIATIN

The art of irony

VLADIMIR TUNIMANOV

In his lectures on the technique of fictional prose, Zamiatin considered humour, laughter and irony to be hallmarks of the new literary trend of 'neo-realism', a term that had been applied to Fedor Sologub, Ilia Erenburg and some of the 'Serapion Brothers' (Lev Lunts, Veniamin Kaverin). Zamiatin emphasised the distinction between the 'neo-realists' and the symbolists, who had 'the courage to depart from life', but who shunned laughter. In his obituary for Anatole France, Zamiatin recalls the words of Aleksandr Blok, which in his opinion exactly captured the suspicious and even hostile attitude of the symbolists towards laughter in general and towards irony in particular: 'Blok said that he could not accept Anatole France: 'he is somehow not genuine, with him everything is irony.' For Blok, France was 'not genuine' because he was a real European to the very end; because out of the two possible solutions to life, Blok and Russia chose the tragic one, with both hatred and love, stopping at nothing, whereas France, also stopping at nothing, chose the ironic solution, with relativism and scepticism'.[1]

Zamiatin's stand against other declarations by Blok was equally pointed: in particular, his stand against the theses formulated in Blok's essay 'Irony', which was first published in 1908 and – notably – republished a further two times, in 1918 and 1919. In the essay, the symbolist-poet wrote about irony as an illness, related to spiritual diseases, about 'destructive, devastating laughter': 'It manifests itself as assaults of stifling laughter, which begins with a diabolically scornful, provocative smile and ends in violence and blasphemy'.[2] To Blok, the 'laughter demon' seemed to possess the vast majority of his contemporaries, who drowned 'their joy and their despair, themselves and their loved ones, their works, their lives and finally their death' in laughter 'as in vodka'.[3] Irony, he concluded, is 'the bite of a vampire'. For him the age was marked by an universal epidemic of destructive irony. 'We were all intoxicated by Heine's provocative irony', writes Blok, including himself also among those who had contracted the disease. Moreover, Blok quotes Heine in order to communicate the very essence of the crisis, calling Heine's words 'a cry for salvation' when he says: '*I am unable to understand where irony ends and where heaven begins!*'.[4]

And for Blok, the more powerful the talent of the artist, the more destructive the effect of the irony. Dostoevsky, Leonid Andreev, Sologub are celebrated 'Russian satirists, unmaskers of social vices and plagues' and their works are, of course, 'useful' in this sense (utilitarian, almost in the spirit of the nihilistic aesthetics of the men of the sixties), but at the same time Blok prays to be preserved 'from their destructive laughter, from their irony'.[5] The necessarily radical and curative medicine which Blok proposes, calling it the 'sacred formula', is, so to speak, made up of three authoritarian precepts: 'There is a sacred formula which is, in one way or another, repeated by all writers: 'Renounce yourself for yourself, but not for Russia' (Gogol). 'In order to be oneself, one must renounce oneself' (Ibsen). 'Individual self-renunciation is not the renunciation of one's *personality*, but a *person*'s renunciation of his or her egoism' (Vl. Soloviev). And that is not simply advice. It is a kind of sermon addressed at contemporaries infected with irony: 'I am convinced that herein lies the cure for "irony", which is a disease of the personality, a disease of "individualism".'[6]

Such a stance was not simply alien to Zamiatin; it aroused his deepest hostility and he rejected it outright. The irony of the neo-realists, Zamiatin emphasised, is art that has been hardened and cooled, stripped of every 'sacred formula' and religious support: 'There are two ways of overcoming the tragedy of life: religion or irony. The neo-realists chose the second method. They believe neither in God, nor in man.'[7] Zamiatin called such a world view 'conscious agnosticism', considering it necessary to stress that he is talking about irony in the highest sense of the word – not 'in centimetres' which is 'pitiful', but about scathing, merciless irony that has no respect for authoritarian and dominant opinions, the irony of Swift, of Anatole France, the deep and tragic irony of Dostoevsky. But at the same time irony is tolerant and opposes all kinds of dogmatism and fanaticism. Zamiatin, in his obituary for France (the author he most respected among his fellow writers), cited the words which were also his own creative creed: 'The irony which I advocate is not cruel; it laughs neither at love, nor at beauty; it teaches us to laugh at the evil and the stupid, whom without it we would hate' (394).

The art of irony in Zamiatin's oeuvre reaches a peak in the novel *We*. Irony permeates all elements of the work's artistic structure, tingeing everything with relativistic-sceptical tones: the past, present and future, social and private life, religion, science, art and politics. Often this irony imperceptibly overflows into self-irony. In its universal penetrability and ubiquity, a potential healing strength lies concealed.

The scale of irony in the novel is already indicated by the title, and the purpose is poignantly and powerfully achieved in the apocalyptic epilogue, which proclaims the inevitable triumph of reason. Zamiatin's irony is polyphonic and polysemantic. The central image of the novel encompassed by the comprehensive pronoun 'we' is notable for its diverse facets and shades. 'We' is, of course, the citizen-numbers of the One State: 'we are a single powerful, million-celled organism ... we are, in the words of the ancient "Gospel", the one Church.' It is the triumph of unanimity and disciplined loyalty: 'I see how everyone votes for the Benefactor; everyone sees how I vote for the Benefactor – and how could it be otherwise, as "everyone" and "I" form the single "We"?'(Entry 24). 'I' is disturbing and the narrator, the rocket engineer D-503, feels obliged to stress that its use is conditional, a kind of tribute to the old language: 'I will try only to note down what I see, what I think – or to be exact, what we think (that's it precisely: we, and let this "WE" be the title of my entries)' (Entry 1). In essence, 'I' should be transposed into a dictionary of abolished and obsolete word-concepts, alongside others in inverted commas: 'mother', 'family', 'spirit', 'love', 'jealousy' 'inspiration', 'apartment', 'grand piano', 'fireplace', 'dreams', 'rain'. 'We', as D-503 persistently informs his 'planetary readers', annihilates the very idea of 'I', thus achieving the dream of absolute equality: 'no-one is *one* but rather *one of.* We are so alike ...' (Entry 2). But such absolute equality even in the One State is an 'ideal', a 'theory' as the conscientious and sincere chronicler has to admit: 'On my right – there she was, slim, sharp, tough and flexible, like a whip: I-330 (I can see her number now): on my left – there was O, totally different, everything about her round, with the childish fold on her arm; and at the end of our circle of four was a masculine number that I didn't know – curved somehow in two places like the letter S. We were all different...' (Entry 2). The thing is that all the 'numbers' in the novel are indeed different, with sharply defined characters and unique, individual features. They are all individuals, including D-503 himself, who having taken the tragic path from loyal number and devout believer in the Table of Hours to that of a rebel with an 'incurable soul' is later transformed into a sterile being, incapable of dreams or 'imagination' after the operation that surgically removes this part of his brain. That is why the hero's pedagogical message, regardless of the sincerity of his intentions, is exploded from inside by the ubiquitous Irony which introduces unwanted elements of parody and the grotesque: 'Our gods are down here with us, in the office, in the kitchen, in the workshop, in the toilet, the gods have become like us: ergo – we've become like the gods. And we're on our way to you, my unknown planetary readers, we're coming to make your lives divinely rational and precise, like ours...' (Entry 12). The ellipsis is significant: the narrator-hero has clearly become entangled and the eulogy, reflecting his confusion, turns into caricature and hostile criticism. The ground has fallen away under his feet (even mathematics has disclosed all its irrational properties and has 'betrayed' him). He has become lost in 'pronouns': 'But who are "they" anyway? And who am I: "they" or "we" – how should I know?' (Entry 25). The hero has been condemned himself to feeling the 'pitiful caged psychology' of the ancients, about whom he has spoken with such irony and disdain. And he can no longer say: 'We have nothing to hide from one another' (Entry 4). It turns out that a lot has to be 'hidden': transparency has disappeared; the glass space allotted to him to 'live' in has been converted into a prison, more nightmarish than the 'prehistoric' dungeons.

M. Iu. Liubimova recently suggested that, in 1920 (the year from which Zamiatin's novel dates), one of Lenin's speeches devoted to the third anniversary of the revolution 'might not only have suggested the title of the novel to the author, but also served as the source for some of the book's ideas and images. The language in which the new power addressed its citizens achieved its final embodiment in this speech by the leader. In Lenin's speech the pronoun "we" is repeated 64 times on the five pages of the text (its derivatives "us", "our" and so on – 43 times). What is more, on 18 occasions, the pronoun "we" begins the sentence. As a rule, the pronoun "we" is accompanied by the verbs "know", "knew" (11 times), "are conquering" or "have conquered" (10 times), and repeatedly by the verbs and verb forms – "can", "must", "are sure", "were right", "were strong and firm".'[8]

Elements of anti-utopia and high lampoon are certainly abundant in the novel. It is an unusually topical and polemical work. Researchers of the novel, with varying degrees of persuasiveness, have pointed out a number of sources that served as a target for Zamiatin's sharp and hard-hitting irony, both in this work and in articles attributed to him. (Here we ought to single out, in particular, the article 'Paradise' with quotations – direct and indirect – from the fantastic social novels – lampoons of France and Wells). The political journalism of the time is parodied in the novel: the speeches of the leaders, the decrees, edicts, newspaper editorials and satirical articles, politicised 'odes' and 'anthems' by the politically engaged literati. Both the high-flown and the servile language of the new era are parodied in the novel. The narrator D-503, as a privileged Number in the One State, has, of course, almost perfect command of both these forms. The articles of the State newspaper (one must suppose the only one in existence) contain examples of the new style. Time and again the hero cites it ecstatically for our edification. It is impossible, however, to single out any one political (or poetic) text that served as starting-point for Zamiatin. The highly compact (and partly encoded) narrative in which integrated images and motifs predominate can by no means be reduced to a topical political and literary polemic. There are several layers of narrative, interwoven and adjoined in a complex way. 'We' are not only the highly developed numbers, constantly counterpointed to their forebears ('they', but you see 'they', too, called themselves 'we' in the old days, remarks D-503, contemptuously slighting his museum predecessors). In the book, there are also other 'they's (from the narrator's point of view): the anarchists, members of the underground society 'Mephi', disciples of eternal revolt and worshippers of energy, who contemplate the permanent destruction of equilibrium, an 'agonisingly-endless movement'. They proudly call themselves 'anti-Christians', opposing those such as the ideological followers of the Table of Hours and the earlier Christians whom they even refuse to acknowledge as their forebears. They worship energy and are filled with energy, but energy that is as destructive and no less cruel in essence than the precautionary-safeguarding measures of the Benefactor and his Bureau. The One State has been created through compulsory measures: 'There was a hollow wail: black endless lines of people were being driven into the city, in order to be saved by force and taught happiness' (Entry 28). But the 'Mephi' conspirators also want to force the numbers to worship energy, and this is declared with a striking single-mindedness by the heroine, who is herself portrayed with great sympathy in the novel. 'You all have to be stripped naked and driven into the forest. You should learn to tremble with fear, with joy, insane rage, cold – you should learn to pray to the fire' (Entry 24). The naive and law-abiding D-503 is introduced to the science of suffering by the predatory and infernal heroine, who deceives and seduces, using him as material for the good of the revolution. The new turns out to be a reworking of the 'old'. The hero dies as a personality, as an individual on the front line of the two opposing 'we's – the rulers and the rebels, dying from the very 'knife', the praises of which he sang in his own confessional diary: 'A knife is the most permanent, the most immortal and the most ingenious of all man's creations. The knife was a guillotine, the knife is a universal means of resolving all conflicts, and the path of paradox lies along the blade of a knife – the only path worthy of a fearless mind. . .' (Entry 20). But the path of paradoxes is dangerous and insidious and far from everyone is granted the gift of possessing fearlessness of mind. With the ellipsis the hero's reasoning once again comes to an abrupt end and he does not manage to fill in this gap.

The rebels are good and in a certain sense 'useful' as necessary ferment and an antidote in a stagnant society approaching the dangerous boundary of decline. They are good at an early selfless and sacrificial stage of revolt. But rebels who have achieved victory seem destined to be transformed into rulers and guardians in their turn, into Grand and small inquisitors, into Benefactors and Benefactresses. Zamiatin wrote in an article 'Scythians?': 'Christ on Golgotha in between two robbers, bleeding profusely drop by drop, is the victor because He is crucified – in practical terms, defeated. But the Christ who has conquered in practice becomes the Grand Inquisitor. And it is worse still when the one who has conquered in practice is this pot-bellied priest in a lilac silk-lined cassock, giving a blessing with the right hand and gathering donations with the left. . . . Such is the irony and such is the wisdom of fate. Wisdom, because the pledge of eternal forward movement lies in this ironic law. The realisation, the falling to the ground, the victory of an idea in practice immediately debases it to a philistine level.'[9]

And in this 'ironic' sense the executed heroine of the novel is the victor. But she foresees a completely different continuation, pledged *a priori* in the 'ironic law' of history, which forces the narrator with much sadness to admit: 'And we know, for the time being, at least, that there is no final number. Maybe we'll forget this. No – it's more than likely that we'll forget this when we get old, just as everything inevitably gets old. At which time we, too, will ultimately go down, just as leaves fall from the tree in the autumn – just as, the day after tomorrow, you will too. . .' (Entry 30). The heroine's confession forms a philosophical counterpoint in the novel, directly recalling Zamiatin's own words in a letter to Iury Annenkov, a prelude to the novel *We*:

> Some wise astronomical professor (I've forgotten his name) recently calculated that the universe, as it turns out, is not infinite at all: its form is spherical and its radius tens of thousands of astronomical light years. But what if you ask him: yes, but if you go beyond the limits of your spherical and finite universe, what then? Further, Annenkov, further, beyond your endless technical progress? Why, you have your delightful public convenience; why, even more delightful, it has music . . .; then finally, you have the only international, delightful, most delightful, sweetest-smelling public convenience, but what then?
>
> Then – everyone will run from these most delightful public conveniences into disorganised and inexpedient bushes'.[10]

Zamiatin was being cunning. He had not, of course, forgotten the name 'of the astronomical professor'. He named him in the sketch 'White Love': 'Einstein, having lost himself in sophisms, calculated that the universe was finite, and its radius equal to so many billion versts. . .' (323). Zamiatin did not forget Einstein's 'sophistry' in the novel *We* either. In a scene where the author's irony reaches particular heights he 'places' the brilliant physicist (laconically portrayed as a scientist, a thinker: 'his forehead was a huge parabola, on which were the yellow, indecipherable lines of his wrinkles') on a seat next to D-503 in one of the most fragrant, sterile public conveniences of the One State. There the scientist, D-503's neighbour, tells him about his discovery: he has already almost calculated that infinity does not exist (he just has to calculate the numerical coefficient), and this means, therefore, that 'philosophical' victory is near. This is already the last 'full stop'. But not so; even at this apocalyptic moment, instead of a full stop or exclamation mark, impertinent and heretical questions are to be heard from the 'philosopher of mathematics' D-503: 'You have to, you have to answer me: there, where your finite universe ends, what is there beyond?' (Entry 39).

In the novel, two world views or rather two religions are constantly juxtaposed, the Bible and the Table of Hours, 'the Law of God' of the ancients and the laws of the One State. The religion and morals of the One State represent a reshaping of ancient social and religious foundations and precepts into a new mechanical and chemical mode. The sterile and 'improved' 'new religion' is genetically linked by the tightest of bonds to the old: 'In the ancient world, this was understood by the Christians, our only (albeit very imperfect) forefathers: humility is a virtue, but pride is a vice; *We* comes from God, *I* from the Devil' (Entry 22). The numbers in the One State, nevertheless, speak of God condescendingly and with contempt, incessantly singing of the final defeat over 'the old God and the old Life': 'The God of the ancients created ancient man, that is to say, a being prone to error, and He, therefore, erred himself. The multiplication table is wiser and more absolute than the ancient God: it never – repeat, never – makes a mistake' (Entry 12). They are proud of the fact that they have 'fastened the sun forever with a chain to the Zenith – we Joshuas, sons of Nun'. Zamiatin masterfully ridicules the crude atheistic propaganda sanctioned by the victorious Bolsheviks. Suffice it to mention the comparison between the new Guardians (the investigation and surveillance services) and the ancient Guardian Angels: 'Who knows – maybe it was precisely them, the Guardians, that ancient man foresaw in his fantasy about the formidably tender 'archangels' that were assigned to every human at birth' (Entry 12). But the new religion without God, love, mystery and tradition is dry and boring, primitively impoverished and elementary as a multiplication table. It is devoid of perspective, it is, so to speak, horizontal, the religion of numbers, imprisoned in a glass cage: 'The ancients knew what was up there: their magnificent, bored, sceptic – God. We know that it's a crystal blue, naked, indecent nothing' (Entry 11). And in a head numbed by methodical and mendacious propaganda he makes a comparison between a blessed and great Christian festival and the terrible Day of Unanimity: "For us I think it's something like "Easter" was for the ancients' (Entry 24).

When speaking about the execution of heretics and free-thinkers by the new court-tribunal, D-503 calls this regulated and cynical arbitrariness 'divine justice, as dreamt of by the people of the stone-house age, illuminated by the rosy naive rays of the dawn of history: Their "God" punished blasphemy against the Holy Church in the same way as he did murder'(Entry 20). Out of all bygone eras, the new religion without God and the resurrection, revoking the soul, love and compassion alike, has enthusiastically assimilated above all the experience of the inquisition. In particular, the sinister figure of the Benefactor, this 'new Jehovah in His aero' throws the despotic substance of the great, divine, precise, wisest 'line of the One State' into relief. The monologues of the Benefactor are a shameless apologia for butchery and cruelty: 'A true algebraic love of mankind is absolutely inhumane, and the indispensable sign of truth is its cruelty' (Entry 36).

Mankind's ancient dream about paradise is turned inside out, dislocated and illuminated in a tragic light of irony. The Benefactor talks about it in the language of a butcher and a jailer:

> I ask this question: What is it that people beg for, dream about, torment themselves for, from the time they leave swaddling clothes? They want someone to tell them, once and for all, what happiness is – and then to bind them to that happiness with a chain. What is it we're doing right now, if not that? The ancient dream of paradise. . . Remember: In paradise they have no knowledge of desires, pity, love – there they are blessed, with their imaginations surgically removed (the only reason why they are blessed); they are angels, the slaves of God . . . And now, at the very moment when we've achieved this dream, when we have seized it like this (He squeezed his hand shut so tight that if a rock had been in it, juice would have shot out), when all that remained was to dress the kill and divide it into portions – at this very moment you – you. (Entry 36)

The most oppressive thing about the Benefactor's monologue is that he speaks in all seriousness when laying down the foundations of this misanthropic religion and explaining the symbol of belief to the heretic lost in the irrational thicket of 'children's' questions. The Benefactor seeks to restore D-503's shaken 'faith' in the infallibility of the One State and his place in it.[11] The extraordinary 'poem of Paradise', the plot of which the poet R-13 outlines to D-503, and which is an echo of Ivan Karamazov's 'poem' about the Grand Inquisitor, is completely different in its mockingly grotesque ironic mode:

> Fetters – that's what the world had always longed for, do you see? . . . We helped God finally overcome the Devil, – it was the Devil who pushed people to break the commandment and taste freedom and be ruined. It was him, the wily serpent. But we crushed his head under our boot – c-c-crack! And it was all over: Paradise once more. And we're simple and innocent again, like Adam and Eve. None of those complications about good and evil: everything is very simple, heavenly, childishly simple. The Benefactor, the Machine, the Cube, the Gas Bell, the Guardians: all of these are good, all are sublime, beautiful, noble, elevated, crystal pure. Because that is what protects our non-freedom, that is to say, our happiness. (Entry 11)[12]

The jokes of his 'friend' annoy the hero: 'Jokes are a bad habit with R-13' (Entry 8). The poet R-13 ironises, parodies, jokes and tries to incite jokes from D-503, but the latter completely fails to understand the jokes and, above all, the subtle taunting and stinging of multi-composite and polysemantic irony.[13] He is afraid that his 'unknown readers' will think that he is 'making wicked jokes', and admits that he is 'not capable of making jokes'. This he regards as a positive feature, since 'the default value of every joke is a lie' (Entry 3). The judgement is deeply unjust: it arises from the confusion of a mathematician-philosopher who has found himself in ironic surroundings; the candid, naive and forever earnest reaction of D-503 to the words of 'the tempters' magnificently sets off the irony, a device used frequently by Zamiatin. R-13's 'poem of Paradise' is pointedly caustic; the words appear to endorse the One State's ideology but invite an opposite interpretation. D-503's simple-minded appreciation, however, brilliantly misses this point: '[R] has such a stupid, asymmetrical appearance, but such a straight-thinking mind' (Entry 11).

The novel concludes tragically. The main heroine I-330 and the poet-conspirator R-13 both die. Many of the numbers, including 'Einstein' and the narrator, 'the philosopher of mathematics', have to undergo operations to cauterise their 'imaginations'. However, the most nightmarish of all is the hero's completely 'optimistic' belief in the victory of reason, in 'our' victory: 'And I hope we will win. More – I'm certain we'll win. Because reason has to win.' The full stop at the end of this sentence, the last words of the novel, is equivalent to death and to the final 'grammatical' victory which the hero already reflected on long before his operation: 'the unknown is in general the enemy of man, and *homo sapiens* – is not fully man until his grammar is absolutely rid of question marks, leaving nothing but exclamation marks, commas and full stops' (Entry 21). The hero has even surpassed this 'ideal', having been saved from emotional exclamation marks alongside desires and fantasies. He has been 'cured' once and for all, and therefore smiles all the time, and cannot help smiling since 'a smile is the normal condition of a normal person'. The blessed smile of an idiot without a mind or imagination, a hollow creature, who has just told the Benefactor everything he knew about the 'enemies of happiness'. Not long before he had smiled completely differently, charmed by 'her' smile: 'She smiles lightly, happily, and I smile. The earth is drunk, merry, light – it's sailing...' (Entry 27)

However, the epilogue to the novel is an appendix written by another person, someone whose 'I' has finally dissolved into 'we'. Those moments when irrational revolt lifted the hero to dizzying heights of genuine, albeit torturous, happiness and when he drunk the air of unseen, but also genuine, freedom are both valuable and unforgettable: 'I felt myself above everyone; I was ... myself, something separate, a world in itself; I stopped being one of many, the way I'd always been, I became one' (Entry 27). But this 'world in itself' of one person, despite all the power of the guardians and benefactors remains as mysterious, secretive and infinite as before. I-330 directly comments on this in the novel: 'A person is a novel: right up until the last page you don't know how it's going to end. Otherwise it wouldn't be worth reading...' (Entry 28). And this time the ellipsis contains within itself a deep symbolic meaning.

The endless, very often polemically pointed, questions do not simply prevail in Zamiatin's novel, they dominate. They clearly triumph aesthetically, psychologically and 'philosophically'. Irony and laughter are the main heroes of the novel. The irony is multi-directional and all-embracing. It is based on both genuine love for mankind and the rejection of cruelty, deception, fraud, demagogy and the many faces of tyranny. The element of laughter is also multi-faceted. Sometimes, sadly not very often, laughter sounds joyful and carefree: 'she burst out laughing and splashed me all over with her laughter, the whole delirium passed, and little bursts of laughter were sparkling and ringing everywhere and how... how wonderful it all was' (Entry 17). Laughter has its own amplitude and an almost palpable form: 'I just saw the laugh with my eyes: the ringing, steep, curve of that laugh, lithe and elastic as a whip' (Entry 7). It might sound contemptuous, challenging, deliberately 'loud – too loud' (Entry 31)). One might laugh 'a desperate, final laugh' (Entry 35) and, finally, as the far too serious, joke-hating hero discovers, laughter is more cunning and terrible than any 'dagger': 'And that was when I learned from my own experience that laughter is the most terrifying weapon there is. With laughter you can kill everything – even murder itself' (Entry 35). And it is this annihilating feature of laughter and of Zamiatin's novel that 'they' appreciated all too keenly in the homeland of the writer – so keenly that nearly seven decades had to pass before it could be published there.

Translated by Hazel Grünewald

12

GODLESS AT THE MACHINE TOOL

Antireligious humoristic journals of the 1920s and 1930s

ANNIE GÉRIN

> A Marxist must be a materialist, i.e., an enemy of religion, but a dialectical materialist, i.e., one who treats the struggle against religion not in an abstract way, not on the basis of remote, purely theoretical, never varying preaching, but in a concrete way, on the basis of the class struggle which is going on *in practice* and is educating the masses more and better than anything else could.
>
> *V.I. Lenin*[1]

IN 1909, Lenin wrote, 'The philosophical basis of Marxism ... is dialectical materialism ... a materialism which is absolutely atheistic and positively hostile to all religion.'[2] He later compared religion to moonshine, blurring the vision of its consumers. These views, shared by a section of the pre-Revolutionary intelligentsia, echo Marx's earlier words: 'Religion is the sign of the oppressed creature, the heart of the heartless world, just as it is the spirit of a spiritless situation. It is the opium of the people.'[3]

In the Marxist-Leninist worldview, hostility towards religion and the more concrete use of propaganda in antireligious campaigns were not peripheral issues. The eradication of religious belief from a population considered backward was deemed key in establishing a socialist culture, divorced from pre-Revolutionary identities, values and practices. Indeed, religion, in its orthodox catholic form, had been one of the main legitimisation tools within the Russian Empire. For hundreds of years, Russian peasants had called themselves *krestianin*, from the word Christian, and a person's religious identity was marked on their official documents until the Revolution. A socialist culture would in turn foster a new social order and provide a free human being, the *novyi chelovek*. The demystification of religions,

Christian, Judaic, Muslim or Buddhist, considered as illusionary forms of human fulfilment, was therefore at the core of communist practice. The same applied to pagan elements, including a sophisticated demonology believed to influence all aspects of life, which survived the import of Christianity, subsumed into the ritual and the practice of everyday life in Russian society.[4]

Disenfranchisement of all ecclesiastical officials soon followed the Revolution; however, the Soviet state was not willing to go beyond this measure. Indeed, chapter five, article thirteen of the RSFSR Constitution asserted that: 'In order to ensure genuine freedom of conscience for the working people, the Church is separate from the State, and the School from the Church: and freedom of religious and antireligious propaganda is recognised for all citizens.'[5] Yet, as Lewis Sieglebaum remarks, like much else at the time, the centre's wishes, if known at all, were ignored in the provinces. Persecutions and killings of priests, looting and desecration of churches and monasteries – all carried out by or at least with the approval of local authorities – were commonplace and were very much part of the Civil War.[6]

Although the 1918 constitution 'secured' freedom of belief, the Church was in fact inhibited by the gradual loss of its resources and privileges. Several practical transformations in social life also made participation in religious activities more difficult. On 30 July 1923, for example, official holidays, which had so far coincided with Church holidays, were transferred to the Julian calendar so that Church holidays became working days and could no longer be appropriately celebrated. Since *holy* days had been so important in marking the tempo of life, the organic cohesion between the religious cycle and the yearly cycle needed to be eroded by the new regime. In addition, an assortment of Soviet holidays was created.[7] The reportedly confusing five-day uninterrupted production week (*nepreryvka*) further complicated the exercise of the cult. Based on a multiple-shift system, the *nepreryvka* (1928) was primarily designed to increase production by keeping factories running continuously during the First Five-Year Plan.

> Previously, the norm was 79 days off per year, consisting of 52 Sundays, 13 holidays and 14 days composed of the two hours off workers received on Saturdays and before holidays. With the introduction of the 5-day week (4 days on and one day off), workers had 73 days off plus 5 revolutionary holidays, or a total of 78 days.[8]

Clearly, while this measure was meant to increase productivity, it also aimed to eliminate the traditional sacred days of Christianity and Judaism by removing from the week both Saturday and Sunday. Consequently, on any traditional day of worship, only one fifth of the Soviet work force was able to attend religious services. And this fraction did not represent the same people every week. In a context where only 20 per cent of the population had any given weekday off, workers reportedly complained about the impossibility of conducting normal family lives. The six-day week (*chestidnevnik*) was established in response to these complaints in 1931, when Saturday was given back to the population as a common day of rest.[9]

As well as being supported by institutional changes such as those previously mentioned, antireligious propaganda benefited from state resources even if it was organised by relatively independent voluntary associations like the *Komsomol* (the communist youth organisation) and competing antireligious militant groups. Strategies included the integration of antireligious slogans in various Soviet parades; State sponsorship of anti-religious films, journals, travelling theatre productions; the creation of numerous museums of world religion and atheism, such as the one located in the former Strastnoi Monastery in Moscow; as well as a vast campaign to denounce the clergy as fraudulent. For instance, challenging the belief that the bodies of saints never decay, relics accumulated by the clergy, bits of bodies miraculously preserved, were exposed and revealed to be wax.[10] However, the lack of cohesion between organisations and propaganda vehicles sometimes caused antireligionists to work at cross-purposes.

A clear example of conflict occurred as a consequence of the first *Komsomol* Christmas, organised on 6 January 1923. The event consisted of a group mockery of the religious holiday, and featured processions of students and young workers dressed as clowns, cantering up and down streets and boulevards. The *Komsomol* sang the *Internationale*, whipping and burning oversized overstuffed religious effigies. This strategy, also used at *Evsektsiia*,[11] which organised a celebration in the Jewish community called *Yom Kippurnik*, was in fact a pre-Revolutionary carnivalesque form. But the specific mischief of the *Komsomol* Christmas sufficiently outraged the sensibilities of believers and non-believers alike to provoke the Central Committee to recommend that the planned *Komsomol* Easter be restricted to the organisation of lectures, movies and plays.

Moreover, a resolution passed by the 12th Party Congress that same year insisted that antireligionists should not 'offend the feelings of believers, since this would only lead to an increase in their religious fanaticism. The deliberately coarse methods . . ., the mocking of objects of the faith and worship, . . . do not expedite but hamper the emancipation of the working masses from religious prejudice.'[12] The declaration also recognised that religious beliefs would continue as long as peasants and some workers remained dependent on *nature* and/or *capitalist* relations. It therefore called for the training of antireligious propagandists in Party schools and workers' circles, the publication of scientific and popular literature on the origin and class nature of religion and on the counter-revolutionary activities the church had engaged in up to that point. This general scheme complied with Lenin's earlier recommendation:

> We must *know how* to combat religion, and in order to do so we must explain the source of faith and religion among the masses *in a materialist way.* The combating of religion cannot be confined to abstract ideological preaching, and it must not be reduced to such preaching. It must be linked up with the concrete practice of the class movement, which aims at eliminating the social root of religion.[13]

It has been observed that the beginning of an organised antireligious campaign corresponds to the inauguration of several periodical publications in 1922 and 1923. These were to compensate for the lack of skilled propagandists, who would have needed to be knowledgeable in both religion and atheism in order to conduct lectures and discussions with a presumably hostile public. Nevertheless, even *à propos* the print medium it shouldn't be said that antireligious propaganda consisted of a coherent or homogenous body of work. Those familiar with the early Soviet period know that government sponsorship and censorship of published matter never guaranteed adherence to the official Party line. Accordingly, the two principal rival factions on the antireligious front both created their own journal, which, in the early 1920s, could be easily distinguished through examination of the linguistic and visual rhetorical tools and strategies they developed.

In December 1922, Emelian Yaroslavsky founded a weekly newspaper titled *Bezbozhnik* (*Godless*).[14] In this paper, national news was juxtaposed with serialised popular-scientific essays on religion. Yaroslavsky's approach was based on a bureaucratised version of the Leninist assumption that exposure to rationalist explanations of natural phenomena as well as the application of scientific, ethical and clean living would naturally demystify religion. Writers who expressed their views in *Bezbozhnik* also contributed to other atheist publications, such as the highbrow *Antireligioznik* (*Antireligious*) and *Nauka i religiia* (*Science and Religion*). *Bezbozhnik* soon became the voice of the Society of Friends of the Godless (founded in 1923 by Yaroslavsky), which became the Godless League in 1925 and was renamed the League of the Militant Godless in 1929.[15] The League's goals were the following. First, to demonstrate to the masses that religion in all its forms had always been the enemy of the workers. Second, to prove that natural science explains everything, and therefore leaves no room for religion. Third, to demonstrate that religion was ethically incompatible with socialism, and therefore represented a sort of disloyalty to the Soviet state. The league devised a Five-Year plan for the total extermination of all religious and paranormal beliefs through scientific enlightenment.[16]

A second approach, considered interventionist and more confrontational, was that of Moscow Party activist Maria Kostelevskaia and her group. Kostelevskaia's strategy was termed by its detractors *popoedstvo* - clergy eating.[17] This bloc of antireligionists had a more mechanistic understanding of religion. While Yaroslavsky considered faith a complex social phenomenon that needed to be explained, Kostelevskaia's followers denounced religious orthodoxy as a direct manifestation of severe exploitation in Russia. Embarking on the socialist path with a clean slate therefore warranted immediate intervention to close churches and briskly rid the landscape of clergy. From within this frame, antireligious activity was considered very different from secularisation. Because Kostelevskaia stressed the external and current characteristics of religion, like ritual, clergy and church, rather than the nature and mechanisms of belief per se, she was accused at the aforementioned 12th Congress of not understanding the social construction of religion.

The principal propaganda organ of Kostelevskaia's group was the monthly illustrated satirical journal *Bezbozhnik u stanka* (*Godless at the machine tool*), published by the Moscow Party Committee between 1923 and 1931, its print-run ranging from 35,000 to 60,000 copies per edition.[18] The journal stood for and repeatedly defended its founder's iconoclastic stance within its pages. For example, in response to a letter from Petrograd asking why the regime was destroying religion without offering a substitute, *Bezbozhnik u stanka* (1924, no. 6) answered:

> Religion is nothing. An illusion. Can you really fill a hole with emptiness? Destroying religion, we say: study science. Science instead of religion. You need to know how nature and human society functions. Only in these conditions is it possible to give meaning to your existence.

The visually alluring publication was aimed at the urban proletariat and was dedicated to establishing the 'antireligious proletarian dictatorship of the atheist city over the countryside.'[19] The prominent Soviet caricaturist Dmitry Moor served as artistic director for most of the life of the publication, which also boasted contributions by caricaturists and Socialist Realist artists such as Aleksandr Deineka, Aleksandr Radakov and the trio Kukryniksy. *Bezbozhnik u stanka* concentrated almost exclusively on contemporary issues, rather than discussing the historical construction of religious belief. It also welcomed testimonies of conversions from religious devotion to atheism and encouraged participation from its readers. 'The most important thing is to write about concrete events from daily life. What type of events? Those that show in the most explicit way the links between the clergy and the interests of the exploiting classes.'[20] The journal also solicited jokes, poems, riddles, songs and games from its readers: 'the funnier, the wittier, the better.'[21] Contributors received an honorarium as well as a six-month subscription to the journal. For the most part, the periodical lampooned the priesthood and all religious faith through humoristic visual material.[22]

An example of the caricatures published in *Bezbozhnik u stanka* mocks not only religion, but also icons, those images of holy propaganda. Indeed, an especially popular type of Russian Christian Orthodox icon was dedicated to the life of saints. In these images, the holy man or woman was generally depicted in the centre of the configuration, framed along its four edges by a sequence of tableaux portraying in chronological order important moments in the saint's life.[23] *Vessel of the Devil* imitates this visual device to tell the story of the devout peasant woman, whose stylised, vessel-like figure occupies the core of the composition. The narrative unfolds as follows: the Devil creates the *baba*[24] in the image of a milk jug, God provides her with arms like handles and a soul like a soup pot. She then fritters her life away bowing to her husband, her children, the *kulak* and the priest, thanking the latter for enslaving her by paying him a tithe.

As well as mocking religiosity in *babas*, this representation sought to encourage women to join the godless movement, a step which would unshackle them from capitalistic exploitation, patriarchy, illiteracy and the clergy, all seen as interdependent evils. This quadruple liberation would answer Krupskaia's famous 1918 call to educate and empower women and thereby 'give Soviet society a new member.'[25] Indeed, women occupied a primary role both as subject and object of antireligious propaganda, since it was believed that they were simultaneously the main victims and guardians of religious belief. An article printed in a 1923 issue of *Bezbozhnik u stanka* clearly expressed this point of view:

> A woman is more religious than a man. It is not her fault... the conditions of life in bourgeois society are such that a worker spends productive time by a machine, interacting with older conscious comrades, participating in the class struggle and generally in political life. But the lot of mothers and female workers is different. Their life is filled with domestic work, kitchen work and sewing, in the company of equally undeveloped girlfriends and neighbours... The male peasant is also not as religious as the female peasant: he travels to town, and participates in village meetings. The female peasant knows only field and domestic work.[26]

Although this view is condescending, to say the least, it illustrates perfectly that the problem antireligionists tried to contend with was considered one of lifestyle, unrelated to questions of fundamental human nature or essence. It was therefore understood that because they traditionally upheld and transmitted social values, if women could free themselves from religion, the liberation of the whole society would ensue.

The strategy of humour coupled with antireligious activity is not specific to *Bezbozhnik u stanka.*[27] Chief Soviet satirical journals *Krokodil, Krasny perets, Krasny voron* and others all depicted the clergy as alcoholics, avaricious parasites, warmongers, sadists, etc. Images printed in these publications testify to the overall campaign's non-denominational anti-theistic stance by concurrently ridiculing clergy of all persuasions. Throughout the twenties, almost no issue of these periodicals appeared without at least one caricature ridiculing the clergy or the church.

One of the key challenges of this media phenomenon corresponds to the creation of a vocabulary and an iconography to deal with the topic of religion in an atheist state. Like other Soviet journals from this period, humoristic publications functioned as laboratories of form, style and propaganda techniques. Indeed, mass publication permitted artists to experiment with visual and narrative *tipazh*, the essence of which was not to reveal typicality, but to type cast, or typicalise new motifs by creating stereotypes.[28] In illustrated journals, the public could familiarise itself with emerging Soviet iconography. Periodicals had the additional role of educating the population by providing them with new codes, symbols and categories from which to interpret the emerging Soviet world.

The concept of a culture creating an iconography divorced from previous social codes (in this case pre-Revolutionary Russia) is quite problematic. Indeed, iconography is generally based on traditional use of visual forms. It is the cumulative use of an image through history that permits the viewer to understand its meaning and cultural function. Yet this was a time of rapid change, and the types of objects available for representation, such as aeroplanes and harvester-combines had no tradition in the history of art. It is also necessary to underscore that the values promoted by the Soviet regime and the specific subtext associated with certain configurations were transformed with the impulse of the Revolution.[29] Artists were therefore deprived of the traditional iconographic model. This question becomes even more complex with the willed creation of an antireligious iconography, which could not attempt to create types, but rather represent the *absence* of religion and superstitions previously accepted as underlying every aspect of the material world.

Many art historians have argued that Soviet artists relied on the principle of allegory to create meaning in their works. Wolfgang Holz further proposes that the lack of iconographic tradition in Soviet art was compensated by the use of this specific semiotic strategy, which he describes as a wide ranging aesthetic current that finds its sources in organised ideology, rather than individual insight or expression. According to Holz, allegory, in the particular context of a society in conflict with its traditional roots, represents one aspect of an institutionalised search for a cultural and political identity in which the nation could collectively believe.[30]

Additional consideration of this rhetorical tool can be enlightening. According to Paul de Man's systematic theory of figural language, allegory differs structurally from symbols in that it designates primarily a distance in relation to its own origin. In other words, while symbols conventionally and unequivocally denote their origin (the referent), the allegory's hidden meaning refers to an idealised past, which can never be fixed in time. 'The meaning constituted by the allegorical sign can then consist only in the *repetition* (in the Kierkegaardian sense of the term) of a previous sign with which it can never coincide, since it is the essence of this previous sign to be pure anteriority.'[31] Because the referent is pure anteriority, then allegorical meaning is constantly deferred. This rhetorical mode therefore renders transcendence or immediate cognition impossible, because it establishes a dialectic between object and subject, in which experience of the object can never be equivalent to truth or essence, but only to a perception constructed by ideology or narrative. This is particularly important in the context of visual antireligious propaganda; allegory defies the synthetic relationship that was believed to occur in the religious or superstitious worldview, where intersubjective relationships could exist between human beings and nature. Indeed, neither materialism nor atheism conceives of intersubjectivity as a possible relationship between a subject and an object. Both clearly assert the radical priority of the subject over the material world, accessible through an ideological or cultural filter.

Most Soviet visual propaganda focused on the future. The famous painting *Kolkhoz Holiday* by Arkadii Piastov (1937), for example, stages the typical exceptions. This expression borrowed from Henri Lefebvre does not denote the banal of daily existence, but signs of the future, appearing progressively in the empirical world.[32] This means that the now of a representation refers to a constantly deferred origin, which in this case happens to be located in a future (and also always deferred) communist world. So, to be precise, one could therefore speak of an inverted or a forward-looking allegory. Holz describes this temporal conflation as the 'illusion of instantaneous progress.'[33]

While images of the future void of religious references abound, very little Socialist Realist painting engages with the theme of religion at all. This is probably because religion was predicted to be absent from the communist world of the future. Antireligious propaganda therefore had to use a different strategy, one that would first deconstruct values and symbols in order to evoke their absence. The tactic chosen by antireligious illustrators was most often irony, a rhetorical mode that says black (or in this case red) when it means white. *People Live...*, a caricature published in *Bezbozhnik u stanka* in 1925 is a perfect example of this strategy. The scene unfolding in an urban dwelling depicts two workers going about their daily activities, while the persistent demons of Russian culture fool around, emerging from the sink, swinging from light fixtures, sitting on the radiator, etc.[34] The caption reads:

> People live, they drink, eat, go to work, but they don't see what goes on around them. And this is what goes on: in the water lives *vodianoi*, in the stove lives *domovoi*, in the lamp lives *paralik*, and *leshii* drops by from the ceiling for a visit. All this happens in broad daylight and nobody notices. This is just how it is.

The humour of this comment is obviously lodged in the mismatch between two worldviews; a past ensconced in a superstitious lifestyle, and a present/future firmly entrenched in materialism.[35] No, the Soviet proletariat certainly wouldn't share its home with *domovoi, leshii, paralik* and *vodianoi.* Paradoxically, because the conception of the world the artist sought to depict is void of gods and demons, in order to express the absence of superstition, he had to resort to a rhetorical mode that says precisely the opposite of what it means.

New Direction functions in a slightly different way. In this image, a striking visual paradox is evoked; two distinct tableaux constitute this centrefold of *Bezbozhnik u stanka.* The smaller one depicts two women dressed in black, kneeling in front of a heavy-set orthodox priest, bearded and robed in black. The scene is set in a darkly lit church, easily identifiable by the religious paraphernalia it contains. The image is a little off kilter and underscored by the following words: 'Slaves of God'. A much larger and colourful image occupies the rest of the composition. Although the relationship between the two images can be understood as one of simultaneity, the second image slightly overlaps the previous one, implying that it depicts a more recent occurrence. In this representation a woman dressed in red stands on a wide elevated stage framed by slogans. A roomful of workers is giving her a standing ovation. The rostrum is brightly lit and the colour red is omnipresent, insisting on the sovieticity of the event. Under this tableau, the artist has inscribed the phrase 'Candidate to the Party', referring to one of the many typical exceptions which characterised the twenties. The lack of temporal stability in this representation is somewhat akin to the divergent worldviews fused in *People Live...*, by the mode of irony. But does this work also employ this rhetorical device?

Irony relies on the cool breaking of social rules. Therefore, this type of humour often refers to tangible examples drawn from the practice of everyday life.[36] For irony to be effective, it needs to be concrete. Let's pause for a moment and reflect on a typical Soviet joke: A worker rents a room near the factory where he works. The room is modestly furnished with a bed, a chair and a small worktable. In a corner lie a framed portrait of Lenin and a framed portrait of Maksim Gorky. A single small rusty nail has been hammered into one of the stark white walls. The lodger asks the worker if the room is to his liking. 'Yes,' he replies. But, he adds pointing to the frames, 'I just can't decide which one to hang, which one to stand against the wall.' If the audience of this yarn is not familiar with the violated rule, then there is no comic effect. The public must understand the double meaning implied in the expressions 'to hang' and 'to stand against the wall.' But most importantly, it must appreciate the rule, which in this case involves the almost sacred nature of images of Lenin and Gorky in the twenties. If, as I just have, the joker needs to explain or restate the rule being broken, then, suggests Umberto Eco, the comic effect is in serious jeopardy.[37]

In this instance, however, the general law of ironic jokes does not translate unequivocally to the Soviet context. This might be because of the previously mentioned iconographic conundrum faced by Socialist Realist artists trying to depict a future absence. In *New Direction* the artist restates the broken rule (the traditional role of women in Russian Society) by depicting it within a temporal dislocation, which he emphasises by a virtual spatial overlap of the images. It is undoubtedly temporal promiscuity that produces the comic effect in *New Direction*. Nonetheless, we should explore another way to look at this before *and* after model, which restates and violates a rule in two distinct frames within a single representation. Instead of seeing this configuration as the juxtaposition of two moments separated by a tangible lapse of time, I suggest we consider them as moments of consciousness in Russian culture or in the ideological life of a Russian/Soviet subject.

Paul De Man argues that the deferred structure of allegory goes hand in hand with that of irony, which he characterises as an instance when the viewer steps back from the now illustrated in order to better perceive the rules he/she participates in being broken by him/herself. The temporal space between the represented now and the removed viewer is the precious moment of both allegory and irony, where the meaning of the representation lies.[38] Bearing in mind that neither the signs of allegory nor irony ever strictly correspond to their origin, one could therefore argue that there are two moments in any allegorical or ironic representation. One moment belongs to a mystified past, while the other is rooted in the present of Soviet living, which happens to be moulded within the projective, deferred mode of Socialist Realism. In *People Live...*, for example, the *Bezbozhnik u stanka* reader must be aware of the superstitious position described; yet, he/she must also be able to perceive him/herself as residing in a moment removed from it if the representation is to be funny and not insulting. The event that separates the two stages of consciousness is a gap, a radical discontinuity... that fantasised by Kostelevskaia's group. In this structure is implied the value judgement of enlightenment, or a sense of superiority for whoever understands the joke. It is the proof of their participation in the new order of things. Irony suggestively proposes a dialectic of identity and difference.

People Live... uses irony to confront superstitious viewers with their own anachronistic belief system, to make them *fall* from superstition, so to speak. The required splitting of the self into two consciousnesses (*dédoublement*) allows the viewer to dissociate him or herself from the pre-Revolutionary worldview by a means that is purely semiotic. This structure imposes in the viewer a more or less conscious relationship between two selves, the old and the new. At the moment that the *novyi chelovek* laughs at itself falling from its mystified position, it is laughing at a mistaken assumption it was previously making about its own position in the world. The moment of humour is when the two subjects are simultaneously present, but have become irreconcilable and disjointed beings as the *dédoublement* occurred.

This *dédoublement* which restates the frame of the broken rule as well as the appropriate frame of reception permits the image to participate in the antireligious struggle in the most concrete way. This didactic temporalisation provides the viewer with a means of dissociation, so that he/she can laugh. However, if irony, as a rhetorical tool, specifically aims to destroy self-mystification, it should be argued that this disjunction is by no means a serene process, despite the fact that it involves laughter.

Illustrated humoristic propaganda became increasingly important throughout the twenties, since it could reach both educated and barely literate audiences. In order to reach even broader publics, in 1924, the journal *Bezbozhnik u stanka* published a brochure entitled *How to Build a Godless Corner*.[39] To the same extent as antireligious publications, godless corners were to compensate for the lack of trained activist. These corners were designed to provide a stable propaganda environment, while constant exposure to antireligious imagery would contribute to the visual and ideological literacy of Soviet workers and schoolchildren. Furthermore, this would anchor the journal's specific approach to antireligious activism to the public sphere. Hence, for the modest sum of two roubles and eighty kopecks the *Godless Corner Kit* could be ordered from *Bezbozhnik u stanka*. The set of antireligious paraphernalia contained the following articles: a *Godless Corner* banner; two posters with antireligious slogans; seven outsized brightly coloured humoristic posters; six back issues of *Bezbozhnik u stanka* from which to cut out additional humoristic propaganda images; and instructions (with a visual map) on how to assemble the corner. Corners were meant to be easily accessible, brightly lit and inviting. 'The godless corner leads continuous mass propaganda. It must attract every worker in every factory. It must catch everyone's eye.'[40] It was also recommended that current antireligious literature should be made accessible to complement the imagery. Whenever possible, antireligionists were encouraged to spend time at the corner and interact with their fellow workers, initiating them to the materials displayed.

Although the Antireligious Committee still supported the scientific approach of the League of the Militant Godless, humoristic images were recognised to be effective with the general public. Indeed, in July 1925, *Bezbozhnik* followed suit and introduced into the antireligious printed media market a free bi-monthly, *Bezbozhnik krokodil*, a two-page humour supplement which used strategies and artworks similar to those featured in *Bezbozhnik u stanka*. In concert, *Bezbozhnik* began to advertise *Bezbozhnik u stanka*'s godless corner kit. Visual devices were to be used more and more from then on by the propagandists of the League:

> It is necessary to draw into antireligious propaganda all sorts of artistic work, bearing in mind that art accomplishes significant results only in the following cases: When production is consistent; when the artistic quality is high. Careless work and crude displays can be counterproductive. They can produce negative effects and provide fertile soil for religious propaganda.[41]

In 1932, *Bezbozhnik u stanka* was absorbed by its rival.[42] Several artists who had contributed images to *Bezbozhnik u stanka* found employment at the revamped *Bezbozhnik.* That same year, an illustrated album entitled *Bezbozhnik is Ten Years Old* appeared in kiosks.[43] The book, introduced by Yaroslavsky, outlined the history of the League and its achievements over ten years. Only marginal (and sarcastic) reference to Kostelevskaia's group and its chief publication *Bezbozhnik u stanka* can be found in the pages of the album. What is most striking, in view of the present discussion on visual strategies, is that black and white versions of full colour caricatures first printed in *Bezbozhnik u stanka* were used throughout the publication, without any noted source, thus implying that the caricatures were drawn from the *Bezbozhnik* humoristic repertory. Several conclusions can be drawn from this sponging feat. Although *Bezbozhnik u stanka* disappeared surreptitiously, the iconography and the humoristic mode it perfected, which relied on a rhetoric of temporality, survived. They survived because in spite of the official directives emitted by the Antireligious Committee, which considered *Bezbozhnik u stanka* crude and ignorant of the social construction of religious sentiments, they were recognised as valuable socialising tools and effective devices that could visually express *absence.* Ironically, this fusion perhaps implicitly confirmed *Bezbozhnik u stanka*'s use of topical humour as closest to Lenin's conception of how to conduct propaganda 'not in an abstract way, not on the basis of remote, purely theoretical, never varying preaching, but in a concrete way, on the basis of the class struggle which is going on in practice and is educating the masses more and better than anything else could.'[44]

13

THE SINGING MASSES AND THE LAUGHING STATE IN THE MUSICAL COMEDY OF THE STALINIST 1930s

The problem of 'popular spirit' in Socialist Realist aesthetics

EVGENY DOBRENKO

'POPULAR spirit' (*narodnost'*) was indisputably one of the key categories of Socialist Realist aesthetics and one radically distinguishing Stalinist culture from the revolutionary culture preceding it. Nowhere else does popular spirit appear in such a pure form as in the comic genres, which were addressed to the widest audiences. This is defined by the fact that popular spirit is itself an image of the masses as the state power would like to see them. The cheerful, laughing and singing masses, depicted by Soviet cinematography of the Stalinist era, conform to just such an image.

We shall examine the dynamics of comic forms in musical film comedies, which synthesise the two dimensions of theatre and music.[1] Here we can see, in fixed patterns, the discrepancy and conflict between the classical and the mass, between the 'high-cultural' and the 'entertaining', a discrepancy characteristic for the Soviet cultural situation from the very start of the period of revolutionary change. The transformations of Socialist Realist popular spirit reflect not only the dynamics of the image of the masses in the eyes of the state power, but also the attempt made to balance the dichotomy indicated. We could say that the discrepancies and conflict registered here became a system-forming factor of internal readjustments inside Socialist Realism, a regulator in the mechanism of changes in strategy by the state power with regard to the masses.

'THE REST, AS THEY SAY, JUST ENDURED IT'

The new consumer of art in the early Soviet era was born as a product of the cultural collapse, when the 'old culture' received a new recipient. The new spectator formed the optics of his perception through the very process of 'being given access to culture'. This was an extraordinarily difficult and painful process. It was accompanied by a serious crisis of all traditional forms of receptive activities and consequently by the totally negative attitude of the masses towards culture in general: towards both the 'old culture' and the new revolutionary counterpart born in the paroxysms of this culture. The rejection of the consumption of art, and the concomitant desire of the masses to create their own art instead, both begin as a result of this process. This very situation regenerated the recipient, making him, first of all, a participant of the 'creative process' and, subsequently, an author.

The new spectator observed that the old culture did not belong to him: 'I don't know who this performance is for,' writes a worker correspondent after visiting a performance in Vakhtangov's studio, 'but since I received the tickets through a workers' organisation, I expected to see factory and plant representatives there. It came as a total surprise to me when I saw only three or four workers scattered among the general masses. The rest of the spectators seemed to be "gentlemen", ladies all dressed up and young ladies, made up and powdered, with rings and bracelets. I felt totally out of place. You have to remember that the performance was free for the first time ever. But if there were no worker-spectators at a free performance, what is it going to be like later when you have to pay for performances?'[2]

The worker did not rush to consume the 'old art' made available to him by the new state. Art itself in its turn did not 'regenerate, rebuild, become Communist art'. The result was dissatisfaction: 'If we look at them from the workers' point-of-view, then none of the performances present anything except the same rotten old stuff. All there is to be seen at performances are lovers, dancing, legs flying around and flimsy skirts puffing about' (p. 43); 'In the daytime I watched a premiere about life in Roman times (*Anthony and Cleopatra* by Shakespeare) and I thought: why does a worker, busy the whole day with hard physical work, need this rotten historical rubbish?'[3]

Approaching the 'old rubbish' as the 'new owner', the worker-spectator denied entire genres and forms of theatrical art the right to existence. This was the case, in particular, with musical theatre. For example, opera and ballet were rejected outright. The reaction of the new mass audience to these forms of musical art was notable for the particularly aggressive rejection of 'aestheticism'.

'Re-shaping of the old culture', in whatever form, is out of the question. The cultural gulf can be seen here: 'Why do they show us workers things that have become obsolete and which don't teach us anything?' objects one worker correspondent after seeing *Evgeny Onegin.* 'All these ladies and gentlemen (Onegin, Lensky, Tatiana) lived at the expense of the serfs, not doing anything and out of sheer idleness not knowing what to do with themselves!' *Swan Lake* is rejected as 'the story of a prince's love for a princess, followed by the dance of the dying swan as a result of his infidelity. This most boring of boring stories, of no use to anyone, ... takes place over the course of four acts.' The state of the worker spectators during the performance reflects their boredom: "Out of seven us, three were permanently asleep and we had to badger them: 'Hey, lads, just don't snore'. The rest, as they say, just endured it." (pp. 73–6)

Significant difficulties were encountered, however, in understanding not only the 'historical rubbish', but also the avant-garde theatrical performances of Meyerhold and Vakhtangov. 'Despite the fact that I intently followed the episodes, I couldn't make any connection between them,' declares one bemused spectator. 'The thing seemed very difficult and muddled to me,' states another. 'In my opinion the thing wasn't written for workers. It is really difficult to understand and wears the spectator out.' Characteristically, the worker, after watching such a play, leaves completely baffled and bewildered, declaring: 'In new performances, there's a lot of nonsense. There's no overall impression' (pp. 45–7).

Factory-plant theatre, which arose 'unaided', aroused by far the greatest interest among the mass audience; here the spectator was involved in the 'production of art' through his or her own authorship and a familiar plot. This is what the worker correspondents wrote:

> The state theatres only serve the town centre, for example, the bourgeoisie and Soviet intelligentsia. The working masses do not go to these 'real' theatres. They only watch performances put on by drama circles in their working-men's clubs. It is these clubs that carry the whole burden of providing the working masses with theatre. . . . 'That's it: that's ours!' the workers say.' The club is described as putting on performances, 'written by the lads themselves under the direction of the club director' and as a result 'the interest of the workers is captivated.[4]

It is clear that the 'mass spectator' was not ready for the understanding of traditional artistic forms, but the desire of the masses themselves to create served as constant sustenance for the rhetoric of those groupings that advocated 'proletarian culture' (Proletcult and, subsequently, RAPP, the Russian Association of Proletarian Writers). Here we can see the chasm between the mass recipient and the cultured recipient of the era. Socialist Realism took upon itself the task of narrowing this chasm by 'pulling in' the masses on the one hand, and art on the other, bringing them together and adapting them to suit each other, thereby giving rise to the specifics of Stalinist culture.

If there were something that attracted the mass spectator and listener in the 'classical heritage', then it was 'opera from the life of the people'. *Carmen, Mazepa* and *Gal' ka* all met with quite a warm reception in the mass auditorium. Above all, judging by the response of the spectators, the 'familiar plot' attracted them and the 'memorable beautiful music'. 'Plotless' symphony music, by contrast, provoked complete rejection. 'I want the association of the Proletarian Musicians to answer me this,' demands a 'new listener':

> Do we need these endless concerts with specific programmes which run in the . . . halls of the conservatoire? Very rarely do you meet the proletariat here or people like us from the Young Communist League. At such concerts they usually end up yawning or doze off completely. From this some people conclude that workers, because they 'get bored' at such concerts, are 'not mature enough', 'not used to' music, 'not accustomed to it'. But that's nonsense! Why do workers like choirs, why do they like contemporary song, or folk melodies?' (p. 80)

The new listener demanded song. This genre was particularly attractive because of its 'familiarity', 'comprehensibility', 'joviality'. The last characteristic is particularly important. Music or theatre that was 'not ours' (whether old, or new and revolutionary) was, above all, boring. 'The lads just endured it', 'dozed off', as the worker correspondents inform us. In the club, on the other hand everyone is cheerful: 'We pay a lot of attention to the song-march, the song-game and song-staging,' recounts a factory club leader, 'and work in this direction proceeds happily, joyfully enthusiastically'. Is it by chance, then, we might ask, that the musical theme was later sanctioned in the Stalinist cinema namely in the jovially enthusiastic comic genre?

The most radical advocates of the new 'proletarian' culture in the 1920s suggested that it was infinitely possible to bring art and the masses together. However, in order to accomplish this task it was necessary to overcome artistic radicalism, something that revolutionary culture was organically incapable of doing. Socialist Realism took this historical mission upon itself. Having dispensed with the avant-garde project, Soviet culture, more consistently than its revolutionary predecessors, went to 'meet the masses'. It had removed the traditional inferiority complex of the masses in the face of 'high-brow art', and now set out to make art more 'worker-friendly'. In this project it rejected 'directors and actors with satiated, perverse intellectual taste' as alien to Soviet culture. 'Satiety and perversion', likewise 'decadence and neurasthenia' became for many years characteristics attributed to Western art in the demonology of Soviet aesthetics. The middle ground was occupied in accordance with a classic Stalinist model: members of the drama circles, remaining at the lathe, became 'Soviet spectators' as was proper for them; 'decadence' was transferred to the West, avant-garde theatre died, and in its place came the art of Socialist Realism 'belonging to the People'.

As opposed to the revolutionary strategy of substitution, Socialist Realism adopted the strategy of absorption-synthesis, the strategy of a real 're-shaping of culture'. This re-shaping was a process of constant balancing and rearrangement of 'high' and 'low' culture, as the image of the masses changed in the eyes of the state, which was itself directing this process of change.

However, the initial situation appeared, in many respects, to have been fixed by the mass 'consumers of art' of the 1920s to the beginning of the 1930s, 'jolly fellows' who had already in many respects become a thing of the past.

GENUINE MUSIC FOR THE 'WIDE WORKING MASSES' (JAZZ)

Three popular songs came out of the musical *The Jolly Fellows* (*Veselye rebiata*, 1934). One is about a song, the two others are about love. Both songs about love are sad; the song about a song is a bravura. The songs about love are closely linked to the plot of the film. The song about a song has a more general character and in contrast to the love songs is not personal; it speaks about 'all of us' and is directed 'at everyone'. Its hero is expressed in the plural: 'We'.

> A cheerful song lightens the heart;
> It always chases off boredom.
> The countryside and villages love a song
> The towns and big cities love it too.
> Songs help us to live and love,
> Like a friend, they call and lead.
> And those who go about life with a song,
> Will be at home anywhere.
> We are going to sing and laugh, like children,
> Amid the constant battle and work.
> You see, this is what we were born for:
> Never to surrender anywhere.

This song only conveys the mood, without becoming the pivot of the plot (as will be the case later in the film *Volga-Volga*). The shepherd Kostia Potekhin does not only sing well, he also takes violin lessons and 'studies Beethoven'. His first appearance 'before the public in a frock-coat' turns into chaos. The holiday makers from the rest-house 'The Black Swan', taking the shepherd to be the Paraguayan conductor Kosta Frankini, at first rapturously receive his playing of the bagpipes, but on realising that he is a shepherd, throw him out of the house: 'A shepherd has nothing to say to my daughter', says the mother of Elena, the singer. Elena and her circle are not in a position to appreciate Kostia's art. The only person able to do so is the maid Dunia. Kostia loves Elena. Dunia loves Kostia. At first, the shepherd cannot recognise Elena's 'philistinism', but the mistake will be corrected at the end. The lovers' plot and the musical plot motivate rather than just accompany one another: Elena is untalented, Dunia is talented.

This musical comedy by Grigory Aleksandrov consciously uses the conventions of the operetta. For example, everyone takes Kostia for the 'foreign conductor', although he speaks Russian with a strong Odessa accent, whereas the real conductor, as later becomes clear, does not speak Russian at all; 'Elena, the singer', striving to reach the Bolshoi theatre, has no voice at all and simply croaks; the plot depends on constant 'chance meetings' between the heroes.

Two spaces oppose each other here at the beginning: the farm 'Crystal Springs' and the rest-house 'The Black Swan'. This almost fairytale counterpoint of the clear spring to the demonic black swan recalls *Swan Lake.* The association presents itself again at the end of the film when the ballerinas in their white tutus encircle Utesov's jazz-orchestra as extras on the stage of the Bolshoi theatre.

The Bolshoi theatre is the goal of both the jazz musicians and 'Elena, the singer'. The path of the jazz musicians to the theatre is depicted by Aleksandrov as a path of happy adventures. But the Bolshoi theatre itself does not appear in the film as any kind of sacred space. On the contrary, the sacredness of 'the serious' (including the classics) is constantly profaned in the film. The herd of animals from the farm wreaks havoc in the rest house, smashing everything to smithereens, from the expensive crockery to the copy of the Venus de Milo. During the concert in the music hall, the conducting of the fake 'maestro' Kostia as opposed to that of the touring artiste is depicted by means of rhythmic changes. There is much running about on stage, falling down stairs, knocking over of bottles and so on. The rehearsal of the orchestra turns into a fight in which musical instruments are used by 'creative workers' as weapons. In the funeral procession the funeral march proceeds as a jazz improvisation. Finally the jazz players, dirty and dressed in rags, along with drunks, a maid and a cab driver all appear on the stage of the Bolshoi Theatre itself.

This clearly met the requirements of the 'mass demand'. Pandemonium on the 'academic stage' and the laughter of the hall, which turns, however into the sound of applause, are supposed to symbolise the victory over the classics. The musical collective 'Friendship' (*Druzhba*) which finally 'takes the stage' of the Bolshoi Theatre is an idiosyncratic model of how the classics can be 'mastered'. This model, however, was already becoming outdated. Here, a 'nihilistic, couldn't-care-less attitude towards classical heritage', unacceptable in Stalinist culture, is still preserved. Music is not differentiated: the conflict between jazz and classics is almost unnoticeable, because the classic is completely dead. It is as if jazz fills all the empty space: nothing opposes it except for the followers of the classic, who are 'the philistines'.

Nonetheless, 'the philistines' are not the heirs of high culture. They 'chase after' such fashions and only need the classic as a spurious sign of refinement, like a copy of the Venus de Milo in the lounge or busts of composers on the grand piano. The classic has no successors and is therefore, as an aesthetic problem 'removed by time itself'. The creators are the 'innovators' (the jazz musicians), Aleksandrov's musical comedy seems to affirm, and it concludes with a familiar vignette. On stage, there is the ragged amateur working-men's ensemble and the cheerful song about a song which 'helps us to live and love', but this is framed by the image of the chariot that tops the portal of the Bolshoi Theatre.

Like Gogol's famous troika from the finale of Part I of *Dead Souls* this vehicle rushes on and . . . does not give an answer.

'OVERCOMING THE NOISE, SCREECHING AND GRINDING OF THE ORCHESTRA'

The answer followed two years later in 1936. The ground rules were laid down in a series of articles, which was the genre chosen by the authorities to express their new aesthetic demands. 'Popular spirit' becomes a hallmark of the new Socialist Realist art. The issue being addressed, however, is not the 'destruction of formalism' (as a direction of revolutionary culture, it had in practice been eliminated from the 'artistic front' at the end of the 1920s). The point at issue is rather the synthesis of the classical heritage with the average taste of the masses. This synthesis gives birth to a new set of stylistics, combining the accessible and 'the beautiful'. Synthesising becomes the main aesthetic strategy of the state power, waging a battle simultaneously on two fronts: against both 'formalism' and 'naturalism'.[5]

Formalism is exemplified by the works of Shostakovich, which are attacked as a 'dissonant, confused current of sounds. . . roll, grind and screech' in which 'singing is replaced by a cry', melody 'by a maze of cacophony', expressiveness 'by furious rhythm' and passion 'by noise'. Such music has deliberately been made 'topsy-turvy'. All of these are decried as signs of 'petty-bourgeois formalist efforts and claims to create originality by means of cheap affectation'.

Alternately, the music of Shostakovich uses jazz, which is now defined as being nothing more than 'nervous, spasmodic, epileptic music', naturalistic music, vibrating 'crudely, primitively, vulgarly': it 'grunts, bangs, puffs and pants'. It is made clear that such music is 'confused and absolutely apolitical', that it reaches 'only those aesthetes who have lost all healthy taste' and that Shostakovich's opera *Lady Macbeth of Mtsensk* can only 'tickle the perverted tastes of bourgeois spectators with its throbbing, loud, neurasthenic music'.

In the meantime, the campaign 'against formalism and naturalism', which broke out in 1936, contained an important, positive idea: here a new aesthetic programme was formulated 'from the opposite'. Because the 'roll, grind and screech' of Shostakovich's music is 'difficult to follow', it is 'impossible to remember it'. There should be singing in opera, not screeching. Instead of cacophony, 'a simple and comprehensible melody' should sound. Instead of 'a furious rhythm' there should be 'expressiveness'. Music made 'topsy-turvy' has to be 'turned the right way around again': into 'symphonic sounds and simple, popular musical discourse'. The music of Shostakovich 'is built upon the principle of negation of opera', but the confirmation of opera is 'simplicity, realism, comprehensibility of image, the natural sound of words'.

The basic aesthetic strategy, expressed in angry party invectives, is the strategy of synthesising, built upon the appeal of a ready-made set of stylistics: accessibility, similarity, 'expressiveness', 'naturalness', all of which are present to the same extent in both classic and folk art. Only their proposed synthesis is able to offer art, loved by 'Soviet audiences'. As such, superimposition, doubling, repetition and tautology occur, exemplified in the title: *Volga-Volga.*

TODAY'S NEW MUSIC (SONG-SONG)

Volga-Volga (1938) is of course a film about the Volga, specifically about how an unknown postwoman writes a wonderful song about the Volga, which everyone admires. Only the refrain of this song is really about the Volga, however: 'Folk beauty, like the full-flowing sea, Like the free Motherland – wide, deep, strong.' The song itself is not about the river:

> Many songs about the Volga have been sung,
> But they haven't yet made one that
> Is warmed by the Soviet sun,
> And that would ring out across the River Volga.
> We burst into song resoundingly and bravely,
> So that our strength lives in it,
> So that it flies to the sun itself
> So that it penetrates the heart itself.
> Many songs have rung out across the Volga
> But the songs did not have the right refrain:
> In them we used to sing of our yearning,
> But now it is of joy we sing.

It is obvious that this is not a song about the Volga, but in fact, a song about a song. The film could have been called 'Song-Song', for it is the problem of the song, that 'most popular' musical genre 'loved by all', that lies at the film's centre.

At the very beginning of the film it becomes clear to the spectator that the most important person in the town of Melkovodsk is Comrade Byvalov. Everyone knows him – from the janitor to the ferryman, from the woodcutter to the water-carrier – although Comrade Byvalov arrived in town only recently and does not have a very responsible post: he is not the head of the town administration, nor a party leader, but simply the administrative director of a small, locally based industry. So where has such nationwide fame come from?

Since everyone in the town has some amateur interest in music (and, as can be seen, does nothing else), Byvalov steps into the role of official conductor of this mass amateur work. He makes no claims to this role: his aim is to move to Moscow. However, finding himself at the head of this 'mass movement', Byvalov finds himself also in a situation of conflict with the 'popular element'.

This opposition is reproduced in a different conflict: the central pair of lovers of Aleksandrov's 'musical comedy' is split into two halves, one of which (the postwoman Strelka) directs the 'popular talents', the other (the accounts clerk Trubyshkin) conducts a classical orchestra. Both collectives are amateur and at the very beginning Strelka says to her beloved accounts clerk: 'Your rehearsal is my rehearsal'. However, then it turns out that Strelka finds his music boring. She says, 'What a colossal bore!' with regard to Wagner and of the 'Death of Isolde' remarks similarly on the tedium: 'What a long time she takes to die.' The accounts clerk responds that this is how it is done 'classically'. These are key definitions: 'classically' and 'a colossal bore'. The accounts clerk suggests that Strelka 'simply does not understand classical music'. This is, however, not the point: Strelka (the masses) is not a performer, but a creator:

> 'Aleshka, did you never want to create something yourself?'
> 'Never.'
> 'If I knew music like you, I would create something all the time.'
> 'You would never be successful.'
> 'Why not?'

'Because you are a postwoman,' replies the accounts clerk-conductor. Comrade Byvalov says roughly the same thing to Strelka several scenes later: 'You need to study for twenty years in order to be able to sing like that.' For Strelka something independently made or done is better than something ready-made: 'But our Uncle Kuzia plays better on the trumpet that he made himself than on a bought one,' she says to the accounts clerk. A bought trumpet, like a bought balalaika, is notoriously bad (the balalaika produced by Byvalov's enterprise, for example, 'sounds like a log'). Classical music is something ready-made and, therefore, in the eyes of Strelka, impaired. For the accounts clerk, on the other hand, all these 'Uncle Kuzias and Aunty Mashas' are 'low farce'. This opposition is, however, not absolute: both aims, apparently opposing one another, are already in a diffused state and the entire conflict of the film leads to their final synthesis. The dialectics of conflict in *Volga-Volga* are, in fact, a dialectics of 'the re-shaping of classical heritage' and the conversion of it into 'the property of the wide working masses'.

On the one hand, 'popular talents' like Strelka prove themselves in part through the performance of classics: the courier Simka, as we recognise, performs the aria of Tatiana from Tchaikovsky's opera wonderfully well, Mishka the engraver can recite the whole of *Demon* off by heart, 'popular talents' perform folk songs which in Soviet culture were elevated to the high musical genres. On the other hand, the 'symphony orchestra' of Trubyshkin 'takes Beethoven, Mozart, Schubert, Wagner to Moscow': this is a list of officially approved classics that are seen as not at all alien to the 'folk masses'.

Thus a general musical locus of the official anthology of the classic, available to the masses, arises at the intersection of the two repertoires. 'Popular talents' like Strelka do not perform anything 'bawdy' and, in turn, the 'Neapolitan orchestra' of the accounts clerk produces none of the formalist 'muddle' or 'trans-sense', but only melodic, memorable music (like Schubert's *Musical Moment* or the march from *Aïda*). The extreme poles are cut off: the spectator enters an entire organic musical space in which the apparent opposition becomes imaginary, and the conflict is playfully-comic.[6]

This apparent opposition develops at the beginning of the film: if the ferry with the 'populists' moves to the sound of folk music, then the steamship with 'the classics' is accompanied by opera. But the folk music of those on the ferry is liked even by Byvalov ('They sing well!'), and the opera music, the well-known march from *Aïda*, is no less popular than the folk song. The musical space preserves its heterogeneity: in it tradition and innovation are dialectically organic. Finally, even the arguing sides understand each other. Having turned up by mistake on different boats (Strelka with the 'classics', Trubyshkin with the 'populists'), they stop their musical 'arguments' and finally create the song.

The song was incomplete. Its first performance by Strelka at the very beginning of the film is still amateur, monologic, too personal. As a result of the fact that they 'set the song to notes' (a synthesis of the classicists and populists) towards the end of the film, it 'matures' very rapidly. Finally the entire musical 'ado' retreats (on the one hand the classic, on the other folk songs) and only the 'Song of the Volga' sounds, the 'Song about a song', a song about itself. This egocentrism of the created work invites us to study it more intently.

The song appears here as a synthesis of the previously opposed elements, absorbing them into itself. At the beginning of the film, the 'populists' played the song on the ferry, using whatever they could get their hands on (a saw, bottles etc.): they played it 'wrongly' ('low farce'). Then the song was performed on violins, flutes and trumpets by the 'classics', who had earlier played 'the wrong thing' ('a colossal bore'). The 'populists' understood that a song was what was needed, and the classicists, perfecting their performance mastery by learning from 'Beethoven, Mozart, Schubert and Wagner', finally understood what they needed to play. The synthesis of the symphony orchestra (which Strelka now conducts) and the folk choir (conducted now by Trubyshkin) gives birth to the work which, indeed, becomes fantastically popular: the holiday makers and the river divers, the woodcutters and even the river planes discover the song. It is performed literally by everyone: from the pioneers to the military brass bands. Eventually the song is converted into a symphony production thanks to a talented pioneer ('Your theme; my orchestration,' he tells Strelka). The final sounding of this 'theme' in the symphonic 'orchestration' raises the song to the status of high culture, converting it into a super-genre.

The song acquires a triumphal-majestic ring, which marks it as a hallowed text. Here, popular and classical culture, music, theatre, cinema and literature (Strelka is not only a composer, but also a poet) all merge. The finale of 'the musical comedy' is a stage backdrop with the emblem of the USSR and flags of the national republics. This closing image reveals to the spectator the 'conversion' of art, the end of its re-shaping in Stalinist culture. This is achieved without the classic being debased to cater for mass taste, nor preference being given to the classics or to popular music (something for which reviewers none the less blamed the director in various ways). Instead, what we have is the birth of a synthesis of arts and styles, of that elevated image of the 'complete work of art' into which the life of the Soviet people was being poured. The song, here, is at one and the same time a film about the Volga, a film about the flourishing of talents in the Soviet Union, and a film about music and theatre: a *Gesamtkunstwerk.*

Volga-Volga represents the historical realisation of Socialist Realist aesthetics in the entire process of its establishment: from the battle with the classic, through 'the taking possession of the classical heritage', right up to the creation of one's own classic, based on the synthesis of the symphony orchestra with the folk choir. It could be said that Aleksandrov's 'musical comedy' is the very manifestation of Socialist Realism and in this sense a pure spectacle of the image of the state power in 1938. This is, however, not yet the end of the Soviet 'musical story'.

THE REAL NEW MUSIC: THE CLASSIC (OPERA AS OPERETTA)

Progressing two years later to *A Musical Story* (*Muzykal'naia istoriia*, 1940), we move at the same time to a new level of the generic hierarchy: to opera. Opera is a symbol of the classic, a symbol of that which is fixed, something to which Stalinist culture aspired. In Aleksandr Ivanovsky's film, opera music resounds constantly. Operas also represent three basic points of the plot: *Carmen* (exposition), *Evgeny Onegin* (culmination), *May Night* (the denouement). The selection of operatic texts is itself telling: foreign opera, Russian opera 'from the old life' and Russian opera 'from folk life'. According to the screenplay by Evgeny Petrov and Georgy Munblit, *Evgeny Onegin* was supposed to be performed again in the finale, but the director stopped at *May Night,* in which choice a definite logic can be seen, for it is simultaneously a classic, an opera, and a folk plot.

The pure operatic stamp is ridiculed in the first scenes of the film when a fat Carmen and José appear on the set, singing out-of-tune and laughing in a schooled, unnatural manner. But *Evgeny Onegin* is an opera loved by all and, of course, well-known to all: the entire hall of the car mechanics' club – from the driver to the senior watchman – now knows the words of the opera, prompting the hero Petia Govorkov by literally chorusing the beginning of Lensky's aria. And, finally, a complete triumph awaits Petia in Rimsky-Korsakov's *May Night* where he performs the part of Levko and dances and sings orchestrated folk songs. It is significant that when Petia (when still a chauffeur) sings folk songs at home, the communal kitchen comes to a standstill: everyone listens to his singing. But when he (now a student at the conservatoire) practises scales at home, it provokes extreme indignation among the residents of the communal flat, his neighbours.

Yet the conservatoire is now presented as an essential part of the 'master craftsman's training': 'talents' are no longer enough. In *The Jolly Fellows* the jazz musicians had appeared directly after the funeral procession in a completely inappropriate state on the stage of the Bolshoi Theatre. In *Volga-Volga* 'the popular talents' had stepped directly onto the Moscow stage from the town square, but no longer onto the academic stage of the Bolshoi, but rather onto the one destined for them: the amateur theatre. In *A Musical Story* the anarchy of *The Jolly Fellows* no longer has any place: it is possible to appear on stage of the Theatre from the garage only by going through the Conservatoire. Therefore, there is none of the former opposition (from *The Jolly Fellows*) between the club and the theatre, but there is a series of steps: Club – Conservatoire – Theatre. For all that, the main vector of movement is preserved: real art comes from below, from the club. The main thing is the full manifestation of talent.

One could say that not only is Ivanovsky's comedy more realistic than the Hollywood buffoonery of Aleksandrov's musicals, but also that it is more realistic both in terms of style and in a conceptual sense. Although the myth about the outstanding talent of the folk masses is preserved, in the end talent only appears as an individual phenomenon (it was not so in *The Jolly Fellows,* nor in *Volga-Volga,* where the talk was always of talents, but not about talent).

Therefore, talent and the conservatoire are two new (or rather recurring old) stages, which one must traverse. However, from film to film this path becomes more and more complicated. Petia Govorkov's teacher Makendonsky, says that 'a lot of serious work is needed', 'opera is hard work'. Such maxims are not taken seriously in *The Jolly Fellows* or in *Volga-Volga,* where the path to the stage is a cheerful journey with singing, dancing and amusing adventures. Maxims of this sort belong in *The Jolly Fellows* to the lovable and funny teacher Karl Ivanovich who speaks with a heavy German accent, and in *Volga-Volga* they are voiced by the bureaucrat Byvalov.

In *The Jolly Fellows* the path towards 'popular art' is towards jazz (with opera as the opposition). *A Musical Story* depicts the path to the operatic stage which has already succeeded in becoming 'popular'. Between the two films lies a gap of only seven years, but, on a general cultural plane, it is a significant fragment of Soviet history, when the classic was integrated in high Soviet culture. There remained no trace of the former opposition.

In *The Jolly Fellows*, opera is associated with the satirically depicted 'bourgeois characters'. The petty bourgeois from *A Musical Story*, Alfred Tarakanov, is completely indifferent to music, whereas a love of classical music is inherent to the positive heroes, who all have come entirely from 'the broad working masses'. Here, what is important is the unifying of the poles, the synthesis, reached in Stalinist culture, on the one hand, by means of simplifying the classic, its 'Tchaikovskisation', and on the other hand, through the academisation of popular music.

A year after *A Musical Story*, Ivanovsky made a film, *Anton Ivanovich Gets Angry* (*Anton Ivanovich serditsia*, 1941), based on this theme. A professor of the conservatoire and a passionate follower of classical music who worships Handel and even considers opera somehow very suspect, someone for whom Puccini already represents 'muddle instead of music' and who fervently protects his daughter from the contagion of the frivolous music of jazz, sees the light towards the end of the film and gives his blessing to his daughter, who is in love with the composer, Mukhin, who writes 'for the people' and states that the people need music of all genres: opera, operetta, variety songs, jazz. As if to counterbalance the prejudices of the father, his talented daughter Simochka takes part in an operetta, playing the main role in Mukhin's musical comedy. All are portrayed sympathetically here: Anton Ivanovich himself, and Simochka, and Mukhin.

Only Kerosinov is not likeable. This satirical model of an untalented, but pompous 'composer', performed by S. Martinson, symbolises 'the face of the formalist'. For the past two years he has been composing some sort of 'physiological symphony' which no-one has heard: only a kind of 'musical muddle' is emitted from his room. 'The physiological symphony', an oxymoron, like 'material spirit', reveals the face of the formalist, who does not want to join in with modernity, to understand and accept 'the demands of life', to be inspired. Instead he creates something cold and, as such, not needed by anyone. Formalism is cold, but creativity is warm. Kerosinov's 'physiological symphony', is by definition cold. A symphony with such a title by a composer with such a name cannot possibly be 'humanly warm' (except by the artificial means of kerosene). Indeed, all genuine creators in Soviet musical film-comedies are, above all, able to create because they are 'warmed by the heat of love'.

The attitude towards music is a sign of 'culturedness' (*kulturnost*). The masses are supposed to perceive music as their own, but at the same time the very content of 'their music' in Stalinist culture constantly changes. Thus, jazz music, operetta, opera, symphony are in turn presented as 'theirs'. Nonetheless, by becoming 'popular', all musical genres average out, and the 'memory of genres' re-writes itself every time. If we acknowledge that popular spirit is the image of the masses, as the state would like to perceive them, then we also ought to acknowledge that the process of erasing 'the memory of genre' is the result of erasing the previous image of the masses.

Just as the bureaucrat represents the former image of the state power, the philistine represents the former image of the masses. Therefore, the opposition philistine/creator is a stable element in musical film-comedy. In *The Jolly Fellows* the philistines are grotesque characters, revealing traits of the profiteers from the period of the New Economic Policy of the 1920s. Their 'bad taste', passion for 'plush curtains' and 'foreign things' become a source of comic situations (for example, in the scene where Elena talks about the 'artificiality' of a live sheep, assuming that it is not real and states that 'they make them better abroad'). Bourgeois 'cultivation' is supposed to underline the discrepancy between the 'philistine' and the role of the 'cultivated person' which he wants to play. The incongruity of this social role is one of the key features of the satirical image. In the case of 'Elena, the singer' this discrepancy, in particular, is important, since she lays claim to the role 'of artistic worker', 'a person of a refined organism', yet at the same time she does not possess the required refinement (as in the scene where she attends the concert of the 'foreign conductor' and takes handfuls of sweets and munches them during the performance), nor the required 'interest in art' (during the concert she does not even look at the stage, preferring to scrutinise those sitting in the boxes). All this is designed to reflect her artificiality (that is why Aleksandrov, apparently, allots her unnatural laughter: vulgar, yet at the same time with claims to being a 'trilling coloratura'). Genuine creators are, on the contrary, natural and unrefined (Kostia and Dunia).

The modern face of the masses is presented in *A Musical Story* in minute detail: they are an artistic, talented and cultured 'mass', one and all in love with the musical classic. If Elena is 'the face of yesterday' of the masses as perceived in 1934 (when the memory of NEP was still vivid), then Tarakanov from *A Musical Story* is 'the face of yesterday' of the masses dating back to the second half of the 1930s. Tarakanov's views on 'cultivation' form an entire encyclopaedia of 'philistinism' as perceived at the end of the 1930s: it is materially-minded in contrast to the romantic elevation of real artists; it is pretentiously-profound and 'bureaucratic'. Tarakanov's speech register is that of the cliché, expressing his lack of sensitivity to the word. The satirical character is (literally) sheer nonsense: everything in him conflicts. This discrepancy is the result of the hero's groundless claims to a social role that is 'not his'

It is not accidental that in Soviet comedy there is a clear demarcation between satirical and humorous characters. In *The Jolly Fellows* Elena and her 'bourgeois circle' are satirical characters, Karl Ivanovich or the Paraguayan touring artiste are humorous characters. Byvalov is a satirical character in *Volga-Volga* and the boatswain is humorous. In *A Musical Story*, Tarakanov is satirically presented, while the fat chairman of the local trade union committee, who constantly wipes sweat from his brow, and the amateur Onegin, are humorous characters.

Such clear marking is linked to the diverse functionality of humour and satire in Soviet comedy. Soviet satire has always been an image of what is announced today by the state as being of 'yesterday'. Hence, the persistent categorisation of 'negative aspects of our reality' as 'vestiges of the past': they are, as it were, still present today, but already marked as 'the past', and by that very fact are being eliminated. The entire potency of the statement is directed at the future in the present ('life in its revolutionary development').

Soviet satirical comedy is a continual process of change in the image of reality over time. In this essay we have focused on the changing image of the masses in the eyes of the state power as illustrated in the way that the musical heritage is portrayed in Soviet musical comedies of the 1930s. The process is one of systematic dialectical removal of oppositions. This is registered in the Soviet musical film comedy, rather like the ring markings on a wooden log: by these means it is possible to reconstruct the process of Socialist Realist popular spirit in the making. This picture is seen here so clearly since it is mapped onto the grid of specific generic forms, in this case musical genres.

14

THE THEORY AND PRACTICE OF 'SCIENTIFIC PARODY' IN EARLY SOVIET RUSSIA

CRAIG BRANDIST

It is well known that early Soviet Russia saw a massive upsurge in theoretical writings on parody and that early Soviet literature often seemed to be dominated by parody of one form or another. However, what have been given rather less attention are the ideas that lie behind the pervasive tendency among literary intellectuals in Russia at the time to assign to parody a quasi-scientific, proto-scientific or even a fully scientific status. This took many forms and was certainly not limited to the enthusiasm for machine technology and overturning literary tradition among certain avant-gardistes and their theoretical supporters. In the 1920s the tendency in most cases was to consider parody the midwife of stylistic analysis because it conspicuously and indeed aggressively selects certain stylistic features for attention. In the 1930s and 40s, however, this was integrated into a more historical account of the rise of modern, critical culture. This paper presents a brief survey of the various forms of the notion of 'scientific parody' and suggests that a common philosophical conception informs them.

SHKLOVSKY, TYNIANOV AND THE AVANT-GARDE

Viktor Shklovsky's famous 1921 analysis of *Tristram Shandy* is the most frequently cited analysis of a text based on the centrality of parodic forms.[1] Parody is here championed as a means of defamiliarising autonomised literary forms and violating literary norms with the effect that our perception of literary form is cleansed of the accumulated deposits of everyday consciousness. The contours of 'literariness' are brought into focus and the Formalist critic then gathers and systematises these contours into a scientific object domain. Shklovsky's work was, of course, closely bound up with the project of the avant-garde at the beginning of the early 1920s and there are certainly too many potential examples of attempts to identify and overcome outmoded literary techniques within the literature of the period to enumerate any representative sample. Nevertheless, right through until the last gasp of the avant-garde at the very end of the 1920s there are recurrent attempts to yoke parody to the scientific investigation and the cleansing of literature. In the OBERIU declaration, for example, it is asserted that 'once its literary and everyday skin is peeled away, the concrete object becomes the property of art . . . Look at the object with naked eyes and you will see it cleansed for the first time of decrepit literary gilding.' The artistic investigation of an object was now given a scientific status with the artist able to 'express the object with the exactness of mechanical technology'.[2]

There were, of course more subtle versions of this type of analysis, and ones that were less closely bound up with the partisan literary struggles of the time. Tynianov was perhaps the most significant Formalist theorist of parody, repeatedly returning to the subject from 1919 until 1929.[3] For him parody was not so much a partisan principle as the starting point for a theory of literary evolution. The incongruity between the planes of the parodying and parodied work again reforms our perception and defamiliarises literary form, but this is now a struggle that drives literary evolution in a 'dialectical play of devices'. Old, worn out devices are displaced by new, vibrant ones. But this is only a particular manifestation of the interaction between literary works. His other famous example was stylisation, in which the two planes of the imitating and imitated works are not incongruous, but nevertheless specific features are selected for analysis. What is clear, however, is that Tynianov sees all literary works interacting in one way or another on the basis of the literary system to which they all belong. Parody is significant for literary scholarship because it reveals this intertextuality, while it is ideologically and politically progressive because, as for Shklovsky and the OBERIUTY it undermines the authority of worn-out tradition and in so doing facilitates a critical approach to literature itself. Parody, along with other forms of literary interaction, once again becomes a tool for a textual science by transforming style into an object of study.

VIKTOR VINOGRADOV

The treatment of parody as a literary-critical tool that can be appropriated by the critic was certainly not limited to the Formalists as narrowly defined, however. Viktor Vinogradov, who was critical of the excesses of Formalist scientism engaged in the same procedure in his *Studies of Gogol's Style*, which was written mainly in 1923.[4] Like Tynianov, some of Vinogradov's most sustained remarks on the nature of parody were developed during an analysis of Gogol's work. Vinogradov, however, takes a slightly different tack, carrying out a stylistic analysis of Gogol's works entirely through the lens of contemporary parodies of them. These parodies are not the progressive interventions that the Formalists championed, rather, they were essentially conservative, for they 'only *indicate* those aspects of an artist's work that struck his contemporaries as unusual and most acutely aroused the mockery and protests of the "old-believers" '. Parodies, he explains, are nevertheless valuable for the critic in that they 'consciously single out, in the style of an hostile writer, a complex of forms that are striking by virtue of their novelty of form.'[5] Working from the parodies Vinogradov is able to present a detailed inventory of the writer's devices from tropes, sentence-structure and phonology to hyperbole and personifications, but he is careful to indicate the limitations of such an approach even in stylistic analysis. It is important for the critic to also identify the 'literary camp' in which a writer stands, in order to show the 'psychic background of apperception' which determined the degree to which the parodic mirror distorted the object of parody. This 'camp' can be seen in the traits of plot, architectonics and style shared with other writers within a historical context. It is also necessary to see the literary devices picked up on by parodists within the overall trajectory of a writer's own evolving stylistic system.

As Robert Maguire notes,[6] Vinogradov's work showed the focus of a linguist, concentrating on various types of discourse (*rech*) in the literary work. He focused on the interaction of classical book-language, folksong, *skaz*-like plebeian conversation, normative and coarse, non-normative discursive forms in Gogol's work. The way in which *skaz* was integrated into the artistic structure to manipulate reader-response to the text was also considered rather more extensively than by the Formalist critics of *skaz* like Eikenbaum. But Vinogradov remained close to the Formalists in one crucial respect: carefully selected poetic form takes precedence over ideological content. The value of parody is that it fixes upon this poetic form, making it an object for the critic then to analyse as part of a linguistic superstructure that rises upon natural language and social discourse.

PARNAS DYBOM (1925)

In 1925 there was a new development: these literary theories were put directly into practice, with the appearance of a textbook of literary stylistics based entirely on parody called *Parnas dybom* (*Parnassus in Turmoil*), the title of which clearly sent up Meyerhold's 1923 agitprop spectacle *Zemlia dybom*. A scan through the MLA bibliography suggests that there have been no articles dedicated to this phenomenon in western scholarship and there has been very little attention in Russian literary journals either. This is all the more surprising since it was massively popular, going through four editions in the years from 1925 to 1927 before sinking into obscurity for another forty.[7] Perhaps it is the very popularity of the book as a collection of literary parodies that obscured its significance in the history of Soviet literary scholarship, and it is generally treated as a mere curiosity in most historical accounts of the literature of the period. The book was, however, written and compiled by the philologists Aleksandr Finkel, Aleksandr Rozenberg and Ester Papernaia, at Kharkov University, the very place where the fathers of Russian philology Veselovsky and Potebnia had taught.[8] The book was published anonymously, with only the initials of the authors appearing on the cover. Instead it bore a list of names from literary history, including several contemporary writers, 'on goats, dogs and Veverlei'. Inside, variants on these themes were presented in styles ranging from the impersonated grandeur of Homeric hexameters to the '*sobachii iazyk*' of Zoshchenko's characters.

If we are to believe the comments of two of the collection's authors in 1966, however, then parody was not their intention: 'we were not and did not want to be parodists, we were stylisers with a cognitive purpose. It was also funny and amusing but this was, so to speak, a side effect (at least that's how it appeared to us). But that effect was more important than our seriousness for both our publishers and readers, they ousted the seriousness.' The main purpose was 'to make science humorous and humour scientific'.[9] Thus, unlike Tynianov, who believed that 'from stylisation to parody is a single step: stylisation when comically motivated or accentuated becomes parody',[10] the authors of *Parnas dybom* considered comic stylisation to be neither serious stylisation nor parody, but a third form. Where parody involves a certain acute quality, a polemical edge or subjectivity of evaluation, stylisation is more a balanced and analytical attempt to capture the essence of a style, to disclose its deeper structure.[11]

VOLOSHINOV AND BAKHTIN

The decade ended with what was in some ways the culmination of the trend: Voloshinov's *Marxism and the Philosophy of Language* and Bakhtin's *Problems of Dostoevsky's Art.* In his 1929 study of Dostoevsky, which, one should remember had none of the reflections on the history of genre or discussion of carnival which was introduced only in 1963, Bakhtin presents parody as a specific mode of discursive objectification. Building on Voloshinov's work on the problem of the transmission of alien discourse (*chuzhoe slovo*) Bakhtin treats parody and stylisation as specific intersections between reporting and reported discourses. Reported discourse, says Voloshinov, is 'discourse within discourse, utterance within utterance, but at the same time also discourse about discourse, utterance about utterance'. The 'soul' of the reported discourse is analysis. Parody, stylisation and the like turns a discourse into an object of study rather than simply an object of experience and it does so by turning direct into some form of indirect discourse. While direct discourse, especially in literature, colourfully presents and paints the speaking characters, personifying standpoints and opinions, indirect discourse divides the sense it encounters into simpler significative elements, and every statement into more elementary linguistic and stylistic features. In the Dostoevsky study Bakhtin gives this a specifically phenomenological colouration: the artist's vision (*vídenie*) is akin to the phenomenological *Wesensschau*, the intuition of essences. However, unlike the Formalists and Vinogradov, Bakhtin sees poetic form and content as components of a single 'science of ideologies' (*nauka ob ideologiiakh*). The essence of the style discerned is not so much its linguistic character but its ideological structure. However, it is important to recognise that by now parody is but one of several modes of reported discourse, it has no claims to a scientific validity over and above its kindred forms.

How are we to understand the remarkable methodological similarity between these otherwise very different positions? This has, I think, philological and philosophical dimensions, both of which relate to the dependence of Russian literary scholarship on German thought.

THE GERMAN BACKGROUND

First, and briefly, the philological context. As usual with the Bakhtin Circle, we gain most insight about the sources of their ideas from the works of Voloshinov and Medvedev who, unlike Bakhtin, actually recorded their references. It is clear that Voloshinov was heavily reliant on the 1922 collection *Idealistische Neuphilologie* in honour of Karl Vossler for much of the material in *Marxism and the Philosophy of Language* pertaining to comparative philology.[12] Here essays by Karl Bühler, Oskar Walzel, Eugen and Gertraud Lerch and Leo Spitzer were of special importance. Bakhtin, unusually, cites Spitzer's book on Italian colloquial speech in both studies of Dostoevsky, though leaving the quotation in German. The quotation itself refers to the ironic-sounding quality of another's words when reported.[13] According to the Vossler School, parody occurs when there is a disjunction between the 'inner form of the word', the intentional content invested by the speaking person, and the 'outer form' or the written marks or articulated sounds. When the original context of utterance has passed away, the forms of language are like an objectified 'sloughed skin' whose relationship with the original inner form has become 'equivocal'.[14] There is little doubt that the Russian Formalists were also profoundly affected by the Vossler School, indeed Tynianov's notion of parody as the intersection of evaluative planes finds many echoes in Vossler's work, though from a rather different philosophical position. While the

Formalists, like the Bakhtin Circle, were alien to the pervasive psychologism of the Vossler School, this did not make the latter's empirical studies in such works as Vossler's 1913 *Frankreichs Kultur im Spiegel seiner Sprachentwicklung* or Spitzer's 1928 *Stilstudien* any less attractive.[15] Spitzer, in particular, was such an eclectic thinker that he was interpreted in several different ways in Russia at the time and his work on particular texts was an important source for thinkers who opposed his theoretical assertions.[16] Thus, while Bakhtin criticises Vossler and his collaborators quite severely, it seems he was heavily influenced by Vossler's and Spitzer's characterisations of Rabelais's parodic word-building, which culminates in Vossler's characterisation of Rabelais's work as a 'lexical carnival'.[17] Vinogradov's relationship to the Vossler School was also rather complicated by such factors, a superficially hostile response obscuring a significant influence. Thus, Vinogradov often criticises the ideas of Vossler and Potebnia in a single breath and he also opposed Vossler's metaphysical system in which the history of language was considered as parallel to the history of poetry. However, as N.I. Konrad notes, Vinogradov and Vossler share a conception of the individual's creative activity as a speaker and writer, while A.P. Chudakov notes that Vinogradov's notion of linguistic consciousness builds upon Vossler's 'history of linguistic taste'.[18] This also informs Vinogradov's reading of Gogol through contemporary parodies.

Certain ideas of the Vossler School were also, however, often combined with those of Oskar Walzel, whose had been championed in Russia by Viktor Zhirmunsky. As Zhirmunsky and Pavel Medvedev recognised, Walzel had translated the principles of the art history of Wilhelm Worringer and Heinrich Wölfflin into literary terms.[19] However, Walzel also built upon the ideas of both Shaftsbury and Goethe to argue that parody was evidence of the 'inner form' of the work of art, the aesthetically embodied 'inner dynamic of life', striving against the outlived conventionality of 'outer form'.[20] The convergence of the Humboldtian idea of the inner form of language and the neo-Platonic idea of the inner form of art as its inner necessity was particularly important for the development of the theory of parody in Russia.[21] This convergence was later given a specific, philosophical interpretation in the work of Ernst Cassirer.[22]

For our purposes it is this philosophical dimension that is most important, and it is this that the Bakhtin Circle brought to prominence. Russian philosophy in the first part of the century had been dominated by neo-Kantianism, and German neo-Kantians were the main source of methodological insight for literary scholars too. This was given a further impulse between 1921 and 1929 when commissions for the Investigation of Problems of Artistic Form and Artistic Terminology, organised under the auspices of the State Academy for Research in to the Arts (GAKhN), were active. These commissions included such influential figures as Gustav Shpet, V.I. Vinokur, A.A. Buslaev and A.F. Losev, and they investigated not only German neo-Kantianism but also the incipient semiotics of the Austrian psychologist Karl Bühler, which was to prove extremely influential on the ideas of Voloshinov and later the Prague School.[23] The main texts Tynianov and Eikhenbaum cited for consultation on methodological matters included Wilhelm Windelband's 'Preludes', Ernst Cassirer's *Substance and Function* and works by Paul Natorp and Max Adler.[24] These were some of the main neo-Kantian works that pertained to the humanities, and many were translated into Russian between 1900 and 1925. A special place is also occupied by the work of the Baden School philosopher Broder Cristiansen, whose 1909 book *Philosophie der Kunst* (Russian translation *Filosofiia iskusstva,* 1911) was massively influential on the Formalists, the Bakhtin Circle, Vinogradov, Boris Engelgardt and many others besides.[25] Meanwhile, Vinogradov quoted part of Cassirer's book in his critique of Tynianov's methodology,[26] and in speaking of the key role of the 'background of apperception' for the literary scholar, showed distinctly neo-Kantian traits. The Bakhtin Circle were also steeped in neo-Kantianism, with Bakhtin noting that he was 'simply captivated by the Marburg School' (Cohen, Natorp, Cassirer) in the 1920s and Voloshinov translating parts of one of Cassirer's later work into Russian.[27]

NEO-KANTIANISM, PARODY AND SCIENCE

Why is all this so significant for a consideration of the scientific status of parody? The answer is methodological. For neo-Kantianism the cognition of an object, and a linguistic utterance is no different here, is essentially tied to the realm of judgment, and judgment does not bear upon the thing in its undifferentiated givenness. Rather, it refers to an object as it is intended. Though of phenomenological pedigree, intentionality as understood by the neo-Kantian is quite different than for the heirs of Franz Brentano, including the early Husserl. What is given to consciousness is now in principle unknowable. For knowledge to be possible the perceived object must be transformed into something created by the mind. The percipient now adopts some point of view from which to apprehend the thing in such a way that the latter becomes dismembered or splintered until it is a manifold of distinct aspects, properties, and features. The object of cognition is then pieced back together with the aid of secondary meaning structures, but it is no longer the thing as it was originally given to sensation. It is, rather, the thing as split apart into a plurality of aspects or properties, all of which can be said to have or carry meaning.[28]

It is for this reason that parody, stylisation, double-voiced discourse, polemics and the like are so valued by the Russian theorists: they are preconditions for the scientific cognition of language and of artistic form. These 'rechevie ustanovki' (discursive 'sets' or orientations) transform the 'given' direct discourse, into an object of knowledge by breaking it up into simpler significative elements, and more elementary linguistic and stylistic features.[29] It does this by adopting a specific position of judgement towards the direct discourse and transforming it into an object of knowledge. The literary scholar is then able to gather and systematise these fragmentary aspects into an analytical whole, perhaps seeking to compensate for the necessarily distorted 'image of a language' that results from parodic dismemberment.

Bakhtin is the least enamoured by parody as opposed to other forms of objectified discourse in the 1920s, but as early as 1934 he is the biggest champion of parody of all of them, and the novel is cast as an essentially parodic genre. The *ustanovka* is now depersonalised and becomes a general force within culture. This move is typical of the neo-Kantian identification of subjectivity with the system of objectifying functions which have their true being in cultural documents. In some notes from the 1940s Bakhtin argues that 'all genres are oriented on myth (the last whole), but only the novel is oriented on philosophy (and science).'[30] Why the big change? One of the reasons is most probably Bakhtin's reading of Cassirer's *Philosophy of Symbolic Forms* and studies of the Renaissance in the intervening period.

As Voloshinov noted, Cassirer's magnum opus on symbolic forms was a new departure on the basis of neo-Kantianism.[31] Here Cassirer argued that the adoption of a scientific attitude is the recognition that we can know nothing about the world as given but that we are constantly engaged in the ethical task of producing an image world of culture. This requires the adoption of a position of radical scepticism toward all claims to have truth of the given world, the very notion of a correspondence theory of truth is a sign of mythical consciousness. Instead, critical thought turns toward the process of the production of the image world of culture with the effect that the production of symbolic forms ultimately becomes the object of symbolic forms. Bakhtin's novel has scientific pretensions to the extent that it is precisely this type of symbolic form. In 'Discourse in the novel' he argues that when the essence of the novel appears in literary history, in the work of Cervantes, Rabelais and the like, then 'heteroglossia in itself becomes heteroglossia for itself,' the socially stratified national language that makes up the objective spirit becomes its own object.[32]

For all Bakhtin's 'body-talk', he is a principled and consistent idealist. The body in Bakhtin's work, just as it is in the work of Foucault later, is the body considered exclusively as an object of knowledge.[33] In his studies of the Renaissance of 1928 and 1932 Cassirer links radical scepticism to the comic spirit of the time. He champions the work of Cervantes, Rabelais, Hans Sachs and others for their use of humour as a 'liberating, life-giving and life-forming power of the soul':

> To the pedant, as to the zealot, freedom of thought is an abomination; for the former takes shelter behind the dignity of knowledge, the latter behind the sanctified authority of religion. When both retrench themselves behind a false gravity, nothing remains but to subject them to the test of ridicule and expose them.[34]

In the novels of the Renaissance the figures of the fool, clown and rogue play exactly this role for Bakhtin. As he puts it at one stage, their activity involves a sort of spontaneous philosophy of discourse, a 'radical scepticism ... bordering on rejection of the very possibility of having a straightforward discourse at all that would not be false'.[35] In 1941 he argues that the 'comic operation of dismemberment' associated with parody and ridicule was a crucial precondition for 'free, scientifically knowable and artistically realistic creativity in European civilization'.[36] Scientific thought and literary parody, share a common identity as types of critical thought as understood by Cassirer: both self-consciously break apart the original unity of the object and then piece it back together in a new way by means of secondary meaning structures, or concepts.

Sure enough, Bakhtin does something new with Cassirer's ideas. He combines them with Henri Bergson's notion of laughter as socially medicinal in correcting rigidity of body and mind,[37] Georg Simmel's idea of an oppressive objective culture that needs to be reunited with the life from which it arises, and he gives it all a populist edge by recasting all of this according to a struggle between official and popular forms of culture.[38] However, there is one more Russian source that is crucial for this to be transformed into Bakhtinian carnival: Olga Freidenberg, whose first publication was a short article of 1925 on the origin of parody.[39] Freidenberg facilitated the Bakhtinian transformation of the parodic *ustanovka* into a primordial cultural force through her contention that parody originates with ritual inversions in prehistory and becomes a crucial element of the culture of the *prazdnik*. All of the crucial examples that Bakhtin marshals in his prehistory of carnival: the Lupercalia and Saturnalia festivals, the parody of liturgy on medieval feast days, the filter through the Greek comic novel and all, they all appear in Freidenberg's article. These are then expanded upon with an elaboration of the ambivalent symbolic structure of fire, birth death in her book on the problems of plot and genre which although completed in 1928 was published only in 1936. The following passage, which Bakhtin underlined in his copy of the book, is ample evidence of Bakhtin's debt to Freidenberg:

> [P]arody itself has a sacral origin and this lives on in folklore right up to modern times: its very cultic-folkloric forms bring to us both tragic elements, in the form of public worship and passion [*strast'*], and comic [elements] in the form of farces and obscenity. Beginning with antiquity, the festival of the new year, there is passion and Births – all days of the new suns and the new births – have a parodic beginning in the form of the

> feast of simpletons [*glupets*], the festival of asses, the feast of fools [*durak*] etc. After all we have said, there are for us no novelties; we are not surprised that the king [*tsar*] is chosen from the jesters, that the clergy swap clothes with the crowd, that public worship is parodied, that churches serve as an arena for obscenity and shame. Neither does it surprise us that we meet parody alongside all the acts of life – marriage, burial, birth, the administration of justice, commerce, government etc. And the main image is alongside the act of eating. Characteristic in this regard is the medieval 'liturgy of gluttons', which permeated the church during public worship: the clergy greedily ate sausage right in front of the altar, played cards right under the nose of the priests conducting a service, threw excrement into the censor and made a stink with it.[40]

Freidenberg is clearly the source of Bakhtin's claims for the cultic roots of parody and for a great deal of empirical material. However, while Bakhtin adopts both this and the Marrist notion of the 'sublimation' of folkloric features in modern culture,[41] he interprets all this in line with his neo-Kantian philosophical principles and populist politics. As a result, parody turns out to have quite the opposite philosophical and ideological significance for him than for Freidenberg.[42]

So why is Bakhtin's version now so much more influential than the others? It is not because of his hitherto exaggerated originality, for it now seems that this lies only in the way the others ideas were fitted together. This is not something so small, by the way. It is, rather, that he was the most accomplished philosopher of them all. He was able to integrate the others' observations into a more substantial philosophical whole that transformed parody into an expression of the perennial and indestructible impulse within culture towards critical thought and democracy. The result is simultaneously a philosophy of culture, of history and of science. But it is purely idealist, and we need to ask ourselves if we are happy with the idea of us knowing nothing of the empirical world in principle, for this is what the granting to parody a scientific status on the basis of neo-Kantian philosophy really means.[43]

15

LAUGHING AT THE HANGMAN

Humorous Portraits of Stalin

KAREN RYAN

A premise widely accepted by theoreticians of satire and humour is that there are some subjects that lie outside the realm of the comedic. Some topics – genocide, famine or serial murder, for example, seem too appalling for humorous or even satirical treatment. Intuitively, we might include Stalinism with its absurd injustices, mass deportations, arrests and executions in this list of inappropriate topics. Certainly Stalinism ranks high among policies or programmes that have caused enormous human misery, exploitation and suffering. Yet in surveying twentieth-century Russian literary humour,[1] we find a surprisingly large number of works that make light of Stalinism and Stalin himself. Analysis of these texts within the framework of Soviet and post-Soviet culture suggests that comedy has been used as a strategy for coping with the oppression of Stalin's regime and his legacy. It is, it seems, a means of coming to terms with lingering questions of guilt, complicity and responsibility for both writers and readers.

The corpus of literary humour that treats Stalinism directly is quite extensive and spans most of the twentieth century. Of course, few of the works in question were published (or even written) during Stalin's reign; the majority date from after his death. But beyond establishing a *terminus a quo* in the 1920s, the composition and publishing history of humorous texts about Stalin is not terribly significant. In considering Stalinism as a theme of literary humour, it is more useful to regard it as a mind set or attitude and as such, it is not directly linked to Stalin's life and death. In some respects, we find that Stalinism is still influential in literary humour in the contemporary period.

Distinguishing between comedy and satire is an inexact science at best; the two modes are close, often intersecting or overlapping. As we might expect, satire about

Stalinism is plentiful, for a pernicious system encourages derision, abuse and ridicule. Comedic works about Stalin, on the other hand, are primarily humorous, not critical or didactic. Instead of attacking the evils of Stalinism, they seem rather to laugh at them. If we accept the premise that these works help writers and readers to deal with questions of responsibility for Stalinism, then we see that a primary function of this literary humour is to reveal the absurdity, the (often laughable) surreal quality of Stalin's tyranny. Literary comedy about Stalinism and Stalin is often reductive, demonstrating the banality and vulgarity of its subject. This is particularly important insofar as several generations of Russians have been compelled to confront issues of guilt and complicity. Humorous treatments of Stalin also serve as blunt, aggressive instruments of exposure. Alternately, they provide a cultural 'pressure valve' for writers and readers, a means of coping with fear and irrationality. Yet another function of literary humour about Stalinism is to express optimism. Treating the horrors of Stalinism, these humorous texts incorporate the material of tragedy and transcend it.[2] Generally, comedy has functioned in twentieth-century Russian culture as in many totalitarian states as anti-univocal instrument. In regard to the role of comedy in oppressive states, Edward Galligan notes that 'a totalitarian order attempts to suppress variety and to impose a single, univocal idea on every aspect of life.'[3] The humorous works examined here demolish Stalinist univocality and indeed challenge the conceit that univocality is possible.

A writer who has been particularly successful at portraying the banality of Stalin's evil is Vladimir Voinovich. In the first and second parts of Voinovich's projected five-part *Life and Extraordinary Adventures of Private Ivan Chonkin* (*Zhizn' i neobychainye prikliucheniia soldata Ivana Chonkina*, 1975), Stalin does not have the status of an independent character, but is nevertheless a major source of humour. Stalinism, of course, pervades the background and setting of the novel, but Stalin also appears directly in two dream sequences. In the first of these, Chonkin is confronted by Stalin: 'At this point Comrade Stalin descended slowly from the sky. He was wearing a woman's dress, with his moustache and with his pipe in his teeth. In his hands he held a rifle.'[4] He advises Chonkin's commanding officer to shoot Chonkin, as he has deserted his post and misplaced his weapon. This dream has intrigued commentators and given rise to a number of explications. On one level, putting Stalin in drag is a means of demonstrating the vulgarity of the world view he represents. Portraying him in a woman's dress suggests that we regard Stalin as a potential androgyne, at least in the framework of this humorous novel. Although the androgyne is often credited with magical powers in other cultures, he occupies a liminal and decidedly negative position in the Russian cultural context. To insinuate that Stalin is an androgynous figure is an especially powerful comedic device, given that his official image is markedly masculine. The appellation frequently applied to him in propaganda – Father of the People (*Otets narodov*) – is distinctly masculine. He is usually pictured visually and verbally with his masculine accoutrement of mustache and pipe and Voinovich's text depends on the familiarity of these markers to enhance the jarring effect of Stalin's appearance. Undercutting Stalin's masculinity effectively diminishes him and renders him laughable. It makes little difference that Voinovich's portrayal is fantastic, a fictive dream, for the official, exaggeratedly masculine picture of Stalin to which it responds is equally fictional.

Stalin makes a second brief appearance in *Ivan Chonkin* in the dream Chonkin has of Niura's and Borka's wedding banquet. Following the trays of *chelovechina* (which are Chonkin's military superiors trussed out for consumption), a tray is brought in with Stalin on it. He is holding his pipe and grinning slyly into his moustache. In this case, there is a threat, some danger associated with Stalin's image, but Voinovich places him in a highly vulnerable, even ridiculous position. We are not told explicitly that Stalin has no clothes on, but the officers who precede him as *chelovechina* have none, so it is implied that he too is naked. The absurd situation Voinovich creates in this dream demonstrates Stalin's banal harmlessness and belies the threatening quality of his persona. He is probably naked (a most ludicrous position) and is potentially food (the prey rather than the predator).

Voinovich's short story 'In a Circle of Friends' ('V krugu druzei,' 1967) relies on popular perceptions of Stalin and his cohorts and exaggerates them humorously. In the course of this story, we learn that Stalin crawls into his bedroom through a safe to foil potential assassins. The act of crawling emphasises Stalin's baseness, his essentially animalistic nature. Moreover, his pastimes – cutting out and rearranging men's and women's heads in pictures in *Ogonek*, working crossword puzzles – are simple-minded and banal. His reasoning about the outbreak of war demonstrates his naivete and his blindness: 'But if war has not been declared, that means there is no war, and that means we Kobaists will not admit and do not accept it, for to accept that which doesn't exist means to slide into the swamp of idealism. Isn't that so, comrades?'[5] Voinovich demonstrates that the leaders' awe before the dictator is misplaced, for Stalin is merely deluding himself and others with rhetoric and absurd logic.

Fazil Iskander, in his allegorical beast tale *Rabbits and Boa Constrictors* (*Kroliki i udavy*, 1982), also treats Stalin and Stalinism as humorously banal. He casts Stalin as a snake, the Great Python who rules over the boa constrictors in his fictional kingdom. The Great Python feigns modesty, but compels the boas to listen to his silly riddles and tedious anecdotes. When he deems it necessary, he organises 'spontaneous' question-and-answer sessions for the edification of his subjects. He perpetuates a myth that has evolved about his swallowing a man by hypnotising him. It is on the basis of this feat that the Great Python was originally chosen tsar of the boas, but in fact (Iskander's narrator reveals) the native was intoxicated and unconscious. Not only does the Great Python fabricate the story of his hypnotising his victim, but he himself comes to believe this version. Stalin is indeed a petty dictator in Iskander's allegory, and it is significant that he ends up stuffed after dying in rather dubious circumstances. Iskander places him in a highly undignified position to make him ludicrous and to render his evil impotent.

This comedic approach – exposing the banality and vulgarity of Stalinist totalitarianism – stresses Stalin's humanity (or sub-humanity). This method relies on the premise that Stalinism is too risible and irrational to be worthy of serious analysis. Stalin and Stalinism are effectively diminished through humour at the hands of Voinovich and Iskander. Moreover, humorous treatment of Stalinism reduces it while supporting the innocence of the Russian people, for those surrounding Stalin may be naive or even complicit, but they are not (in these visions) evil.

A second function of anti-Stalinist humour is as an aggressive weapon of exposure. In an oppressive culture such as that of Stalinism, literary humour may well serve as a form of rebellion. Iuz Aleshkovsky in *Kangaroo* (*Kenguru*, 1981) gives Stalin's right foot a defiant character that reflects humorously on the nature of Stalinism. A long chapter within this novel recounts Stalin's participation in the Yalta Conference of 1945; this chapter is actually an embedded narrative, an independent story.[6] The premise of this episode is that Stalin's right foot stages a revolt and turns on him, excoriating him, cursing him and taunting him with predictions of ignominious death. Stalin makes repeated attempts to silence the foot by stepping on it and rubbing it; he even briefly considers amputation. But the foot persists in singing out the truth in the most vulgar terms: 'Stalin is an asshole and a fool and a pitiful shit! Soon you'll croak and die. Your life is a waste.'[7] The humour of this situation is profoundly hostile; this is the humour of the diatribe or invective. Aleshkovsky creates a fictional situation in which Stalin is helpless, at the mercy of his own limb. It is significant that this comedic weapon is so powerful that it actually evokes some degree of sympathy for Stalin within the text. The narrator (who is privy to the ranting and raving of the right leg) senses the burden of Stalin's monstrous evil and apprehends his utter isolation, his vulnerability. This fact does not mitigate the effectiveness of the strategy; Stalin and his world-view are rendered thoroughly ludicrous through Aleshkovsky's comedic lens.

A second text that utilises humour as an aggressive weapon against Stalinism is Viktor Erofeev's *Russian Beauty* (*Russkaia krasavitsa*). This, of course, is a much later work (published in 1990), but the mechanism of its humour in regard to Stalin is remarkably similar to that of Aleshkovsky's work. The novel includes a long passage on Stalin and Stalinism, as well as peripheral references scattered throughout the text. The narrative point of view is that of Irina, the heroine, and the passage begins with her recounting a debate between Iurii and Egor, two men who are driving her to an ancient battlefield outside of Moscow. Their conversation, as retold by Irina, is a reprise of the traditional pro and contra argument about Stalin. Egor asserts that Stalin is respected by the Russian people for winning the Second World War, while Iurii maintains that they are nostalgic for the iron fist. Irina's summary of the debate is cursory and cynical; it can be recounted in a couple of sentences because it is tediously familiar. Having outlined the substance of their debate, she interrupts it by shifting to speculation about Stalin's sexual proclivities. Her insisting that her companions consider the issue of whether or not Stalin practiced fellatio is deliberately outrageous. It is intended to shock both her interlocutors (on a textual level) and the reader (on an extra-textual level). Erofeev essentially treats Stalinism as an obscene joke; and like an obscene joke, this passage is aggressively derisive. Stalin and the world view he represents are made the butt of the crudest sort of sexual mockery. Erofeev's comedy, like Aleshkovsky's, is patently distorted and unfair. Indeed, fantasy and absurdity are utilised consciously to expose Stalinism as dysfunctional and abnormal.

Literary humour that targets Stalinism may also serve as a sort of pressure valve for both writer and reader. Distinguishing between humour as an aggressive weapon and humour as a means of releasing pressure in these texts is perhaps artificial; there are certainly points of intersection. The latter is close, it seems, to what is called 'gallows humour'. It responds to injustice, oppression and the constant threat of arrest and imprisonment. This threat need not be current, incidentally; this kind of humour can express remembered fear or vestigial fear as well. It may be a psychological coping mechanism in a totalitarian society where no other outlet exists.

One example of this sort of dark comedy is Anatolii Gladilin's 'Rehearsal on Friday' ('Repetitsiia v piatnitsu', 1978). In this story, which takes place in the post-Stalin period, Stalin comes back to life after having been cryogenically preserved. He finds discipline weak and his successors insufficiently decisive. Once again, he is compelled to take power into his own hands and he chides his successors threateningly for the reforms of the Thaw period and the revelations of the Twentieth Party Congress. Times have changed, however, and Stalin is ultimately recognised to be irrelevant. He announces that he will deliver a speech on television, but an important hockey game is on and interrupting it would arouse a very strong negative reaction. It is psychologically satisfying to contemplate the dictator's bewilderment at being relegated to a position inferior in importance to a hockey game. Gladilin relies on the cathartic effect of this kind of humour repeatedly in his story to make Stalin and Stalinism ludicrous.

Ilia Suslov's *Stories About Comrade Stalin and Other Comrades* (*Rasskazy o tovarishche Staline i drugikh tovarishchakh*, 1981) is a rather slight collection of stories, but they bear mention in this context. These stories are essentially textual anecdotes, myths about Stalin and his cohorts that Suslov has transformed into miniature stories. They are quite dark in tonality, evoking the oppressive, fearful atmosphere of Stalinism. In several, Stalin is portrayed as a trickster figure who consigns people to terrible fates when they slip up or fail to please him. In 'Legend About Badaev' ('Legenda o Badaeve'), the old Bolshevik Badaev shames the Party by falling down drunk at a diplomatic reception. Stalin devises a cruel psychological punishment: he sentences Badaev to labour the rest of his life in the brewery that bears his name. In 'Image of the Leader' ('Obraz vozhdia'), the actor Gelovani who frequently played Stalin in films and plays has the temerity to request that he be allowed to study Stalin's life more closely, the better to imitate him dramatically. Stalin decrees: 'The actor Gelovani wants to study my image. He wants to understand the course of my life. That's not a bad thing. Let him begin with exile in Turuhansk.'[8] In several other stories, Suslov demonstrates how chance, luck or Stalin's whim determines an individual's fate. There is a good deal of cosmic irony in this sort of humour, and it provides a way to laugh at tyranny. In 'The Double' ('Dvoinik'), Stalin orders that a man who looks like his twin be shot. But on second thought when Beria suggests it might be simpler just to shave off the man's mustache, Stalin accedes: 'That's alright too' (11). In a very funny story called 'Comrade Stalin Watches the Film "Chapaev"' ('Tovarishch Stalin smotrit fil'm "Chapaev"'), Suslov recounts how a particular scene was retained in the film despite Stalin's initial objection to it. One of the directors is determined to argue against excising the scene but once he is in Stalin's presence, he cannot stand the nervous strain and faints. To which Stalin replies: 'Is this really because of the scene [of the attack by the Whites under Colonel Kappelev]? Oh God, well then let it stay in!' (20). Puns and witty rejoinders are used in some stories by Suslov to demonstrate humorously the threat that hung over everyone. In 'A. M. Gorky Writes an Article' ('Aleksei Maksimovich Gor'kii pishet stat'iu'), Stalin and Yagoda pressure Gorky to produce a propagandistic article. To Gorky's objection that he is too busy to undertake this task, Stalin replies: 'Try . . . An attempt, as my friend Yagoda says, is not torture . . .' (13). Stalin's use of the punning adage '*Popytka ne pytka*' is a very thinly veiled threat, given that torture was a common tool of persuasion under his regime.

Iuz Aleshkovsky's 'Song About Stalin' ('Pesnia o Staline,' 1964) is another good example of humour functioning as a safety valve in anti-Stalinist literature. This song-poem is an extraordinarily sarcastic address to Stalin from a prison camp inmate, expressing his admiration, awe and good wishes. Its comedic tone is indeed dark, as Aleshkovsky mixes Stalinist cliches with the coarser dialect of the camp experience:

> 'And here I sit in the Turukhansk region,
> Where the convoys are as coarse as dogs
> I understand all this, of course,
> as an intensification of the class struggle.'[9]

The effect of this song, which expresses contempt and bitterness through its irony, is certainly cathartic.

A fourth and related function of anti-Stalinist literary humour is the expression of hope. William Lynch develops this notion in his work on the theory of comedy, though he does not use terms like hope or optimism. Rather he sees in comedy a mode that discovers that 'rock-bottom reality in man', 'the most inherently confident rung of the finite. It is ugly and strong.'[10] A fine textual example of this type of anti-Stalinist humour is Evgeny Shvarts's play *The Dragon* (*Drakon*, 1944). While the play is ostensibly anti-Fascist, it has been interpreted as anti-Stalinist as well.[11] In this 'fairy-tale for adults,'[12] a three-headed dragon has terrorised a mythical kingdom for hundreds of years, demanding annual sacrifices of young maidens. A wandering hero named Lancelot arrives in the kingdom, challenges the Dragon and ultimately slays him, but is badly wounded in the battle. When he returns to the kingdom after a long period of recovery, he finds that the former mayor has now become a tyrant, oppressing the townspeople as cruelly as did the Dragon previously. Lancelot concludes that the townspeople need to be saved again, now from the dragon of totalitarianism (and this can be read specifically as Stalinism) which resides within them. There is much that is comedic in this play, including a sly talking cat, buffoonish characters and absurdly contradictory propaganda. The play concludes on a note of genuine optimism, as Lancelot assures Elza that the work of expunging the weeds of slavishness in the townspeople can be accomplished, that there is hope for the future: 'I love you all, my friends. Otherwise why would I trouble myself with you? And since I love you, everything will be lovely. And after long trials and sufferings we will all be happy, very happy at last!'[13]

Iskander's *The Feasts of Belshazzar* (*Piry Valtasara*, (1979)) recounts one of Stalin's famous nocturnal banquets in the mid-thirties. Sandro, the hero of Iskander's epic cycle *Sandro of Chegem* (*Sandro iz Chegema*), is a dancer in a troupe that entertains Stalin and his cohorts at the banquet. The story includes a fantastic digression from Stalin's own point of view about his childhood and a recollected episode from Sandro's youth. This latter embedded tale exposes

Stalin's almost supernatural evil, his demonic nature. It is also a very funny story, demonstrating the fear and obsequiousness that Stalin inspired in those around him and the corruption of Stalinism. Although the humour of the tale is rather dark, it culminates in a profession of faith in the eventual triumph of divine justice:

> The very fact that [Stalin] died of natural causes, if in fact he died of natural causes, inclines me personally to the religious thought that God demanded to see his file with all his deeds, in order to Himself judge him with the supreme judgement and Himself to punish him with the highest punishment.[14]

A final example of anti-Stalinist humour that serves to express optimism is Kornei Chukovsky's poem 'The Big Bad Cockroach' ('Tarakanishche', 1923). This poem was written very early, in 1921, but has been widely read as anti-Stalinist allegory. Lev Loseff's contention that the work targets 'an authoritarian system of rule which later in the century would be designated "Stalinism"'[15] positions it within the broader framework of anti-authoritarian satire. It may well be that it acquired a specifically anti-Stalinist slant only after the fact, but it has, significantly, continued to be read this way. 'The Big Bad Cockroach' is ostensibly a children's poem which tells the story of a harmonious community of animals, birds and sea creatures that is invaded by a terrible, tyrannical cockroach. The cockroach appears mysteriously and establishes himself as a dictator, demanding that the animals deliver up their young for him to consume. They submit in terror until the sparrow observes that the cockroach is merely an insect and gobbles him up. The animals go back to living happily and peacefully. Chukovsky's humour, directed at tyranny generally and perhaps Stalinism specifically, sustains optimism in the possibility of living free of fear.

Stalinism presents, it would seem, better material for tragedy than for comedy. In the context of modern Russian culture, however, humour plays an important role in coming to terms with the evils engendered by this system. Considering the tremendous misery and loss caused by Stalinism, we might well question how comedy about it can be created or appreciated. Edward Galligan's observation about the function of comedy under conditions of injustice is certainly relevant here: 'You make or savour comedy in a world like this precisely because it is a world like this.'[16] That is, ironical humour born out of terrible, tragic experiences is necessary to sustain or regenerate the life of writers, readers and nations. Literary humour that takes Stalin and Stalinism as its subjects fulfills at least four social-psychological functions. It demonstrates the banality and vulgarity of the Stalinist mind set; it serves as an aggressive weapon to expose and counter the evils of Stalinism; it provides a pressure valve in an extremely repressive society; and it expresses hope that Russia can transcend Stalinism. A few observations follow from this analysis and suggest that humour may contribute to the enormous ongoing work of destalinisation. First, it is generally true in these works that those surrounding Stalin (with the exception of his coterie) may be naive, even complicit; nevertheless, they are not actively evil themselves. The Russian people – in these humorous texts and by implication in twentieth-century history – are innocent of the corruption and immorality that Stalinism engendered. These works as a corpus provide a way of encountering Stalinism that reduces and diminishes it. It is, ultimately, too irrational and too ludicrous to harm permanently an essentially healthy culture. For all its irony and sarcasm, this sort of comedy is a strong statement of faith: faith in the human spirit under totalitarianism and faith in the Russian national character.

16

VARIETIES OF REFLEXIVITY IN THE RUSSO-SOVIET *ANEKDOT*

SETH GRAHAM

An early indication that Vladimir Putin's Russia would see a mini-renaissance in popular oral humour was the reappearance of the meta-*anekdot*, the joke about jokes:[1]

> The Russian government has announced that beginning 26 March 2000 [the day Putin was elected president -SG] all *anekdoty* about Vovochka[2] will be considered political.[3]

Those who argue that Russia has entered a new era of stagnation might point out this *anekdot*'s resemblance to one from 1984 about a ban on all '*anekdoty* beginning with the letter "ch": Chapaev, Chukchi, Cheburashka, and Chernenko.'[4] With similarly self-referential texts in mind Andrei Siniavsky (writing as Abram Terts) observed in 1978 that the *anekdot* is a rare example of reflexive – or, in his words, 'self-conscious' – folklore.[5] Siniavsky limits his discussion of textual 'self-consciousness' to meta-jokes, but the philological descriptor 'reflexive' is in fact applicable to a broader variety of *anekdot*, analysis of which reveals how the genre's capacity for self-regard (both by the text and by the discursive source, i.e., the joke-teller) contributed substantially to its prominence in Soviet culture.

Like meta-*anekdoty*, the following joke types employ reflexivity of one sort or another: (1) *anekdoty* that make reference to other specific texts; (2) *anekdoty* that implicitly evaluate the nature and practice of verbal signification; and (3) self-referential ethnic *anekdoty*, i.e., Russian jokes that foreground Russian-ness. This list may seem irresponsibly to conflate two distinct species of reflexivity: meta-textuality, on one hand, and self-reference in the literal sense of an individual or group's discourse about themselves, on the other. Russian jokes about stereotypical behaviours and traits of the Russian (or Russo-Soviet) ethnos, however, *are* intertextual, insofar as they implicate extant *textual representations* of that ethnos. Moreover, their function often overlapped with that of other intertextual *anekdoty*: to engage critically with the normative, inscribed models of social reality that dominated the corpus of texts available for popular consumption. Nevertheless, the present article shall treat only the first two varieties of reflexivity, leaving the third for a separate study of the relationship between popular humour and the Russian ethnic self-image.

During the so-called era of stagnation (coinciding roughly with the Brezhnev period) the *anekdot* was not only a ubiquitous form of discourse; its attention to other constituent texts and genres of Soviet culture made it the medium of choice for popular meta-discourse. While *anekdoty* did, naturally, depict actual personalities, relationships, and events, 'anecdotal' significations of such things had more immediate referential links to previous significations: concrete textual representations of 'real-life' phenomena. One scholar of the genre writes that *anekdoty* were constructed on the basis not of 'realia as such, but those realia that had moved to the level of idea.'[6] Ideas are expressed in the form of discourse and, as Mikhail Bakhtin tells us, every unit of discourse – every utterance – is by definition responsive to previous utterances in the given cultural environment's communicative chain.[7] What was significant about the *anekdot* as a speech genre was its tendency to display its responsive nature, to draw attention to its discursive position vis-a-vis other utterances. *Anekdot*-telling was not merely a response, but a performance of response, just as dance (as Richard Bauman points out) is both movement and a performance of movement.[8] Performance as a cultural practice involves simultaneous use of and commentary on a medium of expression. Its reflective probing of 'the formal features of the communicative system'[9] is thus also reflexive; cultural performance is self-evident meta-communication.

Verbal performance is a reflexive form of discourse in the same way that philology is: the medium – language – is also the referent (although in philological analysis the reference is explicit). While this bootstrapping dilemma has the potential to undermine the objectivity (and therefore the credibility) of a scientific endeavor like philology, reflexivity amplifies the discursive potency of the *anekdot*, a form of utterance that thrived on 'paradoxicality' long before it became the chief medium for parodying the self-contradictions of Soviet ideology.[10] Because it is of the same stuff as its referent, the intertextual *anekdot* is able to assimilate all or part of a text from a different context and re-present it through the prism of the *anekdot*'s own generic logic:

> During a speech by Brezhnev a man in the audience is arrested. He turns out to be a spy. 'How did you know he was a CIA agent?' Brezhnev asks the famous KGB officer, Major Pronin. 'As you constantly remind us, Leonid Il'ich, the enemy never sleeps.'[11]

Such *anekdoty* are a form of ironic oral philology that engages with other texts from a position not of scholarly detachment, but satirical condescension. The Soviet *anekdot* became an outlet for the otherwise restricted meta-discursive impulse of the educated, urban cultural consumer (the intelligentsia). The genre was also, of course, a means of expressing contempt for the source of the restriction – the state's illegitimate monopoly on textual production – and the resulting crisis of representation.

As Siniavsky points out, the *anekdot* itself was not immune to its own predilection for critical meta-discourse. The culture of *anekdot*-telling was a narrative theme in *anekdoty* themselves for the simple reason that it was a part of everyday life, a central medium for the representation of which was the *anekdot*. The meta-*anekdot* is a generic subcategory that exists in several variants. Especially common are variations on the 'numbered *anekdoty*' motif:

> In a prison all the jokes have been told a thousand times, so the inmates number them so as not to waste time.
> '67!' Laughter.
> '52!' Laughter.
> '41!' One inmate starts laughing like mad.
> 'What's with you?'
> 'I've never heard that one before!'[12]

In other versions, a newcomer shouts out a random number, prompting reprimands for telling a dirty joke in the presence of women, a dismissive rebuke that 'he doesn't know how to tell a joke,' or a gestured warning that a hidden microphone or informant is present. The notion of numerical shorthand for *anekdoty* is an implicit commentary on the status of the *anekdot* itself as a sort of shorthand, a distilled observation on a particular aspect of public or private life. The 'jokes by numbers' motif also implies the scarcity, and value, of fresh *anekdoty*, something addressed in the brief *anekdot* 'Why did Cain kill Abel? For telling old jokes.'[13]

Another category depicts *anekdot* (or other folkloric) characters acknowledging their own textual status or telling *anekdoty*; the already tongue-in-cheek pretense of mimesis is explicitly abandoned. Textual self-reference of this sort functioned as an exaggerated corrective to the hyper-mimetic, transparent texts of official culture, which subordinated form to content while rigidly prescribing both. The *anekdot's* formal exhibitionism was anathema to the representational system of socialist realism, which had little tolerance for self-referential art; once a text acknowledges its textuality, its signifying link to reality – and its potential as a medium for the equation of reality with myth – is damaged. The *anekdot*'s playful complication of the relationship between text and reality is sometimes an explicit narrative theme:

Shirlits wakes up in a cell and thinks:
'If a Nazi soldier comes in, I'll say I'm SS officer von Shtirlits. If he's in a Red Army uniform, I'll say I'm Colonel Isaev.'
A Soviet policeman comes in and says:
'Well, comrade Tikhonov, you sure tied one on last night, didn't you?'[14]

Another example of this type of reflexivity is the 'super-*anekdot*' motif, in which a computer is programmed to generate the most typical *anekdot* possible:

Rabinovich asks a Chukchi:
'Vasily Ivanovich, have you been to the visa office?'

'The women there once met Lenin himself.'[15]
A woman is in bed with her lover. The doorbell rings. Vovochka runs to get it and there stand Chapaev and Pet'ka, both Jewish.
Chapaev is walking on Red Square and he meets Lenin. Lenin asks Chapaev (in a Jewish accent), 'So, Abram, isn't it time we left for Israel already!?'[16]

Some meta-*anekdoty* function as generic feedback mechanisms that identify hyper-productive (and/or hackneyed) cycles or motifs by ironically laying bare their textuality:

Pet'ka is walking down the street when he meets Chapaev, covered in puke.
'What happened, Vasily Ivanovich?'
'It's from that last *anekdot*, Pet'ka!'

A Jew is running along Nevsky Avenue. He meets an acquaintance who asks him, 'where are you coming from?' He answers, 'from the *anekdot*! The generals crowded me out!'[17]

Such reflexive treatment of jokelore in danger of losing its novelty served to defamiliarise thematic or compositional patterns that had been repeated in so many permutations that the only remaining direction for innovation was 'up,' to the meta level.

The most extreme example of such generic auto-criticism is the so-called abstract *anekdot*:

Bear and Fox are sitting by the river. Hare comes up and asks:
'Guys! Do you have any glue?'
'No,' they answer.
Hare runs off, comes back with a bottle of glue, and says:
'Here you go.'

Such jokes (akin to Anglophone shaggy dog stories) are reflexive in an etymologically literal sense: they 'turn back on themselves' by inflicting the genre's signature device – a sharp disruption of the logical flow of discourse – on the genre's *own* expected discursive trajectory, towards a punch line. They display awareness of the genre's conventions by ostentatiously violating them. Paradoxically, however, they are no less successful as *anekdoty* than normative texts of the genre; they fulfill the genre's most basic function: to evoke laughter. They are, then, simultaneously generically self critical and generically self-regenerative. Some abstract *anekdoty* feature absurd content in an *anekdot*-shaped shell[18]:

> A guy stands on his balcony with a case of kefir and pours one bottle after another onto the street. A man from the balcony below asks:
> 'You playing chess?'
> 'How'd you guess?'
> 'See that bicycle over there?'[19]
> A customer in a restaurant:
> 'Bring me a pot of soup.' He takes the pot and pours it over his head. The waiter says:
> 'What are you doing? That's soup!'
> 'Oh, I thought it was compote.'[20]
>
> A cow is climbing a tree.
> 'Hey, Cow, where are you going?' asks Crow.
> 'Well, I wanted some apples.'
> 'Apples? That's a birch tree!'
> 'I have some with me.'[21]
>
> Two crocodiles were flying: one red, the other to Africa.

Even absurd *anekdoty* are not immune to becoming hackneyed and formulaic, and thus require periodic, prophylactic *ostranenie.* Consider, for example, the following hyper-absurd, embellished variants on two of the above-cited *anekdoty*:

> A man stands naked in the middle of the street. Every other minute he pours a glass of juice over his head and says 'coo-coo.' Another man comes up and asks:
> 'What are you doing?'
> 'Playing chess.'
> 'Can I play?'
> 'Sure!'
> They stand across from each other saying 'coo-coo!' A third man walks by:
> 'Playing chess?'
> 'How'd you guess?'
> 'Because there's a *zaporozhets* parked around the corner.'[22]
>
> Two crocodiles were flying: one green, the other to the right. How much does a kilogram of herring weigh? (Who the hell knows!).[23]

Such texts fulfill on the level of form the comic utterance's role as, in Barbara Babcock's words, 'a remark on the indignity of any closed system.'[24] Pavel Borodin writes that their purpose is 'to expose the laws of the communicative act.'[25]

Another form of meta-joke – *anekdoty* about the culture of *anekdot*-telling –

were an outlet for the popular impulse not only to violate taboos but to reproduce the pleasure therein in a ritual, symbolic way by *talking* about the violation.[26] Such texts are semantically akin to representations of other illicit activities such as drinking, swearing, and fornication. The Soviet *anekdot* was not only meta-discursive but meta-transgressive, simultaneously a *medium* for depicting taboo-breaking behaviour and *itself* a form of taboo-breaking. A joke circulating in Moscow in 1999 acknowledges the simple truth that talking about transgressive acts can be as appealing as the acts themselves:

> A man is shipwrecked on a desert island with Claudia Schiffer. After a few days, he says to her, 'um, I was wondering. You're a woman, I'm a man. We might be here for years. Why don't we, you know. . . .' She agrees. Afterwards she asks how he liked it. 'Well, it was great,' he answers, 'but. . . .' 'But what? What else do you want?' she says. 'Um, could you do one more thing for me,' he says, 'could you put on my hat? And my suit?' 'What, you don't like women anymore?' she says. 'Please, just put it on,' he implores. She obliges. He looks at her, puts his hand on her shoulder and says, 'Dude! Guess who I just had sex with!'

The association of the *anekdot* with the physical realm is expressed not only thematically, but meta-textually, in the communicative process of joke-telling itself. As Arthur Koestler points out, laughter, uniquely among human reflexes, is a physical response triggered by a cognitive stimulus: the comic.[27] Joke-telling is thus a point of contact between the visceral and the abstract, the mundane and the aesthetic, the realm of the mind and the realm of the mouth. In this sense it is similar to drinking alcohol, another activity that combines the material and the intellectual (and is an obligatory mutual accompaniment to *anekdoty*). Joke-telling and drunkenness – along with other pastimes like sex and fist-fighting – were self-induced reminders of one's physical, ontological reality in the face of the hyper-rational yet absurdly unreal official models of human character and behaviour. Popular behaviours and cultural practices often represented a deep parody of state ideology, which posited in materialist theory an essential link between the physical and the mental/spiritual while producing abstract discursive models that were actually diametrical opposites of lived, physical experience.

The *anekdot* also engaged critically with the obtaining ideology on a more direct, thematic level, of course, and here too its capacity for reflexivity played a role. The genre became grist for its own mill initially as a result of its politicisation by the state, i.e., when arrests for telling or transcribing *anekdoty* became an element of the Soviet popular consciousness and experience. Jokes about the political consequences of careless joke-telling became commonplace in the 1930s, when the sentence for propagating or transcribing *anekdoty* was up to ten years imprisonment. For example: 'The state announces a contest for the best political joke. First prize: fifteen years.'[28] Or: Stalin boasts to an advisor that he himself has a large collection of *anekdoty*, and when asked how large, answers 'two-and-a-half camps worth.' In especially reflexive displays, archetypal *anekdot* protagonists themselves figure in some texts: 'Two Chukchi are sitting on the icy shore of the Pacific. "Want to hear a political joke?" one asks. "Better not," replies the other, "you can get exiled to Siberia for that!"'

While it is clear why such jokes were illegal, the *anekdot* represents a special case among the outlaw texts of Soviet culture; for much of Soviet history the state treated the entire *genre* as inherently anti-Soviet. The official culture industry readily co-opted other folklore genres such as the folktale, the proverb, and even the *chastushka*, encouraging the composition of socialist-oriented fakelore and scholarly emphasis on 'progressive' pre-revolutionary folk texts. The *anekdot*, however, did not yield so easily to ideological colonisation and integration into the Soviet *Ars poetica*.

One reason for the generic embargo was the state's awareness that the *anekdot*'s extreme portability made it an ideal medium for rapid, clandestine propagation of unvetted opinions. Unlike the *chastushka*, which shares the *anekdot*'s brevity and satirical potential but is rhymed and usually sung, the *anekdot* blends easily into conversation; it is both an aesthetic composition and a form of speech. Moreover, because of its traditional role as a medium for popular irreverence towards elites, the *anekdot*'s 'class origins' were simultaneously impeccable and suspect; although its pre-revolutionary value in mocking priests and landowners was clear, its utility as a contemporary genre was problematic, considering the current ruling class. One humour theorist described satire as a natural by-product of a social environment in which 'the intelligentsia has long recognised the inherent emptiness, absurdity, and cultural abnormality of the ruling class, and considers that class's claims on the power to rule society inherently unjustified and therefore ridiculous.' Although this reads like a description of the premise behind the Stagnation-era underground *anekdot*, it is in fact a characterisation of the revolutionary proletariat's satirical impulse written by Soviet Commissar of Enlightenment Anatoly Lunacharsky in the early 1930s, the end of a period of debate over the place of satire in the Revolution.[29]

As popular, oral satire, the *anekdot* was difficult to reconcile with the official view of contemporary folklore as the organic expression of the Soviet People's gratitude and contentment in the new world (Gorky himself wrote that 'pessimism is entirely alien to folklore'[30]). Beginning with the consolidation of Stalinist cultural policy in the 1930s humour and satire were increasingly assigned to the realm of non-folkloric, inscribed forms (film, literature, theatre). Although short comic pieces were published in official periodicals and books throughout the Soviet period, and performed on the variety stage, at amateur, roast-like talent shows [*kapustniki*], and in frequently-televised humour competitions known as the 'club of jolly and witty' [*klub veselykh i nakhodchivykh*, or KVN], they were almost never called *anekdoty*. Instead, they were labeled 'jests' [*shutki*], 'miniatures' [*miniatiury*], 'gags' [*khokhmy*], 'quips for clowns' [*reprizy dlia klounov*], etc. So, when popular cynicism towards state discourse began to peak, it found potent expression in a genre whose very name was anathema to official culture. A taboo-breaking ritual could be initiated with the mere announcement of the genre one was about to perform: '*Anekdot*:...'

A convergence of circumstances fomented the *anekdot*'s rise in the era of 'developed socialism.' With its characteristic reflexivity and irony, the *anekdot* was a form of expression well suited to Soviet society's increasingly cynical, introspective *Zeitgeist*. Among the factors that nourished that *Zeitgeist* were: the state's rollback of the Thaw (culminating in the 1968 invasion of Czechoslovakia, but nascent in cultural politics years before); the relative lull in life-shattering historical cataclysms; and the emerging ubiquity of television. One observer characterises the Stagnation ambience as 'a gentle gloom [in which] it seemed that everything ... had already passed, that you could quietly live your life (saving up for a car, reading *samizdat*, sipping port wine, or combining these and other pleasant activities).'[31]

The new paradigm was in contrast to recent, uncharacteristic episodes of public enthusiasm and consensus: first, the war effort; later, the Thaw with its mass poetry concerts and premium on sincerity and 'joviality' [*veselost'*], to use Petr Vail' and Aleksandr Genis's term.[32] Temporal tropes were changing; a general sense of historical progression, teleology, and/or eschatology had given way to a common perception of time as cyclical, like the work week or the TV schedule (and the *anekdot*). The insular micro-collectives characteristic of the age were highly amenable to *anekdot*-telling. At the same time, those individual, 'cellular' collectives together constituted a larger, abstract popular collective whose cohesion was defined by the uniformity of its members' life experiences, and also by their common exposure – and response – to mass media texts.

Boris Briker and Anatoly Vishevsky identify a common awareness among the educated populace of an abstract paradigm of the typical life of the members of that stratum. They call this model a 'cultural text,' and write that it has an almost

> generic structure ... at the basis of [which] lies a schematic description of the life of... the average person. All the elements of the description are so characteristic of all the participants that any one of them can superimpose it onto their own personal life and see that the two correspond. Moreover, the person will be surprised to discover that even the private,...inimitable features of his life are already programmed into the overall schema.[33]

Language was a crucial medium for this collective. Vladimir Elistratov writes of the tendency of social sub-groups to use linguistic doubles [*iazykovye dvoiniki*] of the standard language.[34] The *anekdot* was an important instantiation of this verbal doppelganger, and the collective used it to comment on – and define itself in relation to institutions associated with – the 'parent' language.

Prominent among the manifestations of mass culture that provoked popular 'anecdotal' responses are several films and television programs of the 1960s and 1970s. They provided thematic, compositional, and linguistic material for topical *anekdot* cycles that to this day account for a large portion of the generic corpus: ballroom lothario Lt. Rzhevsky,[35] Shtirlits, Vinni-pukh (the Russian rendition of Winnie-the-Pooh, which has little in common with the Disney version except being based on Milne's book), the big-eared, fluffy animated character Cheburashka, Sherlock Holmes and Watson, and even (arguably) the Chukchi cycle.[36] The Chapaev cycle, incidentally, also dates from this period; the 1934 film enjoyed a renewed surge of popularity after the celebration of its thirtieth anniversary in 1964.

Although these cycles were inspired by visual texts, the *anekdot*'s engagement with them was primarily meta-linguistic. Visual culture had begun to reflect the resurgent official logocentrism of the post-Thaw years. Moreover, the *anekdot* favored dialogue as its chief compositional form, so it typically co-opted specific examples of dialogue from the source texts (e.g., the famous bedtime chat between Chapaev and Pet'ka). The one major cycle that mostly eschews dialogue between characters – Shtirlits – is based on a different verbal device: Emil Kopel'ian's voice-over narration in *Seventeen Moments of Spring*:

> Shtirlits arrived at Himmler's house in a red Russian shirt carrying an accordion. He played 'Kalinka' and danced squatting while whistling. Kopel'ian's voice over: 'Yes, never before had Shirlits been as close to blowing his cover as on that night.'[37]

Film and television narratives also lent themselves to strip-mining by the *anekdot* because, like it, they are performance genres; the raconteur does not quote from Chapaev or Vinni-pukh; he momentarily becomes Vasily Ivanych or Piglet.[38] Finally, with the rise of television viewership and sky-high cinema attendance, the film and television media – part of an electronic-age phenomenon Walter Ong calls 'secondary orality'[39] – themselves functioned as generators of oral utterances that quickly became common knowledge. In other words, mass culture itself became a prolific source of folkloric material.[40]

A better term than citation or allusion for the *anekdot*'s engagement with material from other texts is abduction. Its most obvious form of abduction is from the realm of irony-deficient solemnity to one of pure irony. This is one reason why certain popular visual texts (e.g., *White Sun of the Desert* [*Beloe solntse pustyni*, 1969], *The Very Same Munchausen* [*Tot samyi Miunkhauzen*, 1979], *The*

Twelve Chairs [*Dvenadtsat' stul'ev*, 1971], and the cartoon series *Just You Wait!* [*Nu pogodi!*, 1970s–1980s]) did not provoke *anekdot* cycles: because they themselves already use the ironic mode.

Some visual texts inspired *anekdot* cycles because they employ common *anekdot* structures and motifs. *Seventeen Moments of Spring*, about a Russian among non-Russians, has a link to comparative ethnic jokes, e.g., about a Frenchman, an Italian, and a Russian on a desert island, etc. The film *Chapaev* is structured as a series of brief episodes with simple dialogues, many of which end with (humorous or non-humorous) 'punch lines.'

The *anekdot's* intertextual links were not limited to aesthetic texts; political discourse figured in the Soviet *anekdot* early in its history. The sub-genre of the 'decoded acronym' [*rasshifrovka*], for example, is well represented in an anthology of early post-revolutionary *anekdoty* published in Munich in 1951:

> VKP(b) [*Vsesoiuznaia Kommunisticheskaia partiia* (*bol'shevikov*)] [All-Union Communist Party (Bolsheviks)] – Vory [Thieves], Kaznokrady [Embezzlers], Prostitutki [Prostitutes] (the 'b' in parentheses clarifies the third, foreign word [implying *bliad'*, 'whore'].[41]

Stalin-era *anekdoty*, like later ones, found material in Soviet leaders' use of language. Unlike Stagnation jokes, however, which tended to portray members of the political elite as incompetent, Ivan-durak-like abusers of language, older ones frequently emphasise the trickster-like or even diabolical nature of official discourse and manipulation of texts:

> Stalin is meeting with Gorky, trying to convince him to write a sequel to *Mother* entitled *Father*: 'It won't hurt you to try. Right, comrade Beria?' [in Russian the proverb is *popytka – ne pytka*, literally 'making an attempt is not torture'].

> [Politburo member Mikhail] Kalinin is giving a speech about industrialisation and animatedly describing for his audience the new twenty-story skyscrapers recently built on Karl Marx Street in Kharkov. Suddenly one of the listeners interrupts him:
> 'Comrade Kalinin, I am from Kharkov. I walk down that street every day, but I have not seen any skyscrapers!'
> 'Comrade,' replies Kalinin, 'instead of loitering on the streets you should read newspapers and find out what's going on in your city.'[42]

Contrast the image of crafty Stalin transforming a proverb into gallows humour to the many jokes about Brezhnev's simultaneous dependence on and incomprehension of texts:

> A knock on Brezhnev's office door. He pulls a piece of paper from his coat pocket and reads: 'come in!'

> Before a state visit to an Islamic nation, Brezhnev is coached in the traditional greeting – 'Salaam aleikum' – and response – 'Aleikum asalaam.' During his speech upon arrival, an anti-Soviet protestor in the crowd yells out 'Gulag archipelago!' to which Brezhnev dutifully replies 'Archipelago Gulag!'

The *anekdot's* critical engagement with state discourse often involved isolating and excising a discrete unit of that discourse (slogan, neologism, acronym, quotation) from its communicative frame (speech at a state ceremony, political banner, socialist realist film or novel, history book) and transplanting it in an incongruous context (Chapaev and Pet'ka in Africa; a Marxist slogan uttered in a brothel; the first line of the 'Internationale' in a telegram addressed to Lenin in the mausoleum). As Mikhail Krongauz points out, Soviet state utterances were particularly susceptible to this basic comic device – incongruity between discursive content and context – because they were maximally reliant on their communicative environments.[43] Thus, even a verbatim quotation of a political utterance amounted to critical reinterpretation of its meaning.

A good example of the popular perception of the political during Stagnation is the well-known *anekdot* about an encyclopedia of the future that contains the following entry: 'Brezhnev, L.I. – Minor political figure of the Pugacheva era,' which Tat'iana Cherednichenko tapped for the subtitle of her 1994 book, *A Typology of Soviet Mass Culture: Between 'Brezhnev' and 'Pugacheva.'* Those two figures, she argues, represent the 'public and private poles of the cultural continuum' during Stagnation.[44] As the joke indicates, the sphere of the 'minor political figure' could not compete for the public's attention with the popular culture realm ruled by icons like Pugacheva. In fact, says Cherednichenko, political texts and images were perceived and consumed by the populace the same way they consumed mass culture: as pure form with non-existent or irrelevant content. It was all, she writes, 'la-la-la.'[45] Another *anekdot* suggests that the Soviet subject's conflation of popular and political culture began in childhood:

> During a class trip to the park the teacher points at a hedgehog and says, 'look, children, this is who I've told you so many stories and sung so many songs about.' One of the kids picks up the hedgehog and says in a sweet voice, 'so *that's* what you look like, Vladimir Il'ich.'[46]

The nature of the *anekdot*'s rehearsal of other texts distinguishes it from traditional, uncritical performances by a 'folk' of its native cultural reservoir. An intertextual *anekdot* removes discourse from its original context in order to exploit it in a new signifying performance. In this respect the *anekdot* is an ironic form of ritual, which according to Richard Schechner is a performance constructed of pieces of other signifying acts (specific movements, gestures, and invocations) that the performer treats 'as a film editor treats strips of film' in order to create a new signifying act.[47] Susan Stewart defines in similar terms the performer of riddles, jokes, and puns, whom she calls a 'bricoleur' who transforms old knowledge in specific ways to produce 'new meanings.'[48] Unlike a shaman, whose ritualistic use of 'recovered behaviours'[49] as material for the new performance typically either affirms the original meaning of the material or uses it unreflectively, the *anekdot* performer's discourse is directed in a triangulated fashion towards the source text and its original referent in order to comment critically on one or both.

Sometimes, however, the *anekdot*'s mobilisation of a past text – especially traditional folklore and pre-revolutionary literature[50] – implies an appreciation of that text as a useful, discursively legitimate tool for socio-political criticism. *Anekdoty* frequently modify folkloric texts such as proverbs and tales, for example, in order to comment on a contemporary issue. This device has been used in the post-Soviet period, as well, for example in the recent proverb/*anekdot* 'if you're afraid of Putin don't go into the outhouse' [*Putina boiat'sia – v sortir ne khodit*], which combines the proverb 'if you're afraid of wolves don't go into the forest' [*volkov boiat'sia – v les ne khodit*] with the new president's public promise to 'waste' [*mochit*] Chechen terrorists 'in the outhouse' [*v sortire*].

A less obvious way in which the *anekdot* challenged official models of cultural discourse was by embodying them more convincingly than state cultural production did. The *anekdot*'s characteristic patterns of propagation and consumption represent a deep-tissue, parodic upstaging of state paradigms of cultural processes in Soviet society. In a scene near the end of Grigory Aleksandrov's 1938 musical *Volga-Volga*, for example, the peasant girl Strelka's 'Song of the Volga' becomes literally the song of the Volga when a storm blows the sheet music (apparently written on water-proof paper) off the ship and into the river. The next day the song is being sung or played by everyone Strelka meets downstream, in various individual arrangements that nevertheless retain the spirit of the original, thus exemplifying the universal appeal of true 'folk' creativity and the people's unanimous receptivity to it. That the *anekdot* accomplished the same, but in reality, indicates that it was not only parody; its very existence exposed state cultural models themselves as naïve self-parodies.

Despite its ostentatious, ludic exposé of signifying practices (including its own), the *anekdot* cannot historically be confined to the project of postmodernism, much of the cultural production of which is premised on language's essential failure to signify anything except other signifiers. As Bauman writes,

> [c]ultural performances may be primary modes of discourse in their own right, casting in sensuous images and performative action rather than in ordered sets of explicit, verbally articulated values or beliefs, people's understandings of ultimate realities and the implications of those realities for action.[51]

Soviet *anekdoty* did impugn the representational capacity of a particular language – the language of official culture – making the genre a sort of 'postmodernism in one country.' However, its symbolic undermining of the representational authority of official discourse was accompanied by a complementary project: composition of an alternative, more credible representation of popular experience. *Anekdoty* were performances of a discursive schism in Soviet culture: the incongruity between official versions of the society's collective life, on one hand, and the popular experience of that life, on the other. Whereas official discourse emphasised brotherhood, unanimity, and the infallible word of the Party, the *anekdot* trafficked in conflict, dialogue, and contradiction. If the official national self-image was marked by exaggerated egoism (which at times served as the justification for righteous sadism), urban folk consciousness found in the reflexive *anekdot* a medium for performative rebuttal, a potent instrument for ironic, symbolic masochism.[52]

17

HUMOUR AND SATIRE ON POST-SOVIET RUSSIAN TELEVISION

JOHN DUNN

IN the closing moments of a programme called *Tushite svet (Turn off the light)*, transmitted on 26 March 2001 and devoted to the first anniversary of Vladimir Putin's victory in the presidential elections, Lev Novozhenov (a well-known television presenter) turns to his co-presenters, Khriun Morzhov (a computer-generated pig) and Stepan Kapusta (an equally virtual hare) with the question: 'What, are there really no jokes about Putin?', to which he receives the following reply: 'In honour of today's anniversary one of the bakeries has come up with a new cake, called the "Putin".' Novozhenov naturally enquires about the recipe and is told: 'It's like a "Napoleon", only without the eggs.' The 'Napoleon' cake is a classic of Russian patisserie, and the joke here depends on a pun: the word for 'eggs' can also mean 'testicles', or 'balls'.

This episode illustrates two points about humour on post-Soviet Russian television: the first is that it can, at least to judge by the reaction of those to whom the joke has been re-told, be extremely funny; the second is that in the right place and at the right time it is (or was then) possible by the standards that have traditionally prevailed in Russia and the Soviet Union to be very rude indeed about the current leadership. As for the programme *Tushite svet*, this embodies several features which are characteristic of post-Soviet television: the humour is political and (mostly) satirical; it could never appear on British television, since no attempt is made at political balance; the programme has not always appeared on the same channel, having moved (without Novozhenov) from NTV to TV-6 after the takeover of the former channel by Gazprom (see below, note 2); the programme is within the wider context of television as a whole self-referential, since it is clearly a 'grown-up' version of the long-running children's programme *Spokoinoi nochi, malyshi*

(Goodnight, Children), with Khriun and Stepan depicted as 'adult' versions of the puppet characters who appeared regularly on that programme.

Tushite svet was first shown in the summer of 2000, and has already managed to acquire something of a cult status.[1] During the following eighteen months or so it was, in the view of the present writer, one of the best of the Russian television programmes then available to him, a formulation chosen not to make the praise appear more faint than it ought to be, but instead to draw attention to two limitations that will inevitably affect this survey of humour and satire on Russian television in the post-Soviet period.

The first limitation is simply that of personal taste: different people find different things funny, and while it is hoped that nothing central to the development of Russian television humour in the last ten years has been omitted from this survey, no claim is made for its being a definitive or all-inclusive account, and no apology is made for any reflection of the author's personal preferences. The second limitation is perhaps more regrettable: it seems highly improbable that even the most assiduous commentator would have seen everything broadcast on all the six main terrestrial channels available in Moscow since 1993,[2] but any observer based outside Russia suffers the further restriction of access to a more limited range of channels, in the present case to only one at any given time. This, however, is less of a handicap than it may at first sight appear: the above-mentioned propensity of programmes to migrate from channel to channel, a change of available channel from ORT to NTV in 1997 and the occasional practice adopted by the international versions of domestic channels (all that is currently available on the north-western fringe of Europe) of showing programmes bought in from elsewhere all mean that it has been possible to view much more material than might be expected. It is also appropriate that I should record here my gratitude to colleagues, especially Galina Kurokhtina, for recording programmes that otherwise would have remained outside my line of sight.

KVN

At the opposite end of the scale of longevity to *Tushite svet* is a programme which can be described as the flagship of Russian television comedy. The initials stand for *Klub veselykh i nakhodchivykh (The Club of the Merry and the Resourceful)*, though the programme is invariably known by the abbreviation. Indeed, so widely used are these initials that they make up the only abbreviation of this structure to be capable of being declined in standard modern Russian. The programme can perhaps best be described for British readers as being a cross between *The Cambridge Footlights* and *University Challenge*, it being student cabaret organised on a competitive basis. *KVN* first appeared in 1961, and, as one of the few live television programmes being shown at the time, it soon acquired great popularity.[3] Although by then the programme was being recorded and thus capable of 'losing' items that were deemed undesirable, S.G. Lapin, who became chairman of the State Committee for Radio and Television in 1970, disliked the whole enterprise, and *KVN* was closed down in 1971. Later, however, it proved to be one of the earliest beneficiaries of the more propitious climate of glasnost, being resurrected in 1986,[4] since when it has gone from strength to strength; it is not quite the longest running programme on Russian television, but out of the well-known programmes associated with the liberalisation which took place in the second half of the 1980s it is the only survivor.

KVN remains curiously impenetrable to the foreign viewer, and no attempt seems ever to have been made to reproduce the format outside the russophone world. Within that world, however, the programme has become a huge and sprawling enterprise, with a structure of leagues more complicated than that run under the auspices of the Russian Football Association; much of the material is written by professionals (usually former participants) and bought in specially; most of it is carefully rehearsed and vetted by the organisers (on grounds of taste).[5] Classic games from the past are repeated regularly on various channels: during the summer of 2001 NTV-International showed games from the Ukrainian league of 2000. As this last example suggests, *KVN* operates on the scale of the former Soviet Union;[6] it is, indeed, sobering to contemplate that as the former Republics of the Union grow ever further apart, it remains just about the last functioning Soviet enterprise. And, like many another Soviet enterprise, it has been successfully and, it would seem, lucratively privatised by its top management: the programme itself and its associated rights and properties are firmly in the hands of an independent production company, AMIK, controlled by the programme's long-serving presenter, Aleksandr Masliakov.

No less a commentator than the august Editor of this volume (in a private communication, June 2001) has suggested that *KVN* belongs firmly to the Odessa tradition of Russian humour, tracing its descent through Ilf and Petrov, and it is true that the so-called Odesskie dzhentl'meny (Gentlemen of Odessa), who were the first winners of the programme in its second incarnation, probably remain the best known team. An alternative way of looking at this problem, however, would be that the already capacious Odessa tradition simply expanded to take in this new form. In any event, according to Iuliia Taratuta's article (see note 5), if the programme was considered by some in the 1970s to be too 'Jewish', it is now widely perceived as being in the hands of a Caucasian 'mafia', largely because some of the most successful teams in recent years have come from Armenia and Azerbaidzhan; it is also the case that in Soviet times Armenia often saw itself as an alternative centre of humour (reflected in the 'Armenian radio' cycle of jokes). Unfortunately the Soviet Union was a great mangler of traditions, and this question may be incapable of resolution.

As might be expected, a number of participants in *KVN* have gone on to make careers in television; prominent among these are Leonid Iakubovich (presenter of the popular game show *Pole chudes [Field of Miracles])* and Iuly Gusman (presenter of the talk show *Tema [Topic]*);[7] Mikhail Lesin, Minister for the Press, Broadcasting and Mass Communications, is also a 'graduate' of the programme,[8] as in a pleasing piece of symmetry are the two producers of *Tushite svet.*[9] A group formed from the Odesskie dzhentl'meny put together a programme of that name which migrated from channel to channel during the 1990s. This compilation of sketches and *anekdoty* (i.e. jokes) was of variable quality, but the programme merits a mention on two grounds. Many of the sketches were not surprisingly set in Odessa, which makes this the only comedy programme on Russian television with a distinct regional basis, albeit one which is heavily stylised and semi-mythological. The programme is also noteworthy for a rare nod in the direction of political correctness: the heroes of what are normally known as Chukchi jokes are more generically and presumably less offensively described as *zhiteli krainego severa (inhabitants of the far north).*

THE REST OF THE SOVIET INHERITANCE

Though Soviet radio and television had a department of humour and satire, it existed for specific purposes and operated in specific conditions which ceased to have any relevance immediately upon the collapse of the August coup in 1991. In these circumstances it is perhaps more surprising that *KVN* survived at all than that it provides almost the only real element of continuity between the Soviet and the post-Soviet eras. Humorists and satirists of what in this context may be termed the older generation are not totally banished from television, but the appearances of the likes of Evgeny Petrosian, Gennady Khazanov and Mikhail Zhvanetsky tend to be presented as exercises in nostalgia: in the 1999–2001 NTV has shown a cycle of programmes by Gennady Khazanov consisting largely of reminiscences and entitled *Zhil-byl ia (Once upon a time there was me)* and a series called *Ves' Zhvanetskii (The Whole of Zhvanetsky).* The format of the latter consisted of Zhvanetsky reading his work to an audience in what looked like a University lecture theatre, this being interspersed with extracts from a filmed interview with the producer Leonid Parfenov. This does not make ideal television, but while it is true that the texts were not generally written for and are often not particularly suitable for that medium, it is interesting that no-one considered it worthwhile employing a couple of actors and an imaginative director to make the series somewhat more viewer-friendly. It is also significant that Zhvanetsky has now decided that he wishes to be known as a humorist, rather than as a satirist.[10]

OBA-NA

One day towards the end of 1990 Gorky Street in the centre of Moscow was closed off for a funeral procession. What made the event unusual was that the procession was made up of vans normally used for delivery of bread and meat, and that the obsequies were being performed not for some great dignitary, but for food itself.[11] Subsequently the funeral procession for food was shown on a programme called *Oba-na*, which formed part of a block of programmes put together by one of the Soviet Union's first independent production companies, Avtorskoe televidenie (ATV); this was the first of a number of scandalising events to be associated with *Oba-na* and its main instigator, Igor Ugolnikov. A potentially more serious incident followed a year later when Ugolnikov brought together a number of rock singers and cabaret artists to perform a rather unusual version of *Gimn Sovetskogo Soiuza* (i.e. the national anthem of the Soviet Union). The resultant video clip, enhanced by carefully chosen images, was prepared to mark the anniversary of the October Revolution and was shown in *Oba-na* as part of the ATV block of programmes on 25 November 1991.

The series of *Oba-na* which ran from the end of 1990 to the summer of 1992 forms a bridge between the late Soviet and the post-Soviet periods, at the same time introducing certain trends into Russian television. The first of these is linguistic: this was one of the first programmes to include non-standard language, such as words taken from criminal and youth slang.[12] The second is that of using television itself as a starting point for its humour. The travesty of the Soviet national anthem was preceded by a long parody of another ATV programme called *Budka glasnosti (The Glasnost booth)*, and the editions of 23 March 1992 and 27 April 1992 were devoted to parodies of current television advertisements and a whole range of television programmes respectively.

The main importance of *Oba-na*, however, lies in its role in breaking down taboos. These taboos were not only political and linguistic, but also included areas that were unacceptable under the previous dispensation on grounds of *poshlost'* (a compendious term of disapprobation sometimes translated as 'vulgarity'), such as scatological references and sexual innuendo. There is, it is true, an element of sleight-of-hand about this procedure. In the first place Ugolnikov and his colleagues were for the most part pushing at an open door: in the period immediately the collapse of the August *putsch* the mockery of even the most sacred of Soviet institutions (Ugolnikov's imitation of Lenin was first seen on 2 September 1991) went with, rather than against the grain of at least that part of popular sentiment which was reflected on state television, while the euphoria generated by the sudden release from the bounds of Soviet-style censorship, which on television continued right up to the end of the *putsch*, created a climate unsympathetic to complaints about even the more extreme forms of non-political humour.[13] In the second place it is unclear how many people watched these taboos being broken down. ATV's programmes were transmitted in a block late on a Monday evening, and the fact that ATV was widely known as a repository of experimental and unorthodox programming meant that it was easy for those who were likely to be offended by *Oba-na*'s brand of humour not to be watching in the first place. Nevertheless, once Lenin and the Soviet national anthem had been travestied, once the words *bliadina* (a taboo word for prostitute) and *fuck* had been uttered,[14] once a man had been shown sitting on a toilet and a woman shown sitting naked in the metro, once men had been shown dressed up as women, *Monty Python*-style, no one on television ever again had to do anything merely to demonstrate that it was possible to do it.

There is, however, one taboo which was not broken by *Oba-na* and that is the parodying of a living Russian or Soviet politican while still in office. The credit for this small, but significant step for *homo (post-)soveticus* appears to belong to Valery Komissarov (ironically himself now a politician), who found an actor capable of producing a perfect imitation of Mikhail Gorbachev's voice and then conducted him on a 'tour of inspection' of a Moscow eating establishment. The episode was shown as part of a short film called 'Iz Rossii na vse sluchai zhizni' ('From Russia for all life's eventualities'), broadcast on ATV's *Press-klub* on 2 December 1991, when Gorbachev was still President of the USSR.

STEB

Igor Ugolnikov's travesty of the Soviet national anthem marks the apotheosis of a linguistic and cultural phenomenon known as *steb* (from the verb stebat', meaning 'to whip'). This term, which apparently originated among Leningrad and Moscow underground intellectuals in the 1970s,[15] has been defined as follows: 'A type of intellectual mischief-making in which symbols are openly (i.e. in print) deflated by their demonstrative use in contexts of parody.'[16]

Steb is essentially an exercise in subverting linguistic and cultural hierarchies, and in order to achieve its full effect *steb* would seem to require the existence of a clearly defined hierarchy of values which is universally known and widely accepted, but which is not so universally accepted or so effectively imposed that it is beyond public mockery. It is thus a phenomenon which is likely to be particularly effective in periods of political and cultural transition, such as occurred in Russia after August 1991.

ATV was the natural home of *steb*, and in addition to *Oba-na* the phenomenon surfaced in other of their programmes, most notably some of the sketches on Dmitry Dibrov and Andrei Stoliarov's *Montazh* and a number of spoof items shown in *Press-klub*, such as the 'newsreel' 'SSSR, kotoryi my poteriali' ('The USSR which we have lost'), transmitted on 3 May 1993, and the 'party political broadcast' for Sub-tropicheskaia Rossiia (Sub-Tropical Russia), shown during the 1993 election campaign on 6 December.[17] Elements of *steb* can also be found in the ironical use of Soviet language and symbols in the 1995 election broadcasts of two parties, Partiia liubitelei piva (The Beer-lovers' Party) and Blok nezavisimykh (Block of Independents), as well as in some of the set designs for Aleksandr Liubimov's (mostly) serious debate programme *Odin na odin (One against One)*.[18]

As with many other cultural phenomena, the boundaries of *steb* are somewhat fluid, and it is not always entirely clear what should be included under this heading. Certainly, with a few exceptions, such as those noted above from the 1995 election campaign, the ironical use of Sovietisms and Soviet symbolism had become much less prominent after 1993, and after that date the survival of a widely accepted hierarchy of values becomes distinctly problematic. Nevertheless, for some the question of *steb* remained a live issue, as is demonstrated by this exchange from an interview with Sergei Blagovolin, the first Director-General of ORT:

> 'What do you think of the currently fashionable "steb" style?'
> 'I don't like *steb*, and I don't think we'll be having any of it on our channel.'[19]

If the *steb* tradition is to be discerned anywhere on present-day Russian television, it is perhaps in the work of Viktor Shenderovich, and especially his programme *Itogo (In Total)*, which was broadcast on NTV and later TV-6 between April 1997 and January 2002. Here, however, the values being subverted in the author's ironical comments on current events were those of the post-Soviet political world, including serious news analysis programmes, such as NTV's *Itogi (Summing up)*.[20]

KUKLY

The most important programme in the post-*steb* era of Russian television satire is undoubtedly *Kukly (Puppets)*. This is the brainchild of its French-based producer Vasily Grigoriev, and the programme, with its use of latex puppets to represent politicians and other prominent figures in public life, clearly belongs to the same tradition as the British *Spitting Image* (apparently the originator of the genre), the French *Les Guignols de l'info* (the most probable direct inspiration for the Russian version) and others. It is probably the only comedy programme on Russian television with a format borrowed from abroad,[21] but it does none the less have some specifically Russian features.

The first is that whereas in *Spitting Image* each edition consisted of a series of more or less disconnected sketches, each broadcast of *Kukly* (the running time is normally about eleven minutes) consists of a single episode which is usually adapted from what to a Russian audience would be a well-known work of literature, film or television programme. This structural device has an important consequence, since each of the puppet 'characters' each week plays a dual role: that of the politician he (only occasionally she)[22] is representing, but also that determined by the logic of the individual episode. Thus one week the characters may be drivers trying to bribe a policeman to allow their vehicles to pass the annual inspection ('Tekhosmotr-97' ['Technical Inspection'], 10 August 1997), while another week they might be Louis XIII, Cardinal Richelieu and assorted musketeers ('Stseny iz frantsuzskoi zhizni' ['Scenes from French Life'], 14 June 1997); on several occasions they have been either criminals of one sort or another or residents of a communal flat.[23] This rather complicated role-playing means that in each episode the speech and behaviour of each 'character' must not only reflect the characteristic features associated with the particular politician being represented, but must also be adapted to suit the requirements of the situation depicted. It is arguably this element of dual role-playing that provided in the earlier days of the programme its most subversive element, since Russian viewers were not used to seeing a recognisable depiction of their President speaking and behaving like a criminal.[24]

The second distinguishing feature is that each episode is written by an individual, rather than by a team of scriptwriters. In fact, the great majority of episodes since the programme began in 1995 have been written by Viktor Shenderovich (See p. 187), who has published two volumes of his scripts.[25] The third distinguishing feature, which is in part a consequence of the second, though it also reflects the peculiarities of the quasi-legal framework in which Russian television operates, is that the programme is under no requirement to maintain a political balance. This does not mean that all editions necessarily display an automatic bias, and politicians representing all possible tendencies have at one time or another been depicted in puppet form. Nevertheless, someone who watched *Kukly* over a long period of time would probably discern a particular ideology which can in general terms be described as liberal and pro-western. This not surprisingly matches, or matched the ideology of Shenderovich, as reflected in his programme *Itogo* and that of NTV itself, as reflected in its flagship news analysis programme *Itogi.*

The lack of balance was particularly striking in the two instances where the programme was used as part of a political campaign. In the presidential campaign of 1996 the main function of *Kukly* seems to have been not so much to support the re-election of Yeltsin, as to promote opposition to certain figures in Yeltsin's entourage, above all the head of the presidential security service, Aleksandr Korzhakov, with whom the then owner of NTV, Vladimir Gusinsky, had a long-standing quarrel.[26] In one bizarre episode, however, the puppets from *Kukly* played a direct part in Yeltsin's campaign, when they were recruited to play the 'contestants' in what purported an edition of *Pole chudes*, transmitted on 14 June 1996, the Friday preceding the first round of voting.[27] After the presidential elections in 2000 *Kukly* adopted a distinctly hostile attitude to President Putin, which reflected the increasingly acrimonious dispute between NTV and the presidential administration.

It is an interesting reflection on the state of free speech in post-Soviet Russia that notwithstanding the novelty of the format both to audiences and to officialdom and the distinctly unflattering depiction of most of Russia's leading politicians the programme appears to have been subject to rather less pressure from the authorities than might have been expected. It is true that in the programme's early days an attempt was made by the prosecutor's office to initiate criminal proceedings, but these were dropped at an early stage.[28] Another episode is altogether more curious: shortly after Putin's inauguration it was rumoured that a request had reached NTV from the Kremlin that the puppet depicting the new President should be removed from the programme. In the closing moments of the edition of *Itogi* broadcast on 21 May 2000 the presenter, Evgeny Kiselev, confirmed that this was indeed the case and that in his capacity of Director-General of the channel he would ask Shenderovich to ensure that the puppet 'Putin' was absent from the following week's episode. Sure enough, the puppet representation of Vladimir Putin did not figure in the episode transmitted on 28 May, entitled 'Usilenie vertikali' ('The Strengthening of the Vertical Axis'),[29] though since the action was based on the bringing down of the Ten Commandments from Mount Sinai, it is not difficult to work out the role played by the unnamable and invisible 'President'. Subsequently, however, some doubt has been cast on this incident: Vasily Grigoriev claimed in an interview that no request to remove 'Putin' was ever received and described the whole matter as a piece of flirting ('informatsionnyi flirt').[30]

After the take-over by Gazprom *Kukly* remained on NTV, but without the services of Shenderovich. Episodes broadcast since the take-over were markedly less pro-western that before, but were in other respects conspicuously lacking in sharpness. It may be that this is not just a consequence of a changed political atmosphere at the station following the removal of Gusinsky's influence, but also a reflection of the nature of politics and politicians in Putin's Russia: the format of the programme, ideally suited for caricaturing the colourful and often rather *louche* figures of the Yeltsin era, works less well with the somewhat monotone Putin entourage.[31]

AND THE REST . . .

All the programmes mentioned up to now have involved, either partly or wholly, humour which is political and which would be generally accepted as being satirical. Humour with no political overtones whatsoever seems to have played very little part in Soviet public (or even private) discourse,[32] and the development of a completely apolitical strand of humour on post-Soviet Russian television has been a slow and not particularly glorious process. It is revealing that perhaps the most successful in this area has been TV-6's *Raz v nedeliu (Once a week)* (later *O.S.P.- Studiia [O.S.P.- Studio]*), which consists of parodies of other television programmes,[33] though in 2000–2001 RTR's *Gorodok (Small Town)* has achieved a reasonably level of quality. For the the rest, it is difficult to dissent from Alla Bossart's description of two long-running programmes, the sketch show *Kalambur* (literally *Pun*, though there is no verbal humour) and the slapstick *Maski-shou*, as 'lezhalyi musor' ('rubbish that has lying around for too long'),[34] in which case the chief merit of the more short-lived predecessors of these programmes, including most of Igor Ugolnikov's work since 1992, is that they are no longer lying around.

One genre to which Russia has remained largely immune is the situation comedy, and apart from a somewhat frantic and surreal effort by Igor Ugolnikov, which ran for three episodes in 1995,[35] the only attempt noted is the hospital-based *Uskorennaia pomoshch' (Quicker than first aid)*;[36] to judge by the copyright caption this was first broadcast on ORT in 1999. There have, however, been one or two imported examples of the genre, notably the American (and ubiquitous) *Friends* and a French student sitcom called *Hélène et les garçons*.

It is in the area of apolitical comedy that foreign influences are most likely to be found. This is a difficult area, and the present writer cannot claim to have seen by any means all the relevant programmes, whether they are donors or recipients of influence; nevertheless, it would seem clear that NTV's *Zastava (Picket)* and elements of *Gorodok* are derived directly or indirectly from *Candid Camera*, while *Maski-shou* and others are probably at least partly influenced by *The Benny Hill Show*, a programme which to the total bewilderment of British observers is as popular in Russia as elsewhere in Europe. Given the near simultaniety of their first appearances, however, the uncanny resemblances between *Gorodok*, with its two male protagonists and its use of running jokes, to the BBC's *Chewin' the Fat* must be pure coincidence.

It would not be fitting to conclude this survey without mentioning Nikolai Fomenko, who was a member of the *Oba-na* team from 1991 to 1992 and who has gone on to devote himself single-mindedly to the cause of dumbing down Russian television. His style is best illustrated by a programme called *Imperiia strasti*

(Empire of Passion), which at one time was shown on NTV: this is a game-show, in which losing contestants face a forfeit of having to remove a pre-determined number of items of clothing, until one of them is stark naked. Fomenko seems to have an inexhaustible capacity to devise formats for light entertainment, though by no means all of his considerable output falls within the category of comedy even at its most capacious definition. His work is normally apolitical, though his attempt, with the help of a studio audience, to devise an instant national anthem for Russia falls within the *steb* tradition.[37]

CONCLUSION

In one sense there can be no conclusion to these observations, since what is being described here is a continuing process, and one where significant changes may occur (and indeed have occurred) even in the interval between writing and publication. Nevertheless, a few general points can be made.

The first, which comes close to being a truism, is that humour and satire on Russian television is something very distinctive and relatively free from foreign influences. For those who argue that Russia is always a special case, this may come as further confirmation of their views, but matters are not as simple as that: in many other respects, ranging from the wholesale importing of Latin American soap operas to the copying of American mannerisms in news presentation, Russian television has been remarkably open to foreign influences. The important factor is that of all the television genres comedy is the one that travels the least well, and, as the example of *The Benny Hill Show* demonstrates, those that do travel well can sometimes occasion surprise. Even in the anglophone world British comedy formats usually have to undergo significant changes to make them acceptable to American audiences, and while some anglophone comedy programmes (*Friends, Monty Python's Flying Circus, Fawlty Towers, Absolutely Fabulous*) have been shown in some West European countries, movement in the reverse direction is non-existent. In this respect therefore Russia is merely conforming to the international norm, just as it is conforming to the international norm in its extensive use of television itself as an inspiration for various forms of humour.

The most important of the distinctive features of Russian television humour is its political orientation and the major role played by satire. In the light of Russia's cultural history this is not surprising; it also helps to confirm the view expressed elsewhere by the present writer that on television politics plays the same role in post-Soviet Russia as football does in Western Europe.[38] It would seem that the first term of the Putin presidency has seen the beginnings of a certain depoliticisation of Russian television, which is perhaps due to several factors: the consistently high standing of the President in public opinion polls and the absence of any clear and consistent opposition to his administration; the perceived political background to the events concerning NTV and TV-6;[39] the enthusiasm which greeted Russia's first foray into 'reality television' in the autumn of 2001.[40] Certainly in August 2002 *Izvestiia* considered it worth asking whether political satire in Russian was dead,[41] though with Shenderovich and *Tushite svet* continuing to flourish, it still seems premature to assume that this form of humour is about to disappear from Russian television. At any event, given the way in which Russian television has during the 1990s embraced with enthusiasm most other non-serious genres, and, with the help of Nikolai Fomenko, has even invented a few of its own, the slow and hitherto relatively unsuccessful development of a stream of non-political humour is worthy of note.

The final point may come as a surprise to some, but since the days of *Oba-na* there has, provided one knows where, when and how to say or do it, been very little that cannot be said or done somewhere on Russian television. The proviso is important: the greater part of Russian television, as with other national television systems, reflects a fairly limited cultural spectrum, and the qualified wording is used because there are some untrodden paths (the travestying of senior clerics of the Russian Orthodox Church perhaps or direct expressions of support for the Chechen rebels) that really are closed off; it may, moreover, be the case that this state of affairs is due less to any positive act of policy than to the lack of a proper regulatory framework for television and a chronically divided body politic, and there are signs that the first attempts to remedy these shortcomings are proving a distinctly mixed blessing. None the less it is, given the history of Russia in this respect, a quite remarkable achievement and one which those of us writing in a country where the prime minister has recently been quoted a saying that there are limits to satire[42] may wish to contemplate with special awe.

NOTES

Chapter 1: Introduction

1. Howard Jacobson, *Seriously Funny: From the Ridiculous to the Sublime* (London: Viking, 1997), 97.
2. Ibid., 7.
3. D. S. Likhachev, A. M. Panchenko, '*Smekhovoi mir' drevnei Rusi* (Leningrad: Nauka, 1976).
4. Ibid., 97.
5. Jostein Børtnes, 'The Literature of Old Russia 988–1730', in *The Cambridge History of Russian Literature*, ed. Charles A. Moser, Revised Edition (Cambridge: Cambridge University Press, 1992), 36–7.
6. D. S. Mirsky, *A History of Russian Literature*, ed. Francis J. Whitfield (London: Routledge and Kegan Paul, 1968), 109.
7. Jacobson, *Seriously Funny*, 92.
8. Ranjit Bolt, 'Tsar Nikita and His Daughters', in *After Pushkin: Versions of the Poems of Alexander Sergeevich Pushkin by Contemporary Poets*, edited and introduced by Elaine Feinstein (London: The Folio Society, 1999), 32–8. For the Russian text see 'Tsar Nikita i sorok ego docherei', Aleksandr Pushkin, *Polnoe sobranie sochinenii*, vol. 2, part 1 (Moscow: Izdatel'stvo Akademiia nauk SSSR, 1947), 248–54.
9. Pushkin, *PSS*, vol. 2, part 2, 1113–14.
10. T. J. Binyon, *Pushkin: A Biography* (London: HarperCollins, 2002), 138–9.
11. Jacobson, *Seriously Funny*, 134.
12. Mikhail Bakhtin, *Rabelais and His World*, translated by Hélène Iswolsky (Cambridge, Mass.: The MIT Press, 1968), 45.
13. Elizabeth Bibesco, nee Asquith (1897–1945), was a daughter of the English statesman Herbert Henry Asquith by his second marriage. In 1919 she married Prince Antoine

Bibesco, who became a diplomat of the Romanian legation in Paris. He is known to posterity as a correspondent of Marcel Proust. Elizabeth Bibesco herself is known as an aphorist and the author of lively novels.

14. See Lesley Milne, 'Nationalism, anti-Semitism and Bulgakov', in *Bulgakov: The Novelist-Playwright* (Luxembourg: Harwood Academic Publishers, 1995), 62, 64.
15. Svetlana McMillin and Arnold McMillin, 'Any colour, so long as it is black: cruel and gallows humour in contemporary Russian jokes, anecdotes and folklore', *Rusistika* (2001), 23, Spring: 6–10.
16. Jacobson, *Seriously Funny*, 137.
17. See the chapter by J. A. Dunn in this volume, 'Humour and Satire on post-Soviet Television', footnote 6.
18. The description of Il'f and Petrov's novel's as 'foundation-laying','a basic grammar of Soviet humour' is that of Iurii Shcheglov in his introduction to I. Il'f, E.Petrov, *Dvenadtsat' stul'ev* (Moscow: Panorama, 1995), 22.

Chapter 2: Tragicomic principles in Pushkin's Drama 'The Covetous Knight'

1. N. N. Minskii, 'Skupoi rytsar'', in *Pushkin: biblioteka velikikh pisatelei*, ed. S. A. Vengerov (St. Petersburg, 1909), vol. 3, 104.
2. N. Skatov, *Pushkin: Russkii genii* (Moscow, 1999), 472.
3. D. P. Iakubovich, 'Skupoi rytsar'', in *Pushkin: Polnoe sobranie sochinenii. Dramaticheskie proizvedeniia* (Moscow and Leningrad, 1935), vol. 7, 521
4. G. A. Gukovskii, *Pushkin i problema realisticheskogo stilia* (Moscow, 1957), 320.
5. V. G. Belinskii, *Sobranie sochinenii v 9 tomakh* (Moscow, 1981), vol. 6, 476.
6. V. Ia. Propp, *Problema komizma i smekha* (Moscow, 1976), 109. This book by Propp, published posthumously, was never completed by the author. Undoubtedly, whilst working on it, the author would have introduced further corrections of some kind. But in the basic lines of his theory of the comic, outlined here, there would scarcely have been anything to correct. In our view, it merits serious attention, not excluding polemics on certain questions. In the current work I use this theory as support.
7. Ibid. Propp also talks about the baron's usury. I believe that this opinion is unfounded and is tribute to a popular delusion. For a refutation of it, see V. E. Vetlovskaia, 'Problemy Novogo vremeni v ponimanii Pushkina. Tema deneg v tragedii *Skupoi rytsar*'', in *Literatura i istoriia (Istoricheskii protsess v tvorcheskom soznanii russkikh pisatelei i myslitelei XVIII-XX vv)*, 2 (St Petersburg, 1997), 61–2.
8. V. Ia. Propp, *Problema komizma i smekha*, pp. 16–17 and passim. For Aristotle, 'the comic is [simply] part of the ugly or formless. In fact, the comic consists of certain mistakes and deformities, but ones which are painless and harmless.' Aristotel', *Poetika*, in *Sochineniia v 4 t.* (Moscow, 1983), vol. 4, 650.
9. Aristotel', *Poetika*, 660.
10. Propp, *Problema komizma i smekha*, 8.
11. As Gogol said in Chapter 7 of *Dead Souls*, Part 1:'and for a long time to come I am destined by miraculous powers to walk hand in hand with my strange heroes, to view the whole of this colossal life rushing past, to view it through laughter that is seen by the

world and through tears that are unseen and unknown to it.' N. V. Gogol, *Polnoe sobranie sochinenii* (Moscow and Leningrad, 1951), vol. 6, 134.

12. The subtitle, as well as the reference to 'Shenstone', did not appear straight away. See D. P. Iakubovich, 'Skupoi rytsar'', 506–7.
13. Propp, *Problema komizma i smekha*, 16.
14. Ibid., 145. See also: 'Laughter is given to us as a punishment by nature for some kind of hidden but suddenly revealed inferiority inherent in man.' Ibid., 29. And further: 'Something beautiful can never be funny, the comic is a deviation from this. Man has certain instincts of what is necessary, what he considers to be norms. The norms concern both the external appearance of man and the norms of moral and intellectual life.' Ibid., 43.
15. A. S. Pushkin, *Polnoe sobranie sochinenii* (Moscow: Nauka, 1948), vol. 7, 99–120 (p. 106, ll. 100–108). References to page and line numbers will henceforth appear in the text. Translations of the text are taken from Alexander Pushkin, *Mozart and Salieri: The Little Tragedies*, trans. Anthony Wood, revised edition (London: Angel; Chester Springs: Dufour, 1987), 19–34.
16. Propp points out that in order to evaluate puns and anecdotes, one also has to carry out some sort of intellectual operation. *Problema komizma i smekha*, 26.
17. Ibid., 91.
18. Ibid., 39.
19. F. Nietzsche, *Zlaia mudrost': aforizmy i izrecheniia* (Moscow, 1993), 109.
20. '... choosing what seems to be best and for the best': Aristotel', *Bol'shaia etika*, *Sochineniia*, 4, 315. And further, 'all knowledge and every conscious choice is directed towards one good or another': Aristotel', *Nikomakova etika*, *Sochineniia*, 4, 56–7.
21. Belinskii, op. cit., p. 478.
22. Ibid., 477.
23. Aristotel', *Bol'shaia etika*, 315.
24. According to Aristotle, error lies at the base of both comedy and tragedy. He states, 'the comic consists of certain mistakes and deformities, but ones which are painless and harmless.' Later, discussing tragic heroes, he emphasises that they must be 'men who are not distinguished by either virtue or righteousness, and who fall into misfortune not because of any depravity or baseness, but because of some sort of mistake, ... having until this point lived in great glory and happiness, like Oedipus, Thyestes and other such prominent men of that type', *Poetika*, 650, 658–9. M. L. Gasparov's commentary to Aristotle's *Poetics* states that 'a 'mistake' in Aristotle's terms is a false step, taken not out of base intentions but because of ignorance ...; thus, Oedipus killed his father and Thyestes ate the flesh of his children': Aristotel', *Poetika*, 782. However, Aristotle also defines 'mistakes' another way: 'a mistake always consists of an [erroneous] combination' (meaning combination of ideas). See Aristotle, 'O dushe', Ibid., v. 1, 436.
25. Propp writes, 'irony is very close to paradox ...' If with paradox ideas which are excluded from mutual understanding are united in spite of their incompatibility ['all wise men are fools, and only fools are wise' is Propp's example – V. V.], then with irony one meaning is spoken, but another, opposite meaning is implied, but not voiced directly.

In the words that are spoken a positive meaning is suggested, but they are to be understood in the opposite sense, negatively. Through these means irony allegorically exposes the faults of the subject. It represents a type of mockery, and as such it can be defined as comic. *Problema komizma i smekha*, 99–100.

26. V. E. Vetlovskaia, 'Problema Novogo vremeni v ponimanii Pushkina. . .', 83–9.
27. A. S. Pushkin, *Polnoe sobranie sochinenii* (Moscow and Leningrad, 1949), vol. 12, 232.
28. Propp, *Problema komizma i smekha*, 117.
29. Plautus, 'Amphitryo', in *The Rope and Other Plays*, trans. E. F. Watling (Harmondsworth: Penguin, 1964), 221–84 (p. 230).
30. See I. I. Vinkel'man, *Istoriia iskusstva drevnosti. Malye sochineniia* (St Petersburg, 2000), 96, 538 (commentary).

Chapter 3: Gogol as a Narrator of Anecdotes

1. M. N. Loginov, 'Vospominanie o Gogole', *Gogol' v vospominaniiakh sovremennikov* (Moscow, 1952), 71–2.
2. I. I. Panaev, 'Vospominanie o Belinskom', *Gogol' v vospominaniiakh sovremennikov*, 218.
3. A. O. Smirnova-Rosset, *Dnevnik: Vospominaniia* (Moscow, 1989), 72.
4. 'Pis'mo N. V. Gogolia k A. S. Danilevskomy ot 20 dek. 1832', *Perepiska Gogolia: v 2 tomakh* (Moscow, 1988), vol. I, 47.
5. V. A. Sollogub, *Povesti: Vospominaniia* (Leningrad, 1998), 551–2.
6. Khodzha Nasreddin (or Mullah Nasreddin) is the hero of folk tales among the peoples of Azerbaijan, Persia, Tadjikistan and the north Caucasus, and is popular also in Romania, Serbia, Greece and Armenia (*Bol'shaia sovetskaia entsiklopedia*, 2nd edition, vol. 46, 256).
7. *Dvadsat' chetyre Nasreddina*, compiled, with introduction, notes and index by M. S. Kharitonov (Moscow, 1986), 93.
8. Smirnova-Rosset, *Dnevnik: Vospominaniia*, 57.
9. Ibid., 454.
10. Ibid., 454.
11. Ibid., 57.
12. *Biblioteka dlia chteniia*, 1864, February, 7.
13. F. V. Chizhov, 'Memuary' , in A. Kulish, *Zapiski o zhizni N. V. Gogolia* (St Petersburg, 1856), vol. 1, 326.
14. L. I. Arnol'di, 'Moe znakomstvo s Gogolem', *Russkii vestnik*, 1862, vol. 37, 63.
15. M. Minskii, 'Ostroumie i logika kognitivnogo bessoznatel'nogo', *Novoe v zarubezhnoi lingvistike*, issue XXIII, Moscow, 1988, 282.
16. Sollogub, *Povesti: Vospominaniia*, 441–2.
17. 'Iz vospominanii baronessy M. P. Freriks', *Istoricheskii vestnik*, 1898, no. 1, 82.
18. Sollogub, *Povesti: Vospominaniia*, 436.
19. Sollogub, *Povesti: Vospominaniia*, 441–2.
20. Published in the book: E. Ia. Kurganov, *Anekdot kak zhanr* (Moscow, 1997), 112–13.
21. V. I. Shenrok, *Materialy dlia biografii Gogolia*, vol. IV (Moscow, 1897), 43.

22. Smirnova-Rosset, *Dnevnik: Vospominaniia*, 27–28. [Editor's note: Gogol, a prodigious traveller, had indeed once invented a trip to Spain. See Vladimir Nabokov, *Nikolai Gogol* (New York: New Directions Paperback, 1959), 131.]
23. V. I. Shenrok, *Materialy k biografii Gogolia* (Moscow, 1892), vol. I, 336–7.
24. Ibid., 336.
25. Smirnova-Rosset, *Dnevnik: Vospominaniia*, 43.
26. *Gogol' v vospominaniiakh sovremennikov* (Moscow, 1952), 77.
27. N. V Gogol', *Polnoe sobranie sochinenii*, 14 vols (Leningrad, 1952), vol. VII, 64.

Chapter 4: Antony Pogorelsky and A. K. Tolstoi: the Origins of Kozma Prutkov

1. Koz'ma Prutkov, *Polnoe sobranie sochinenii* (Biblioteka poeta: Bol'shaia seriia, 2oe izdanie. Moscow-Leningrad: Sovetskii pisatel', 1965), 121. For a selection of Prutkov's aphorisms in translation, see Laurence Senelick, 'Kozma Prutkov: *The Fruits of Meditation: Thoughts and Aphorisms (Selections)*', *Russian Literature Triquarterly* (1976), Winter, 14: 300–1.
2. 'Proekt: O vvedenii edinomysliia v Rossii', *Polnoe sobranie sochinenii*, 151–4. Translated by Senelick, 'Kozma Prutkov: *Project: Towards Creating Unanimity of Opinion in Russia*', *Russian Literature Triquarterly* (1976), Winter,14: 297–9.
3. Rosamund Bartlett, 'Koz'ma Petrovich Prutkov 1803–1863: Fictitious poet and prose writer', in Neil Cornwell, ed., *Reference Guide to Russian Literature* (London-Chicago: Fitzroy Dearborn Publishers, 1998), 673–4.
4. D. S. Mirsky, *A History of Russian Literature*, edited and abridged by Francis J. Whitfield (London: Routledge and Kegan Paul, 1968), 223.
5. O. A. Roninson, 'Istoki iazykovoi i literaturnoi pozitsii sozdatelei Koz'my Prutkova'. Avtoref. dis. na soisk. uch. st. kand. filolog. nauk. Tartu, 1988, 3. Roninson's dissertation is one of the few works devoted to the 'Arzamasskian' branch in the Prutkovian 'genealogy', but it deals only with the linguistic-stylistic aspect of the problem – and only with respect to Aleksei Zhemchuznikov.
6. For information on the Arzamas group see *The Cambridge History of Russian Literature*, ed. Charles A Moser, Revised edition (Cambridge, 1992), 129–31.
7. Cf: V. E. Vatsuro, *V preddverii pushkinskoi epokhi: 'Arzamas'*, 2 vols (Moscow, 1994), vol. 1, 5–10; M. I. Gillel'son, *Molodoi Pushkin i arzamasskoe bratstvo*, (Leningrad, 1974), 3–4, 142–3.
8. See: Iu. M. Lotman, *Poeziia 1790–1810-kh godov: Poety 1790–1810-kh godov* (Leningrad, 1971), 25–6; V. E. Vatsuro, *V preddverii pushkinskoi epokhi: 'Arzamas'* vol. 1, 7.
9. P. Viazemskii, *Staraia zapisnaia knizhka* (Leningrad, 1929), 118.
10. Letter from 25 May and about the middle of June 1825, *Perepiska A. S. Pushkina*, 2 vols (Moscow, 1983), vol. 1. 205. [Le chantre de la merde – the bard of muck.]
11. P. N. Berkov, 'Koz'ma Prutkov (Literaturnaia biografiia)', in Koz'ma Prutkov, *Polnoe sobranie sochinenii* (Moscow-Leningrad, 1933), 12.
12. See: Antonii Pogorel'skii, *Izbrannoe*, (Moscow, 1985), 366–7; 414–15.
13. The manuscript department of the Russian State Library. Fond Kiselevykh. Fond 129. No. 204, L. 63.

14. Antonii Pogorel'skii, *Izbrannoe*, 397.
15. *Ostaf'evskii arkhiv kniazei Viazemskikh*, vol. 1 (St. Petersburg, 1899), 136.
16. Antonii Pogorel'skii, *Izbrannoe*, 372–90, 416–20.
17. A. S. Pushkin. *Polnoe sobranie sochinenii*, vol. XIII (Moscow-Leningrad, 1937), p. 21; vol. IV, 282.
18. See: V. V. Vinogradov, *Stil' Pushkina*, (Moscow, 1941), 507.
19. Letter of 27 March 1825, in A. S. Pushkin, *Polnoe sobranie sochinenii*, vol. XIII, 157.
20. E. N. Penskaia, 'Genezis parodiinoi maski Koz'my Prutkova v russkoi literature XVIII-XIX vv.'. Avtoref. dis. na soisk. uch. st. kand. filolog. nauk. Moscow, 1989, 17.
21. *Ostaf'evskii arkhiv kniazei Viazemskikh*, vol. 3.(St. Petersburg., 1899), 220–1.
22. A. K. Tolstoi, *Sobranie sochinenii v 4-kh tomakh*, vol. 4 (Moscow, 1964), 423.
23. See, for example the letters from A. K. Tolstoi to S. A. Miller, 22 August 1851 and 6 January 1853, Ibid., 51, 60.
24. Ibid., 22 ff.
25. Letter of 27/15 June/July?/, no year indicated. Otdel rukopisei Rossiiskoi national'noi biblioteki. F. 539/ V. F. Odoevskogo/. op. 2. No. 1003. L. 21 i ob. This was not Sobolevskii's first visit to Rome and since there is no year on the letter it is difficult to state with absolute certainty that it had not been written the previous year. This, however, does not alter the crux of the matter.
26. A. K. Tolstoi, *Sobranie sochinenii v 4-kh tomakh*, vol. 4, 460.
27. A. A. Kondrat'ev, *Graf A. K. Tolstoi* (St Petersburg, 1912), 12. D. Zhukov, *Koz'ma Prutkov i ego druz'ia* (Moscow, 1983), 145.
28. Antonii Pogorel'skii, *Izbrannoe*, 402. Tolstoi had had the opportuity to become engrossed in antiquities in the library on the Pogorel'tsy estate. Much later, describing the library to N. M. Zhemchuznikov, he wrote: '... there are good and rare publications, for example, a large description of Egypt, compiled on the instructions of Napoleon ...' (A. K. Tolstoi, *Sobranie sochinenii v 4-kh tomakh*, vol. 4, 98).
29. Antonii Pogorel'skii, *Izbrannoe*, 14, 128–9.
30. 'Drevnii plasticheskii grek', 'Pis'mo iz Korinfa' in: Koz'ma Prutkov, *Polnoe sobranie sochinenii* (Moscow-Leningrad: Biblioteka poeta, Bol'shaia seriia, 1965), 72,70.
31. A. K. Tolstoi, *Sobranie sochinenii v 4-kh tomakh*, vol. 4. 46.
32. Koz'ma Prutkov, *Polnoe sobranie sochinenii*, 59.
33. Zhukov, *Koz'ma Prutkov i ego druz'ia*, 58–60.
34. A. K. Tolstoi, *Sobranie sochinenii*, vol. 1 (St Petersburg, 1914), 489. The poem is well known in several copies. In Tolstoi's lifetime it was banned by the censor, which considered it to be 'extremely cynical and indecent and extremely offensive to the Head of the Roman Catholic Church'. See also: A. K. Tolstoi, *Sobranie stikhotvorenii v 2-kh tomakh*, vol. 1 (Leningrad, 1984), 320–4, 581.
35. V. V. Vatsuro. 'Skazka o zolotom petushke' (opyt analiza siuzhetnoi semantiki), *in Pushkin. Issledovaniia i materialy*, vol. XV (St Petersburg, 1995), 132.
36. See *The Cambridge History of Russian Literature*, (Revised edition), 129–31.
37. See: I. M. Sukiasova, *Iazyk i stil' parodii Koz'my Prutkova* (Tbilisi, 1961).

Chapter 5: Comedy between the Poles of Humour and Tragedy, Beauty and Ugliness

1. P. M. Bitsilli, *Izbrannye trudy po filologii* (Moscow 1996), 504.
2. I. I. Lapshin, 'Komicheskoe v proizvedeniiakh Dostoevskogo', in *O Dostoevskom: sbornik statei*, ed. A. L. Bem (Prague, 1933), vol. 2, 34.
3. See N. M. Chirkov, *O stile Dostoevskogo* (Moscow, 1963), 144–53; R. G. Nazirov, 'Iumor Dostoevskogo.' In *Russkaia literatura 1870–1890 godov* (Sverdlovsk, no date), vol. 10, 47–8.
4. Chirkov, *O stile Dostoevskogo*, 146.
5. M. M. Bakhtin, *Problemy poetiki Dostoevskogo* (Moscow, 1963), 142. Translated as *Problems of Dostoevsky's Poetics*, ed. and trans. Caryl Emerson (Manchester: Manchester University Press, 1984).
6. For a fundamental survey of literature addressing problems of the comic in Dostoevsky's works, see A. E. Kunil'skii, *Smekh v mire Dostoevskogo* (Petrozavodsk, 1994), 5–22.
7. M. M. Bakhtin, 'Iz zametok o komicheskom.' In *Den' poezii 1986* (Moscow, 1986), 223.
8. Bakhtin: *Problemy poetiki Dostoevskogo*, 38; *Problems of Dostoevsky's Poetics*, 28.
9. See T. Kasatkina, 'Krik osla,' in *Roman Dostoevskogo 'Idiot': Razdum'ia, problemy*, Mezhvuzovskii sbornik nauchnikh trudov (Ivanovo, 1999), 146–8.
10. Olga Meerson noted the consistently manifested attempts by Dostoevsky to 'conceal' biblical reminiscences (O. Meerson, 'Bibleiskie interteksty u Dostoevskogo. Koshchunstvo ili bogoslovie liubvi?', in *Dostoevskii i mirovaia kul'tura*, 12. Moscow 1999, 40. A great deal of recent research has uncovered numerous biblical references not noted in earlier commentaries. There is potentially an even more significant number of such discoveries to be made, precisely because we have grown accustomed to these references being 'fused' and hidden within the artistic text.
11. M. M. Bakhtin. 'Rabelais i Gogol,' in M. M. Bakhtin, *Voprosy literatury i estetiki* (Moscow, 1975), 493.
12. Translation taken from *The Notebooks for 'The Idiot'*, ed. Edward Wasiolek, trans. Katherine Strelsky (Chicago and London: University of Chicago Press, 1967), 193–4.
13. M. Jones, 'K ponimaniiu obraza kniazia Myshkina,' in *Dostoevskii: materialy i issledovaniia*, vol. 2 (Leningrad: Nauka, 1976), 106–12. See also M. V. Jones, *Dostoevsky: the Novel of Discord* (London: Elek, 1976), 90–127.
14. See V. A. Kotel'nikov, 'Kenozis kak tvorcheskii motiv u Dostoevskogo.' In *Dostoevskii: materialy i issledovaniia*, vol. 13. (St Petersburg: Nauka, 1996), 194–200.

Chapter 6: The Young Lev Tolstoi and Laurence Sterne's *A Sentimental Journey*

1. Tolstoi, L. N., *Polnoe sobranie sochinenii*: In 90 vols. vol. 46 (Moscow-Leningrad, 1934), 269. References to this edition will subsequently be given in the text with the volume and pages indicated.
2. Stern, Lorens, *Sentimental'noe puteshestvie. Vospominaniia. Pis'ma. Dnevnik.* Perevod A. Frankovskogo (Moscow, 1940), 38. Laurence Sterne, *A Sentimental Journey*, edited with an introduction by Ian Jack (Oxford: Oxford University Press, 1984), 34.

3. *Sentimental'noe puteshestvie,* 24–25; *A Sentimental Journey,* 22. The chapter 'The Remise Door' containing this quoted text was another of those that Tolstoi chose to translate.
4. [Editor's note].The writings of Benjamin Franklin (1706–90) were well known in Russia and highly regarded. (Ernest J. Simmons, *Leo Tolstoy,* New York: Vintage Books, 1960), vol. 1, 78). Tolstoi had begun a special column in his diary, in which he would record his weaknesses 'in the manner of Benjamin Franklin' (Henri Troyat, *Tolstoy,* Harmondsworth: Penguin Books, 1970), 99.
5. *Sentimental' noe puteshestvie,* 38; *A Sentimental Journey,* 34.
6. See the edition: Sterne, L., *A Sentimental Journey through France and Italy* (Paris, 1851), 60.
7. Tsitseron, Mark Tulii, *Tuskulanskie besedy,* in Tsitseron, Mark Tulii, *Izbrannye sochineniia* (Moscow, 1975), 297–323.
8. See: G. L. Galagan, *Tolstoi. Khudozhestvenno-eticheskie iskaniia* (Leningrad, 1981).
9. See also: G. Galagan, 'Dnevnik molodogo L. Tolstogo i ego filosofsko-istoricheskaia kontseptsiia', *Mir filologii* (Moscow, 2000), 188–94.

Chapter 7: Fashioning Life

1. June Sochen, 'Introduction', *Women's Comic Visions,* ed. June Sochen (Detroit: Wayne State University Press, 1991), 9.
2. J. B. Priestley, *English Humor* (New York: Stein and Day, 1976), 126. Quoted by Regina Barreca, 'Introduction', *Last Laughs: Perspectives on Women and Comedy,* ed. Regina Barreca (New York: Gordon and Breach, 1988), 4.
3. See, for example, Nancy Walker, 'Toward Solidarity: Women's Humor and Group Identity', in Sochen, ed., *Women's Comic Visions,* 57–81. For a generous sample of Anglo-American women's humour, see the anthologies: Nancy Walker and Zita Dresner, ed., *Redressing the Balance: American Women's Literary Humor from Colonial Times to the 1980s* (Jackson, Miss.: University of Mississippi Press, 1988); Regina Barreca, ed., *The Penguin Book of Women's Humor* (New York: Penguin, 1996).
4. Paul McGhee, 'The Role of Laugher and Humor in Growing Up Female', in *Becoming Female: Perspectives in Development,* ed. Claire B. Kopp (New York: Plenum, 1979), 183–4.
5. See Sochen, 'Introduction', 12.
6. Walker, 'Toward Solidarity', 58.
7. Ibid., 59.
8. Walker notes that both the women's suffrage movement of the early twentieth century and the women's movement beginning in the 1960s facilitated the growth of women's humour (Ibid., 69).
9. See Richard Stites, *The Women's Liberation Movement in Russia: Feminism, Nihilism, and Bolshevism, 1860–1930* (Princeton, N. J.: Princeton University Press, 1978), 191–232.
10. N. A. Teffi, Letter to Waleria Grabowska, Jan. 16, 1946, Nadezhda Aleksandrovna Teffi Papers, Bakhmeteff Archive of Russian and East European History and Culture,

Columbia University. For more detailed biographical information, see Edythe Haber, 'Nadezhda Teffi', *Russian Literature Triquarterly*, no. 9 (Spring, 1974): 454–72; Elizabeth B. Neatrour, 'Tèffi', *Dictionary of Russian Women Writers*, ed. Marina Ledkovsky, Charlotte Rosenthal, and Mary Zirin (Westport, Conn.: Greenwood, 1994), 640–43; E. M. Trubilova, 'Teffi (1872–1952)', in *Literatura russkogo zarubezh'ia: 1920–1940*, ed. O. N. Mikhailov (Moscow: Nasledie, 1993), 241–63.

11. 'Zhenskii vopros: Fantasticheskaia shutka v 1-m deistvii', in N. A. Teffi, *Iumoristicheskie rasskazy* (Moscow: Khudozhestvennaia literatura, 1990), 375. Translation here and elsewhere is my own. This collection will hereafter be cited as *Iu. r.* (1990). 'Zhenskii vopros' was first staged in 1907 at the St. Petersburg Maly Theatre. It was published in Teffi, *Vosem' miniatiur* (St. Petersburg: M. G. Kornfel'd, Teatral'naia biblioteka 'Satirikona', 1913), 43–67; Teffi, *P'esy* (Paris: Vozrozhdenie, 1934), 75–91. For an English translation, see: 'The Woman Question: A Fantastical Farce in One Act', trans. Elizabeth Neatrour, in *An Anthology of Russian Women's Writing, 1777–1992*, ed. Catriona Kelly (Oxford: Oxford University Press 1994), 174–92.
12. 'Zhenskii vopros', *Iu. r.* (1990), 388.
13. N. A. Teffi, 'Muzhskoi s''ezd', Censor's copy. Censorship stamp, Apr. 21, 1909. Rukopisnyi otdel, Sankt-Peterburgskaia Teatral'naia biblioteka. For information on the Women's Congress, see Stites, *The Women's Liberation Movement*, 215.
14. Rachel M. Brownstein, 'Jane Austen: Irony and Authority', in Barreca, ed., *Last Laughs*, 58–9.
15. 'Veselaia vecherinka', *Iu. r.* (1990), 50. Originally published in the newspaper *Birzhevye vedomosti, Utrennii vypusk*, no. 183 (11 [24] Apr. 1904), 2–3. The story was included in Teffi's first prose collection, *Iumoristicheskie rasskazy. Kniga pervaia* (St. Petersburg: Shipovnik, 1910). Hereafter cited as *Iu. r. Bk. 1.*
16. 'Kurort', *Iu. r.* (1990), 36. Originally published in *Iu. r. Bk. 1.*
17. 'Duraki', in N. A. Teffi, *Sobranie sochinenii*, ed. D. D. Nikolaev and E. M. Trubilova (Moscow: Lakom, 1997-) vol. 1, 306. Hereafter cited as *Sob. soch.* followed by the volume number. The story originally appeared in *I stalo tak ...: Iumoristicheskie rasskazy* (St. Petersburg: M. G. Kornfel'd, 1912). Hereafter cited as *I stalo tak.*
18. 'Duraki', *Sob. soch.*. 1, 309.
19. 'Prichiny i sledstviia', *Iu. r.* (1990), 285–86. Originally published in *Iumoristicheskie rasskazy, Kniga vtoraia: Chelovekoobraznye* (St. Petersburg: Shipovnik, 1911). Hereafter cited as *Iu .r. Bk. 2.*
20. In 1905 Teffi, together with various members of the literary avant-garde, contributed to the first legal Bolshevik journal *Novaia Zhizn'*. (See Teffi's reminiscences of this collaboration: '45 let', *Vozrozhdenie*, no. 49 [Jan., 1956], 92–102; 'On i oni', *Vozrozhdenie*, no. 50 [Feb. 1956], 82–8.) Among the other journals in which her political satire, in prose and verse, appeared between 1905 and 1908 are *Krasnyi smekh, Seryi volk, Zarnitsy, Zritel', Signal, Rus'*. Teffi also wrote some political satire during the revolutionary years of 1917 and 1918. See, for example 'Nemnozhko o Lenine', *Russkoe slovo*, no. 141 (23 June, 1918), 1; 'Dobryi krasnoogvardeets', *Novyi Satirikon*, 1918, no. 3, p. 12.

    In general the assertion that women did not write satire on large political and social issues may require modification in the Russian context, perhaps in part because of the active role women played in revolutionary activities of the nineteenth and early twentieth centuries. There is the case, for example, of Anna Pavlovna Barykova (1839–93), an active supporter of revolutionary groups who, in such poems as 'Tale of How the Tsar Akhreian Went to God to Complain' (1883) expresses solidarity with the oppressed. (See Jane Costlow, 'Barykova, Anna Pavlovna', in *Dictionary of Russian Women Writers*, 60–61; Rymvidas Švilbajoris, 'Anna Barykova', in *Russian Women Writers*, ed. Christine D. Tomei, vol. 1 [New York: Garland, 1999], 199–205.) An older contemporary of Teffi who also wrote political satire during the 1905 revolution is Ol'ga Chiumina (1862–1909). (See A. M. Grachëva, 'Chiumina, Ol'ga Nikolaevna', in *Dictionary of Russian Women Writers*, 131–2.) I am grateful to Charlotte Rosenthal for calling my attention to these writers.

21. 'Broshechka', *Iu. r.* (1990), 186. Originally published in *Iu. r. Bk. 2*. Teffi also adapted the story for the stage. See 'Broshechka', *8 miniatiur*, 103–16; *P'esy*, 39–49.
22. Yurii Lotman, *Kul'tura i vzryv* (Moscow: Gnozis/Progress, 1992), 126. Quoted by Helena Goscilo, 'Keeping A-Breast of the Waist-land: Women's Fashion in Early-Nineteenth-Century Russia', in *Russia. Women. Culture*, ed. Helena Goscilo and Beth Holmgren (Bloomington: Indiana University Press, 1996), 32.
23. See Beth Holmgren, 'Gendering the Icon: Marketing Women Writers in Fin-de-siècle Russia', *Russia. Women. Culture*, 321–46.
24. 'V magazinakh', *Sob. soch.* 1, 356. Originally published in *I stalo tak*.
25. 'Fabrika krasoty', *Sob. soch.* 1, 269, 271. Originally published in *I stalo tak*.
26. 'Bez stilia', *Sob. soch.*. 5, 101. Originally published in *Karusel'* (St. Petersburg: Novyi Satirikon, 1914).
27. 'Vesel'e', *Nichego podobnogo* (Petrograd: Novyi Satirikon, 1915), 125–6.
28. 'Zhizn' i vorotnik', *Iu. r.* (1990), 127. Originally published in *Iu. r. Bk. 1*
29. Ibid., 129.
30. Ash (A. E. Shaikevich), 'Peterburgskie katakomby', *Teatr* (Berlin), no. 14 (1922), 4. Quoted in B. M. Prilezhaeva-Barskaia, 'Brodiachaia sobaka', ed. R. D. Timenchik, *Minuvshee: Istoricheskii al'manakh*, no. 23 (St. Petersburg: Atheneum-Feniks, 1998), 411, n. 34.
31. 'Zinaida Gippius', *Vozrozhdenie*, no. 435 (July, 1955), 94.
32. 'Demonicheskaia zhenshchina', *Sob. soch.* 5, 218. Originally published in *Dym bez ognia* (St. Petersburg: Novyi Satirikon, 1914).
33. Ibid., 220.
34. 'Rubin Printsessy', *Literaturnoe i populiarno-nauchnoe prilozhenie 'Nivy'*, Feb., 1905, 331–50; 'Utkonos', *Niva*, Dec. 17, 1905, 961–66. 'Rubin Printsessy' is reprinted in *Sob. soch.* 2, 20–37.
35. 'Zelenyi prazdnik', *Sob. soch.* 2,138. Originally published in *Nezhivoi zver'* (Petrograd: Novyi Satirikon, 1916).
36. Ibid., 140.
37. 'Rozovyi student', *Nichego podobnogo*, 103. Further references to this edition will be included in the text.

38. M. M. Zoshchenko, 'N. Teffi', ed. V. V. Zoshchenko, *Ezhegodnik Rukopisnogo otdela Pushkinskogo doma na 1972 god* (Leningrad: Nauka, 1974), 140.
39. Barreca, 'Introduction', 8.
40. Virginia Woolf, *A Room of One's Own* (1929; New York: Harcourt Brace Jovanovich, 1940), 170, 181.

Chapter 8: Two Facets of Comedic Space in Russian Literature of the Modern Period

1. Hans Günther, 'Iurodstvo i "um" kak protivopolozhnye tochki zreniia u Andreia Platonova', *Sprache und Erzählhaltung bei Andrej Platonov*, eds. Robert Hodel and Jan Peter Locher, Slavica Helvetica, Bd. 58 (Bern: Peter Lang, 1998), 117–31.
2. Lesley Milne, 'Tvorchestvo M. A. Bulgakova v evropeiskikh traditsiiakh shutovstva', *Diskurs* (1998), 7: 55–9.
3. M. M. Bakhtin, *Tvorchestvo Fransua Rable i narodnaia ku'ltura srednevekov'ia i Renessansa* (Moscow: 1965). A Ia. Gurevich, *Problemy srednevekovoi narodnoi kul'tury* (Moscow, 1981). D. -R. Moser, *Fastnacht – Fasching – Karneval: Das Fest der 'Verkehrten Welt'* (Graz–Wein–Köln, 1986).
4. D. S. Likhachev, A. M. Panchenko, *'Smekhovoi mir' drevnei Rusi* (Leningrad,1976), 114–16.
5. Likhachev and Panchenko, 101.
6. Ioann Kovalevskii, *Iurodstvo o Khriste i Khrista radi iurodivye* (Moscow, 1900).
7. B. A. Uspenskii, *Izbrannye trudy*, vol. 1, *Semiotika istorii. Semiotika kul'tury* (Moscow, 1994), 327.
8. M. M. Bakhtin, *Problemy poetiki Dostoevskogo* (Moscow, 1963), 170.
9. Ibid.
10. Lesley Milne (op. cit.) draws a distinction between the 'dirty' and 'pure' buffoon. She also cites the classic study by Enid Welsford, *The Fool. His Social and Literary History* (London: Faber and Faber, 1935), which notes the kinship between the European tradition of the jester and the Christian paradox. Milne makes the point that Welsford's study shares common features with Bakhtin's research of the same period.
11. This Russian cultural aspect is why Mikhail Bulgakov took as such an insult Viktor Shklovskii's comparison of him to a 'clown-buffoon' in *Gamburgskii schet.* Milne (op. cit.) offers an interesting commentary on this fact.
12. Likhachev and Panchenko, 120.
13. Filofei, *Zhitie i deianiia Savvy Novogo* (Moscow, 1915), 167.
14. Bakhtin, *Problemy poetiki Dostoevskogo,* 167.
15. The 'game' that many Soviet writers played in their relations to Stalin does indeed seem to belong to the category of buffoonish behaviour. In her article Milne cites Mikhail Bulgakov as an example. However, such buffoonery could not preserve the writer's personal sense of dignity, precisely because the buffoon is so tightly linked to the dominant cultural system and therefore is dependent on it, unlike the holy fool.
16. See I. A. Esaluov, *Kategoriia sobornosti v russkoi literature* (Petrozavodsk, 1995).
17. Likhachev and Panchenko, 93–94.

18. L. Silard [Szilard], 'Ot *Besov* k *Peterburgu*: mezhdu poliusami iurodstva i shutovstva (nabrosok temy)', *Studies in Twentieth-century Russian Prose* (Stockholm, 1982), 82–4.
19. V. Shklovskii, *Zhili-byli* (Moscow, 1966), 256.
20. Ibid.
21. See *Pamiatniki literatury Drevnei Rusi: XII vek* (Moscow, 1980), 166–82.
22. M. M. Bulgakov, *Master i Margarita, Sobranie sochinenii v 5 tomakh*, vol. 5 (Moscow: 1990), 350. Quoted in the translation by Richard Pevear and Larissa Volkhovsky, *The Master and Margarita* (London: Penguin Books, 1997), 361.
23. *Master i Margarita*, 372; *The Master and Margarita*, translated by Mikhail Glenny (London; Fontana Books, 1969), 403. [The Glenny translation is cited because it carries the argument here better than does the Pevear and Volkhonskii version. L. M.]
24. See Paleia Tolkovaia, *Filosofskie i bogoslovskie idei v pamiatnikakh drevnerusskoi mysli* (Moscow: 2000), 150, 153.
25. *Master i Margarita*, 349–50; *The Master and Margarita* (Pevear and Volkonskii), 360.
26. *Master i Margarita*, 372; *The Master and Margarita* (Pevear and Volkonskii), 384.
27. *Master i Margarita*, 368; *The Master and Margarita* (Pevear and Volkonskii), 379–80.
28. Szilard, 92.
29. Szilard, 95.
30. Szilard, 100.
31. Editor's footnote: The quotation in English is from Psalm 93, verse 1. In the Russian Orthodox *Psaltyr'* the quotation is from Psalm 92, verse 1 and Psalm 95, verse 10.
32. A. F. Losev, *Filosofiia. Mifologiia. Kul'tura* (Moscow, 1991), 31.
33. Losev, 69.
34. Losev, 80.
35. Losev, 130.
36. Ibid.
37. Ibid.
38. Maksimilian Voloshin, *Demony glukhonemye* (Kharkov, 1919). Henceforward page references to this edition will given in brackets in the text.
39. See I. A. Esaulov, 'Paskhal'nyi arkhetip v poetike Dostoevskogo' in *Evangel'skii tekst v russkoi literature XVIII–XX vv.: Tsitata, reministsentsiia, motiv, siuzhet, zhanr*, vyp. 2 (Petrozavodsk, 1998). I. A. Esaulov, 'Paskhal'nyi arkhetip russkoi literatury i struktura romana *Doktor Zhivago*' in *Evangel'skii tekst v russkoi literature XVIII–XX vv.: Tsitata, reministsentsiia, motiv, siuzhet, zhanr*, vyp. 3 (Petrozavodsk, 2001).
40. On the question of binary opposites in Russian culture see Iu.M. Lotman, *Kul'tura i vzryv* (Moscow, 1992).

Chapter 9: Jokers, Rogues and Innocents

1. M. Bakhtin, 'Forms of time and chronotope in the novel', in *The Dialogic Imagination: Four Essays by M. M. Bakhtin*, ed. Mikhail Holquist, trans. Caryl Emerson and Michael Holquist (Austin: University of Texas Press, 1981), 165. Russian quoted from M. Bakhtin, *Voprosy literatury i estetiki* (Moscow, 1975), 314.

2. Peter Trudgill, *Sociolinguistics. An Introduction to Language and Society* (Harmondsworth: Penguin Books, Revised Edition 1995), 13–15.
3. Lesley Milne, *Mikhail Bulgakov. A Critical Biography* (Cambridge: Cambridge University Press, 1990), 184.
4. See Milne, *Mikhail Bulgakov*, 183–8, 268–74, and J. A. E. Curtis, *Manscripts Don't Burn. Mikhail Bulgakov: A Life in Letters and Diaries* (London; Bloomsbury, 1991), 103–14.
5. Anna Akhmatova, *Sochineniia* (2 vols, Munich and New York; Inter-Language Literary Associates, 1965–68), vol. 2, 141–2. A translation of the first verse is given in J. A. E. Curtis, *Bulgakov's Last Decade* (Cambridge: Cambridge University Press, 1987), 208.
6. In their account of their American travels, *Odnoetazhnaia Amerika* (published in English translation under the title *Little Golden America*, but perhaps best rendered as *Bungalow America*), insecurity of employment and the high cost of health care are singled out as negative aspects of American capitalism.
7. Il'ia Il'f, Evgenii Petrov, *Sobranie sochinenii*, 5 vols. (Moscow: Gosudarstvennoe izdatel'stvo khudozhestvennoi literatury, 1961): 'My Robinzony', II, 414–18; 'Pravedniki i mucheniki', II, 475–7.
8. Konstantin Mochulsky, *Dostoevsky. His Life and Work*, translated by Michael A. Minihan (Princeton: Princeton University Press, 1967), 312.
9. 'Rabochii kostium', in Mikhail Zoshchenko, *Sobranie sochinenii v 3 tomakh* (Leningrad: Khudozhestvennaia literatura, 1986–87), vol. 1, 302–3.
10. 'Meshchanskii uklon', ibid., 360–2.
11. Vladislav Khodasevich, 'Uvazhaemye grazhdane', in Iu.V. Tomashevskii, *Litso i maska Mikhaila Zoshchenko* (Moscow: Olimp.PPP, 1994), 148.
12. This is described by Zoshchenko himself in *Pered voskhodom solntsa* (*Before Sunrise*), in Chapter 2, entitled 'I Am Unhappy and I Don't Know Why'.
13. N. Adasheva, 'Prinial na sebia', in *Vspominaia Mikhaila Zoshchenko*, ed. Iu. V. Tomashevskii, (Leningrad: Khudozhestvennaia literatura, 1990), 383–7. Nadezhda Mandel'shtam, *Vospominaniia* (New York: Izdatel'stvo imeni Chekhova, 1970), 93, 337.
14. L. Miklashevskaia, 'On skazal, chto druzei v bede ne ostavliaiut', *Zvezda* (1994), 8:43–52.
15. Linda Scatton, *Mikhail Zoshchenko. Evolution of a Writer* (Cambridge: Cambridge University Press, 1993), 38–42.
16. Scatton, *Mikhail Zoshchenko*, 42–52.
17. Vladimir Voinovich, *Zhizn' i prikliucheniia soldata Ivana Chonkina* (Paris: YMCA Press, 1975).
18. Vladimir Voinovich, *Pretendent na prestol* (Paris: YMCA Press, 1979).
19. Author's introduction to *Sandro iz Chegema*, vol. 1 (Moscow: Moskovskii rabochii, 1989), 3.
20. 'Piry Valtasara' (Belshazzar's Feast), *Sandro iz Chegema*, vol. 1, 225 and 235–6.
21. 'Piry Valtasara', 261.
22. Fazil' Iskander, *Sandro iz Chegema* (Ann Arbor: Ardis, 1979).

23. These periods were recalled by Iskander in an interview with me in October 1994. He experienced particular difficulty after his participation in the almanac *Metropol'* (1979), which issued a challenge to the Soviet system of censorship.
24. Viktor Pelevin, *Generation II* (Moscow: Vagrius, 1999). The novel has been translated into English by Andrew Bromfield under the title *Babylon.* (London: Faber and Faber, 2000).
25. It was noted by Sally Dalton-Brown in her article 'Ludic nonchalance or Ludicrous despair? Viktor Pelevin and Russian postmodernist prose', *Slavonic and East European Review,* 75 (1997), 2: 216–33, especially pp. 227–8.
26. The 'film star' popularity was mentioned in an interview with Pelevin: *The Observer,* Review Section (Books), 30 April 2000, p. 13. The July 1999 Russian edition of *Playboy* greeted *Generation II* as a watershed work that had changed perceptions of the surrounding reality (p. 89).
27. This is a personal observation of the reactions to the novel of distinguished Russian literary scholars attending a conference in Nottingham University in July 2000.
28. Viktor Pelevin, The Books Interview, *The Observer,* Review Section, 30 April 2000, p. 13.

Chapter 10: Escaping the Past?

1. Boris Fillipov and Vadim Medish, eds, *Iumor i satira poslerevoliutsionnoi Rossii,* 2 vols (London, 1983).
2. M. Keith Booker and Dubravka Juraga, *Bakhtin, Stalin, and Modern Russian Fiction.* (Westport, CT, 1995).
3. Marc Slonim, *Soviet Russian Literature: Writers and Problems* (New York, 1964), 92.
4. Richard Chapple, *Soviet Satire of the Twenties* (Gainesville, 1980), 7.
5. For more details on Zoshchenko's reception, see Gregory Carleton, *The Politics of Reception: Cultural Constructions of Mikhail Zoshchenko* (Evanston, 1998).
6. I. Ilinskii, 'Bytovye perezhitki pered litsom sovetskogo suda,' *Krasnaia nov'* 7(1926): 189–203.
7. Lev Trotskii, 'Rol' pechati v kul'turnom stroitel'stve,' *Sochineniia,* vol. 21 (Moscow, 1927), 199.
8. *Zapiski Terentiia Zabytogo* was originally published in *Dve povesti* (Krug, 1923); references are to its reprint in *Opal'nye povesti,* ed. Vera Aleksandrova, (New York, 1955).
9. Valeriia Gerasimova, 'Nenastoiashchie,' *Molodaia gvardiia* (1923) 6: 3–21.
10. See, for example, the internal dispute regarding Malashkin's *Moon on the Right* in TsKhDMO, fond 1, op. 23, delo 588 and delo 736.
11. 'Iz dokladnoi zapiski P. I. Lebedeva-Polianskogo "O deiatel'nosti Glavlita" Orgbiuro TsK VKP(b),' *Schast'e literatury: gosudarstvo i pisateli, 1925–1938. Dokumenty,* ed. D. L. Babichenko (Moscow, 1997), 29–40.
12. 'O pisateliakh iz molodezhi,' *Komsomol'skaia Pravda* 19 June, 1926, p. 3.
13. See also, for example, Cathy Popkin, *The Pragmatics of Insignificance: Chekhov, Zoshchenko and Gogol* (Stanford, 1993); Rachel May, 'Superego as Literary Subtext:

Story and Structure in Mikhail Zoshchenko's *Before Sunrise,*' *Slavic Review* 55.1 (1996): 106–24; and Berngard Ruben, *Alibi Mikhaila Zoshchenko* (Moscow, 2001). In post-Soviet Russia, particularly in the first half of the 1990s, the image of Zoshchenko as an anti-Soviet writer was effectively canonised in introductions to republications of his work and a number of articles focusing on the tragic final years of his life and the relevance of his stories in helping understand current conditions in Russia. Exceptions to this trend would be Linda Scatton, *Mikhail Zoshchenko: Evolution of a Writer* (Cambridge, 1993); Boris Paramonov, *Sniskhozhdenie Orfeia: Russkie pisateli i kommunizm* (Tallinn, 1997); and Aleksandr Zholkovskii, *Mikhail Zoshchenko: Poetika nedoveriia* (Moscow, 1999).

Chapter 11: Evgeny Zamiatin

1. E. Zamiatin, 'Anatol' Frans. (Nekrolog)' in Evgenii Zamiatin, *Sochineniia* (Moscow, 1988), 393. Henceforward references to this edition will be given as page numbers in the text. References to the novel will be given according to the diary entry.
2. A. Blok, *Sobranie sochinenii,* 8 vols (Moscow-Leningrad, 1960–1963), vol. 5, 345.
3. Ibid., 346.
4. Ibid., 349. Georgii Chulkov, remembering the mood of the times in the book *Gody stranstvii* (The Years of Wandering), cites this article by Blok, which had become impressed upon the minds of his contemporaries (alongside the words of Heine). In the same spirit Chulkov writes about irony as the illness of the century, 'the illness of late romanticism', an illness gripping all – destructive and 'terrifying': 'This terrifying irony, which is always present in romantic poetry, was cultivated by us all in the Petersburg-decadent era. This irony seemed necessary, like salt and food. Without it, it was impossible to write poetry, to give a paper, to converse with friends at dinner. Even falling in love without irony seemed to many vulgar and indecent. It was . . . the epoch of endless puns and mystic nonsense' (G. Chulkov. *Gody stranstvii,* Moscow , 1999, pp. 174, 156–7).
5. Blok, *Sobranie sochinenii,* vol. 5, 348.
6. Ibid., 349.
7. *Literaturnaia ucheba* (1988), 5: 133.
8. M. Iu. Liubimov, 'Tvorcheskoe nasledie E. I. Zamiatin v istorii kul'tury XX veka', Avtoreferat na soiskanie uchenoi stepeni doktora kul'turologii (St Petersburg, 2000), p. 26.
9. E. Zamiatin, *Ia boius'* (Moscow, 1999), 26.
10. *Literaturnaia ucheba* (1989), 5: 119.
11. 'At the moment, I don't know what's there. I've learned too much. Knowledge, which is absolutely certain that it's infallible – is faith. I had firm faith in myself, I believed I knew everything about myself. And then . . .' (Entry 11).
12. Freedom and happiness, in accordance with the new religion, are concepts that are incompatible with one another. Happiness is what is inculcated by force; the numbers are linked by 'beneficial tenets of happiness', 'hand and foot'. Freedom leads to crime,

the two are tied by indissoluble bonds. Freedom is the great delusion, which ruined the lives of the former savages and ancients. In freedom there is something which goes against human nature: 'the instinct of oppression from the earliest times was organically inherent to man'. R-13 ironically summarises the main commandment of the Table of Hours (pure sophism): 'Either happiness without freedom, or freedom without happiness, nothing else' (Entry 11). Naturally, it is difficult for the wild extraterrestrials to understand and accept the 'mathematically faultless happiness' straightaway, the 'wise, eternal happiness of the multiplication table'; therefore 'our duty is to force them to be happy' (Entry 1). And every number is obliged uncomplainingly to carry 'the heavy burden of unavoidable happiness' (Entry 15). One day D-503 made a slip in speaking and the slip draws attention to the dramatic character of the antimony 'freedom and happiness': 'and I'm free once again, or rather, I was once more confined within the orderly, endless Assyrian ranks' (Entry 22).

13. Zamiatin considered irony to be a European weapon which only with difficulty establishes itself in Russia: 'It was with some justification that history credited Russia with inventing and patenting the *knout* [a kind of scourge or whip – *LMM*], but only on the *knout* made from belts: irony and satire in Russian literature were introduced from the West. And although there's no soil more productive than our black earth for satire – up to now only three or four full-weight ears have ripened...' (325).

Chapter 12: Godless at the Machine Tool

1. V. I. Lenin, 'The Attitude of the Worker's Party to Religion', in V. I. Lenin, *Collected Works*, vol. 15 (Moscow: Foreign Languages Publishing House, 1963), 407.
2. Lenin, p. 402. Lenin conceived of religion as an instrument of the bourgeoisie, which served to defend and promote the exploitation of the working class.
3. Karl Marx, 'Contribution to the Critique of Hegel's Philosophy of Right', in K. Marx and F. Engels, *K. Marx and F. Engels on Religion* (Moscow: Progress Publishers, 1975) 38.
4. The *domovoi* lived with people in their house, the *leshii* in the forest, the *vodianoi* in streams, etc. These small demons adapted well to urban life. It was not unheard of that a *domovoi* took residence in a communal apartment and that a *vodianoi* chose to immerse itself in tap water.
5. Constitution of the Russian Soviet Federated Socialist Republic, 10 July 1918.
6. Lewis H. Siegelbaum, *Soviet State and Society Between Revolutions* (Cambridge: Cambridge University Press, 1992), 157.
7. May Day, International Cooperation Day, International Women's Day, International Youth Day, Anniversary of the October Revolution, etc. In an article entitled 'About Drunken Holidays', N. Amosov states that: 'Religious holidays harm the working people enormously. For each celebration, gigantic resources are wasted in order to organise festive gluttony and drunkenness.' N. Amosov, 'O pianykh prazdnikakh,' in A. T. Lukachevskii (ed.), *Antireligioznii Sbornik na 1929 god s materialym dlia antirozhdestveskoi kampanii* (Moscow: Bezbozhnik, 1929), 22.

8. William Chase and Lewis Siegelbaum, 'Worktime and Industrialization in the USSR, 1917–1941,' in Gary Cross (ed.), *Worktime and Industrialization: An International History* (Philadelphia: Temple University Press, 1988), 203. On the five-day week see also Eviatar Zerubavel, *The Seven Day Circle: The History and Meaning of the Week* (New York: Free Press, 1985), 35–43.
9. In 1940, efforts to reach some kind of peace with the Orthodox Church led to the reintroduction of Sundays and the seven-day week.
10. Siegelbaum, 158.
11. The Jewish section of the Party.
12. Quoted in George L. Kline, *Religious and Antireligious Thought in Russia* (Chicago: The University of Chicago Press, 1968), 150.
13. Lenin, 405.
14. *Bezbozhnik* appeared in 1922 with a print-run of 15,000, which reached 200,000 in 1932. The number of readers was presumably much larger than the print-run noted above.
15. Daniel Peris traces the chaotic history of the Committee on the Execution of the Decree Separating Church and State (also known as the Antireligious Committee), and the League of the Militant Godless in *Storming the Heavens: The Soviet League of the Militant Godless* (Ithaca: Cornell University Press, 1998). While in 1928 the membership of the League was a modest 123,000, it reached 5 ½ million in 1932, and had the grandiose objective of numbering 15 million five years later. See N. S. Timasheff, *Religion in Soviet Russia 1917–1942* (London: Sheed & Ward, 1944), 34. Yaroslavskii became a central figure in the antireligious debate when he was appointed chairman of the Antireligious Committee in 1923.
16. The Five-Year plan was drawn as a complement to Stalin's First Five-Year plan, which marked the beginning of the centralised industrialisation of the country.
17. In the mid-1920s, the pejorative *pop* referred to all clergy.
18. Originally simply titled *Bezbozhnik*, the journal appeared in 1923 under the editorship of Kostelovskaia. Although the Antireligious commission failed in its original efforts to have this journal merged with Yaroslavskii's newspaper, the Moscow publication either was compelled or chose to add '*u stanka*' to its title in order to differentiate itself from the newspaper *Bezbozhnik* and to suggest an urban worker orientation.
19. This catchphrase appeared regularly on the cover of the journal.
20. 'O chem i kak pisat' v Bezbozhnike u stanka' *Bezbozhnik u stanka*, no 9 (1925), p. 23.
21. *Op. cit.*
22. The word humoristic is here used in its broadest possible sense. In order to understand how humour functions as a rhetorical and ideological tool, we should provide a straightforward definition of the term. Unfortunately, from Freud to Bergson to Bakhtin, every attempt to understand what is humoristic seems challenged by the fact that humour is a general term which comprises a hotchpotch of heterogeneous phenomena, such as the grotesque, parody, satire, wit, irony, carnivalesque and so on. All these involve different levels of sympathy, concern with social rules, and function within different semiotic structures.

23. During the same period, this visual metaphor was also used to promote the cult of Lenin. It then depicted the Leader at the centre of the image, his life and the history of the Revolution unfolding around him.
24. Pejorative for woman implying backwardness.
25. From the First All-Union Russian Congress of Women (1918), quoted in Richard Stites, *The Woman's Liberation Movement in Russia: Feminism, Nihilism, Bolshevism 1860–1930* (Princeton: Princeton University Press, 1978), 330.
26. *Bezbozhnik u stanka* (1929), 8:6. The Second Congress also reached the conclusion that propaganda directed to women needed to address specific problems. 'Dependence on their family (especially in the countryside), the enslavement on petty domestic tasks, the constant catering to others, the low cultural level, and the religiosity that springs from these call for special forms of antireligious propaganda.' Tsentralnyi Soviet Soiuza Voinstvuiushchikh Bezbozhnikov SSSR, *Rezoliutsii Vtorogo Vsesoiuznogo S"ezda Voinstvuiushchikh Bezbozhnikov* (Moscow: Bezbozhnik), 75.
27. Humour, in the political context, is most often understood as a rebellious, 'avant-garde' practice. George Orwell's often-repeated statement that every joke is a small revolution indeed implies that humour is a potent tool against institutionalised power. However Soviet antireligious humoristic propaganda was devised by the regime for political purposes and yet maintained its avant-garde revolutionary potential in that it constantly challenged the social status quo. In *Mythologies* [1957] (Paris: Seuil, 1970), Roland Barthes opposes mythologies to political speech, which aims at transforming society, and is produced in revolutionary periods. Disillusioned with the Soviet Union and the Stalinist system, Barthes condemns the latter as a producer of weak myths through *zhdanovism*, the cultural policy espoused by the Soviet Union in 1946, which aimed to homogenise and neutralise all cultural production through massive censorship and imposed style and iconography. The static principles of *zhdanovism* are based on the struggle for the creation of meaning and new relations actively waged in the twenties and thirties in art and publications such as *Bezbozhnik u stanka. Zhdanovism* was indeed about securing the status quo and would therefore enter Barthes' definition of a myth-making structure. However, during the 1917–1941 period, speech, art and humour were still political and not yet mythical, precisely because the regime was still struggling to create codes and, as the inconsistencies in antireligious propaganda highlight, had not reached any kind of stable mythological order.
28. See Victoria Bonnell, *Iconography of Power* (Berkeley: University of California Press, 1997), 105.
29. For example, still-lifes were divorced from the art historical tradition of the *momento mori* to represent abundance under the rule of the Communist Party. The configuration of a woman and child, most often associated with the Virgin Mary before the Revolution, was secularised, and the use of the colour red lost all pre-Revolutionary religious or symbolic connotations, now signifying the sovieticity of any object or being clad in this colour.
30. Wolgang Holz, 'Allegory and Iconography in Socialist Realist Painting', in Matthew Cullerne Bown and Brandon Taylor (eds), *Art of the Soviets: Painting, Sculpture and*

Architecture in a One-Party State, 1917–1992 (Manchester: Manchester University Press, date?), 73–85.

31. Paul De Man, 'The Rhetoric of Temporality', in *Blindness and Insight: Essays in the Rhetoric of Contemporary Criticism* (Minneapolis: University of Minnesota Press, 1983), 187–228.
32. In *Kolkhoz Holiday* a combine-harvester serves as the background for a celebration. While these machines were present in much Socialist Realist art of the 1930s, very few had actually made their way to Soviet fields. They were certainly not a common feature in communal and state farms.
33. Holz, 74.
34. The woman is identifiable as a worker for two reasons. First, she is dressed in a red shirt and kerchief. The artist painted even her face in the symbolic colour of the Soviet state. In other word, she is colour-coded as a Soviet being. Second, her headscarf is tied at the nape of her neck (instead of under her chin) like factory workers did during this period.
35. For Soviet Marxists, and especially Soviet antireligionists, coexistence of materialism and religiosity is strictly impossible. This juxtaposition should therefore not be confused with *dvoeverie* (double-faith) or *mnogoverie* (multiple-faith), concepts which refer to the more or less harmonious coexistence of more than one belief system in an individual mind or in a culture.
36. In the case of Soviet irony, the typical exception can be included in this category.
37. Umberto Eco, 'The Frames of Comic Freedom,' in Umberto Eco, V. V. Ivanov and Monica Rector, *Carnival!* (New York: Mouton Publishers, 1984), 5.
38. De Man, 207.
39. *Kak ustroit' ugolok bezbozhnika* (Moscow: Bezbozhnik u stanka, 1924). The concept of the godless corner was drawn directly from the Russian Orthodox tradition. It mimicked corners, which held icons and other religious artefacts erected in people's homes. Nina Tumarkin notes that Lenin corners, red corners and godless corners appeared more or less simultaneously. Nina Tumarkin, *Lenin Lives!* (Cambridge: Cambridge University Press, 1983), 243.
40. *Kak ustroit' ugolok bezbozhnika,* p. 2. In an article on antireligious propaganda directed at children, N. Amosov discusses the installation of godless corners in schools. Their format is meant to be identical to that of godless corners erected in factories, but slogans and caricature must focus on themes of particular interest to children. See N. Amosov, 'Antireligioznaya kampaniya v shkole', in Lukachevskii, 43–5.
41. Resolutions adopted at the Second Congress of the Militant League of the Godless. Tsentralnyi Soviet Soiuza Voinstvuiushchikh Bezbozhnikov SSSR, pp. 72–3.
42. Alluding to Yaroslavskii's affiliation with Stalin and Kostelevskaia's past friendship with Trotsky, Daniel Peris speaks of personal and political conflicts between Yaroslavskii and Kostelevskaia, which led to the latter's removal from the antireligious commission in 1925, and probably paved the way for the absorption of *Bezbozhnik u stanka* into *Bezbozhnik.* See Peris, 48–54. Oddly enough, the merger and its possible causes are not mentioned in Yaroslavskii's personal files at the Central Party

Archive (RTsKhIDNI, f. 89, op. 4) or in the files of the redaction of *Bezbozhnik,* located at the Government Archive of the Russian Federation (GARF, f. 5407). The *Bezbozhnik u stanka* redaction files are absent from the archives of the Moscow Party Committee, the organisation that published the journal.

43. Tsentralnyi Soviet Soyuza Voinstvuyushchikh Bezbozhnikov SSSR, *Bezbozhnik X Let: Antireligioznyi albom-kniga,* Moscow: GAIZ, 1932. The album mentions the merger but does not explain or comment on it. Neither journal warned their readers of the merger. The event was never subsequently acknowledged in *Bezbozhnik. Bezbozhnik* survived until 1941.
44. Lenin, 407.

Chapter 13: The Singing Masses and the Laughing State in the Musical Comedy of the Stalinist 1930s

1. Important aspects of strictly musical cinema conforming to the genre of film-concert are examined in a study by Miron Chernenko, '"My budem pet' i smeiat'sia, kak deti": Tipologiia, ideologiia fil'ma-kontserta v sovetskom kino', *Iskusstvo kino* (1990), no. 11.
2. S. Krylova, L. Lebedinskii, Ra-be (A. Bek), L. Toom, *Rabochie o literature, teatre i muzyke* (Leningrad, 1926), 34–35. Hereafter, references to reviews by worker correspondents about theatre and music quoted from this publication will be made in the body of the text, with page numbers indicated.
3. M. Alatyrtsev, 'Pochva pod nogami', *Literaturnyi ezhnedel'nik,* Petrograd (1923), 8: 12.
4. See: S. Krylova *et al.*, *Rabochie o literature,* 56.
5. See *Protiv formalizma i naturalizma v iskusstve: Sbornik statei* (Moscow, 1937). This is the source for subsequent quotations in this section relating to the campaign.
6. The critics reacted to these circumstances as follows: 'The director-producer had to overcome serious inadequacies of the script. The main flaw of the initial scenario was the harmful opposition of modern art to the classical heritage. The author of the film successfully avoided the nihilistic, devil-may-care attitude to the musical classic' (A. Korchagin. '*Volga, Volga*', *Moskovskii ekran,* 1938, no. 6). Only four years had passed since *The Jolly Fellows.*

Chapter 14: The Theory and Practice of 'Scientific Parody' in Early Soviet Russia

1. V. Shklovskii, *Tristram Shandy Sterna i teoriia romana* (Petrograd, 1921).
2. D. Kharms *et al.*, 'Oberiu (deklaratsiia)' in K. Vaginov *et al.*, *Vanna Arkhimeda* (Leningrad: Khudozhestvennaia literatura, 1991), 456–62, 458.
3. Iu. N. Tynianov, 'Dostoevskii i Gogol' (k teorii parodii)', 'O parodii' in *Poetika, istoriia literatury, kino* (Moscow: Nauka, 1977), 198–226, 284–309.
4. V. V. Vinogradov, 'Etiudy o stile Gogolia' in *Poetiki russkoi literatury* (Moscow: Nauka, 1976), 230–368.
5. V. V. Vinogradov, 'Etiudy o stile Gogolia' in *Poetika russkoi literatury,* Moscow: Nauka, 1976), 230–366, 239.

6. Robert A. Maguire, 'The Formalists on Gogol' in R. J. Jackson and S. Rudy (eds) *Russian Formalism: A Retrospective Glance* (New Haven: Yale Centre for International and Area Studies, 1985), 213–30, 217ff.
7. *Parnas dybom*, sost. E. S. P., A. G. P. i A. M. F., (Kharkov: Kosmos, 1927). Around two-thirds of the texts were republished in two consecutive issues of the journal *Nauka i zhizn'* (11 and 12, 1968).
8. This information was first made available in E. Papernaia i A. Finkel', 'Kak sozdavalsia "Parnas dybom" ', *Voprosy literatury* 7, 1966, 234–41; republished in E. S. Papernaia, A. G. Rozenburg i A. M. Finkel', *Parnas dybom* (Moscow: Khudozhestvennaia literatura, 1990), 121–3.
9. 'Kak sozdavalsia "Parnas dybom"', 122, 121.
10. Iu. N. Tynianov, 'Dostoevskii i Gogol'' 201.
11. O. B. Kushlina, 'Nauchnoe vesel'e' in *Russkaia literatura XX veka v zerkale parodii* ed. O. B. Kushlina (Moscow: Vysshaia shkola, 1993), 216–20, 220.
12. *Idealistische Neuphilologie*, ed. Victor Klemperer and Eugen Lerch (Heidelberg: Carl Winter, 1922). Klemperer and Lerch went on to establish the short lived *Jahrbuch für Philologie* as the organ of the idealist school.
13. M. M. Bakhtin, *Problemy tvorchestva/ poetiki Dostoevskogo* (Kiev: Next, 1994), 93–4, 409–10. Bakhtin's notes from Spitzer's *Italienische Umgangsprache* (Bonn and Leipzig: Kurt Schroeder 1922) have now been published as 'Opisanie konspektov, prednaznachennykh dlia ispol'zovaniia v knige "Problemy tvorchestva Dostoevskogo' in M. M. Bakhtin, *Sobranie sochinenii*, tom 2 (Moscow: Russkie slovari, 2000), 735–58.
14. Karl Vossler, *The Spirit of Language in Civilization*, trans. Oeser, (London: Kegan Paul, 1932),181–2.
15. Victor Erlich is much too categorical in his assessment of the Formalists' being 'well-nigh immune to the "neo-idealistic" school of Karl Vossler and Leo Spitzer'. *Russian Formalism: History – Doctrine* (The Hague: Mouton 1969), 230.
16. M. P. Odesskii, 'K voprosu o literaturovedcheskom metode L. Shpitsera' in V. V. Kuskova and L. V. Zlatoystovoi, *Teoriia i praktika literaturovedcheskikh i literaturovedcheskikh issledovanii*, (Moscow: MGU, 1988), 54–60.
17. Leo Spitzer, *Die Wortbildung als stilistisches Mittel, exempliziert an Rabelais* (Halle: Max Niemeyer 1910); Karl Vossler, *Frankreichs Kultur im Spiegel seiner Sprachwicklung* (Heidelberg: Carl Winter, 1913). On this see Galin Tihanov, *The Master and the Slave: Lukács, Bakhtin and the Ideas of their Time* (Oxford: Oxford University Press, 2000), 266. A summary of Spitzer's views on parody in Rabelais appeared in Russian as 'Slovesnoe iskusstvo i nauka o iazyke', trans. T. N. Zhirmunskii, in V. Zhirmunskii (ed.) *Problemy literaturnoi formy* (Petersburg: Academia, 1928), 191–222, 195.
18. See A. B. Muratov, *Izuchenie iazyka khudozhestvennoi literatury kak metodologicheskaia problema (O trudakh V. V. Vinogradova 1920-kh godov)* (St. Petersburg, Izd. S-Peterburgskogo universiteta 1999), 14. See also V. V. Vinogradov, *O iazyke khudozhestvennoi prozy* (Moscow: Nauka, 1980), 65ff, and Nina Perlina, 'A dialogue on the Dialogue: The Baxtin-Vinogradov Exchange (1924–65)', *Slavic and East European Review* 32 (1988), 4: 526–41.

19. P. N. Medvedev, *Formal'nyi metod v literaturovedenii* in M. M. Bakhtin, *Tetralogiia* (Moscow: Labirint, 1998), 110–297, 163; V. M. Zhirmunskii, 'Predislovie', in *Problemy literaturnoi formy*, vi.
20. O. Val'tsel', 'Khudozhestvennaia forma v proizvedeniiakh Gete i nemetskikh romantikov' in *Problemy literaturnoi formy*, 70–104.
21. In 'Lichnoe delo V. N. Voloshinova', *Dialog. Karnaval. Khronotop* (1995), 2: 70–99, 88, Voloshinov argues that the key figure in this connection between the two notions of inner form was the Brentanian theorist of language Anton Marty. There is certainly little doubt that Marty, along with Bühler, played a crucial role in the development of the Bakhtin Circle's notions of dialogue and the utterance. On this see my 'Voloshinov's Dilemma: On the Philosophical Sources of the Dialogic Theory of the Utterance' in Brandist (*et al.*, eds) *The Bakhtin Circle: In The Master's Absence* (Manchester: Manchester University Press, 2004).
22. Ernst Cassirer, *The Platonic Renaissance in England*, trans. J. Pettegrove (London: Nelson, 1953), 200ff.
23. On the GAKhN commission see Erika Freiberger-Sheikoleslami, 'Forgotten Pioneers of Soviet Semiotics' in *Semiotics 1980*, eds M. Herzfeld and M. D. Lenhart, (New York and London: 1982), 155–63. The influence of Bühler on Voloshinov, which suggests possibilities within the work of the Bakhtin Circle in opposition to Bakhtin's own neo-Kantian idealism is discussed in my 'Voloshinov's Dilemma'.
24. Tynianov, *Poetika, istoriia literatury, kino*, 455. On Tynianov's relation to Cassirer see also Peter Steiner, *Russian Formalism: A Metapoetics* (Ithaca: Cornell University Press, 1984), 101–2.
25. Ladislav Matejka, 'Deconstructing Bakhtin' in C. A. Mihailescu and W. Hamarneh, *Fiction Updated: Theories of Fictionality, Narratology and Poetics* (Toronto: University of Toronto Press, 1996), 257–66; A. B. Muratov, *Fenomenologicheskaia estetika nachala XX veka i teoriia slovesnosti (B. M. Engel gardt)* (St. Petersburg, Izd. C-Peterburskogo universiteta 1996), 10ff; A. B. *Muratov Izuchenie Iazyka khydozhestvennoi literatury kak metodologicheskaia problema*; Peter Steiner, *Russian Formalism: a Metapoetics*, 104–5.
26. Vinogradov, *O iazyke*, 88.
27. *Besedy V. D. Duvakina s M. M. Bakhtina* (Moscow: Progress 1996) 39ff; V. N. Voloshinov, 'Lichnoe delo V. N. Voloshinova' *Dialog. Karnaval. Khronotop* (1995), 2: 70–99, 75.
28. Karl Schuhmann and Barry Smith, 'Two Idealisms: Lask and Husserl', *Kant-Studien* (1993), 83: 448–66, 461.
29. Eugeniusz Czaplejewicz, 'A Type of Reflection and the Literary Genre', *Reflection on Literature in Eastern and Western Cultures*, eds E. Czaplejewicz and M. Melanowicz (Warsaw: Wydawnictwa Universitetu Warsawskiego, 1990), 7–52, 46.
30. 'K stilistike romana', *Sobranie sochinenii* 5, (Moscow: Russkie slovary, 1996), 138–40, 138.
31. Voloshinov, 'Lichnoe delo', 87–8.

32. 'Slovo v romane', *Voprosy literatury i estetiki* (Moscow: Khudozhestvennaia literatura, 1975), 72–234, 211.
33. Craig Brandist, 'Neo-Kantianism in Cultural Theory: Bakhtin, Derrida and Foucault', *Radical Philosophy* (2000), 102; 6–16.
34. Cassirer, *The Platonic Renaissance in England*, 183–4.
35. Bakhtin, 'Slovo', 212.
36. M. M. Bakhtin 'Epos i roman' in *Voprosy*, 477–83, 466.
37. Galin Tihanov, *The Master and the Slave*, 274–5.
38. Craig Brandist, 'Bakhtin, Marxism and Russian Populism' in *Materializing Bakhtin: The Bakhtin Circle and Social Theory* (London: Macmillan, 2000), 70–94.
39. O. M. Freidenberg, 'Proiskhozhdenie parodii' in *Russkaia literatura XX veka v zerkale parodii*, 392–404. It was originally published as 'Idea parodii (nabrosok k rabote)' in *Sbornik statei v chest' S. A. Zhebeleva* (Leningrad 1926) 378–96. Voloshinov may have heard Freidenberg lecture at this very time while studying at ILIaZV in Leningrad. It seems they definitely met in 1930. On this see Kevin Moss, 'Introduction' in Olga Freidenberg, *Image and Concept: Mythopoetic roots of Literature* (Amsterdam: Harwood Academic Publishers 1997), 1–27, 21–2. Meanwhile, Iurii Medvedev has shown that Pavel Medvedev was planning a joint project with Freidenberg and Frank-Kamenetskii on which see Iu. P. Medvedev, 'Na puti k sozdaniiu sotsiologicheskoi poetiki', *Dialog. Karnaval. Khronotop*, 2: 5–57, 31.
40. O. M. Freidenberg, *Poetika siuzheta i zhanra* (Moscow: Labirint, 1997), 275. The passages Bakhtin underlined in his own copy of this book are recorded and discussed in O. E. Osovskii, '"Iz sovetskikh rabot bol'shuiu tsennost' imeet kniga O. Freidenberg": Bakhtinskie marginalii na stranitsakh "Poetiki siuzheta i zhanra"' in V. L. Makhlin (ed.) *Bakhtinskii sbornik IV* (Saransk: M.G.P.I., 2000), 128–34.
41. Tihanov, *Master and Slave*, 160. On Freidenberg and Marrism see also Kevin Moss, 'Ol'ga Freidenberg i marrizm,' *Voprosy iazykoznaniia* (1994), 5 (Sept–Oct.): 98–106.
42. Kevin Moss, 'Introduction', 20–4. It is worth noting that Cassirer's work on myth was actually a significant influence on both the Marrists' 'japhetic theory' and on Freidenberg. See her *Poetika siuzheta i zhanra*, 31–7.
43. I am indebted to Galin Tihanov for his comments on an earlier version of this paper.

Chapter 15: Laughing at the Hangman

1. This study concentrates on literary comedy rather than on oral forms such as jokes or anecdotes; the functionality of literary humour is very different from that of oral forms and that functionality is of central importance in a reading of humour as a strategy of reconciliation. Considerable scholarly attention has been devoted to oral humour about Stalinism by Iurii Borev, Emil Draitser and others. See Iurii Borev, *Staliniada* (Moskva: Sovetskii pisatel', 1990); Emil Draitser, *Forbidden Laughter: Soviet Underground Jokes* (Los Angeles: Almanac, 1978); Emil Draitser, *Taking Penguins to the Movies: Ethnic Humor in Russia* (Detroit: Wayne State University Press, 1998).
2. Northrop Frye in *Anatomy of Criticism* (Princeton: Princeton University Press, 1957) argues that comedy includes but moves beyond the stuff of tragedy. Tragedy, he asserts,

deals with only a portion of the cycle of myth, while comedy encounters the entire cycle.

3. Edward L. Galligan, *The Comic Vision in Literature* (Athens: University of Georgia Press, 1984), 28.
4. Vladimir Voinovich, *Zhizn' i neobychainye prikliucheniia soldata Ivana Chonkina* (Moskva: Knizhnaia palata, 1990), 45. This and all subsequent translations are the present author's.
5. Vladimir Voinovich, 'V krugu druzei', in *Zapakh shokolada. Povesti i rasskazy* (Moskva: Vagrius, 1997), 225.
6. This chapter of *Kangaroo*, written in 1974–75 and entitled 'The Leg' ('Noga'), was originally published as a story: 'Noga: Iz romana *Kenguru*', *Ekho* (1979), 1: 6–29.
7. Iuz Aleshkovskii, *Kenguru* (Voronezh: AMKO, 1992), 147.
8. Il'ia Suslov, *Rasskazy o tovarishche Staline i drugikh tovarishchakh* (Ann Arbor: Hermitage, 1981), 11. The page numbers of additional quotations from this work will be indicated in parentheses.
9. Iuz Aleshkovskii, '"Ne unyvai, zimoi dadut svidanie..." ', *Novyi mir* (1988), 12: 122.
10. William Lynch, *Christ and Apollo: The Dimensions of the Literary Imagination* (New York: Sheed and Ward, 1960), 91.
11. See, for example, Norris Houghton, *Return Engagement* (New York: Holt, Rinehart and Winston, 1962), 47; Veniamin Kaverin, 'Shvarts i soprotivlenie', *Literaturnoe obozrenie* (1989), 2: 77; Lev Loseff, *On the Beneficence of Censorship. Aesopian Language in Modern Russian Literature* (München: Otto Sagner, 1984), 136–37.
12. For a discussion of the generic characteristics of Shvarts's works, see Irina H. Corten, 'Evgenii Shvarts as an Adapter of Hans Christian Andersen and Charles Perrault', *The Russian Review* 37 (January 1978); Amanda J. Metcalf, *Evgenii Shvarts and His Fairy-Tales for Adults* (Birmingham: Birmingham Slavonic Monographs, 1979).
13. Evgenii Shvarts, *Drakon*, in *Drakon, Klad, Ten', Dva klena, Obyknovennoe chudo i drugie proizvedeniia* (Moskva: Gud'ial, 1998), 339.
14. Fazil' Iskander, *Piry Valtasara*, in *Sandro iz Chegema* (Moskva: Eksmo-Press, 1998), 339.
15. Loseff, *The Beneficence of Censorship*, 199.
16. Galligan, *The Comic Vision in Literature*, 152.

Chapter 16: Varieties of Reflexivity in the Russo-Soviet *Anekdot*

1. Although the *anekdot* and the joke share many features, their dissimilar cultural environments make the terms far from synonymous, even in the post-Soviet era (to say nothing of the geopolitically bipolar period that preceded it). Nevertheless, for stylistic reasons I occasionally use 'joke'.
2. Vovochka is the traditional naughty schoolboy of Russian jokelore. His name is a short form of 'Vladimir', one reason for the comparisons to Putin. Other reasons include Putin's impish appearance (short stature, protruding ears, beady eyes) and past Soviet-era jokeloric connections between Vovochka and another Kremlin occupant, Lenin (also a Vladimir) (on this see A. F. Belousov, 'Vovochka', *Anti-mir russkoi kul'tury: Iazyk. Fol'klor. Literatura*, ed. N. Bogomolov [Moscow: Ladomir, 1996], 165–86).

Putin has also been compared to another *anekdot* protagonist, Shtirlits, due to Putin's experience as a KGB agent in East Germany in the 1970s (see Mark Lipovetskii, 'Prezident Shtirlits', *Iskusstvo kino* [2000], 11: 73–6).

3. All translations are mine. Quoted *anekdot* texts for which no source is cited were transcribed orally and translated.
4. These four words, all beginning with the Russian letter *ch*, refer to popular joke subjects between the 1960s and the 1980s: Vasilii Ivanovich Chapaev was a Russian Civil War commander of peasant stock whose exploits and heroic death were the subject of the 1934 film *Chapaev*; the Chukchi are an indigenous people inhabiting the arctic northeast corner of Siberia; Cheburashka is a small, big-eared, furry character from a 1972 animated film; Konstantin Chernenko was general secretary of the Soviet Communist Party in 1984–5.
5. Abram Terts, 'Anekdot v anekdote', *Sintaksis* (1978),1: 77–95.
6. Olga Chirkova, *Poetika sovremennogo narodnogo anekdota*, PhD dissertation, Volgograd U, 1997, p. 8.
7. Mikhail Bakhtin, 'The Problem of Speech Genres', *Speech Genres and Other Late Essays*, trans. Vern W. McGee, eds Caryl Emerson and Michael Holquist (Austin: University of Texas Press, 1986), 60–102, 68.
8. Richard Bauman, 'Performance', *Folklore, Cultural Performances, and Popular Entertainments: A Communications-centered Handbook*, ed. Bauman (NY: Oxford UP, 1992), 41–9, 47.
9. Ibid.
10. E. M. Meletinskii, 'Skazka-anekdot v sisteme fol'klornykh zhanrov', *Izbrannye stat'i. Vospominaniia* (Moscow: RGGU, 1998), 318–33, 319.
11. Iurii Sokolov, 'Vernyi anekdot', *Zhurnalist* (1991), 4 : 94–5, p. 95.
12. Zara Abdullaeva, 'Vse my vyshli iz anekdota', *Znanie – sila* (1993),2: 113–20, 119.
13. Vladimir Bakhtin, 'Anekdoty nas spasali vsegda', *Samizdat veka*, comp. Anatolii Strelianyi, Genrikh Sapgir, Vladimir Bakhtin, and Nikita Ordynskii (Minsk/Moscow: Polifakt, 1997), 799–818, 799.
14. Evgenii Petrosian, *Evgenii Petrosian v strane anekdotov* (Moscow: Tsentr Estradnoi Iumoristiki, 1995), 5. The large Shtirlits cycle is based on the popular 1973 television mini-series *17 Moments of Spring* [*Semnadtsat' mgnovenii vesny*], which depicted the heroic adventures of a Red Army colonel posing as an SS officer in Nazi Germany. Colonel Isaev is Shtirlits' actual identity in the film. Viacheslav Tikhonov is the actor who played Shtirlits/Isaev.
15. L. A. Barskii, *Eto prosto smeshno* (Moscow: Kh.G.S., 1992), 32.
16. Terts, 90.
17. There was a wave of stupidity jokes about Soviet generals and their wives in the 1950s.
18. The abstract *anekdot* was not, incidentally, the only form of contemporary folklore to use the absurd to do violence to its own fundamental genetic code. Consider the 'misfit *chastushka*' [*chastushka-neskladukha*], for example:

   A brick crawls up the wall,
   Hairy as gasoline.

This is a song of love.
Hooray for the Red Army!

(V. Bakhtin, 'Po stene polzet kirpich, ili Kak podvodnaia lodka v stepiakh Ukrainy pogibla v zhestokom vozdushnom boiu', interview with Mikhail Grigor'ev, *Trud* 21 Apr. 1995, p. 9).

19. P. A. Borodin, 'Abstraktnyi anekdot kak sotsiokul'turnyi fenomen', *Material mezhdunarodnoi konferentsii 'Fol'klor i sovremennost'', posviashchennoi pamiati professora N. I. Savushkinoi (20–22 oktiabria 1994 goda)* (Moscow: Moskovskii gorodskoi dvorets tvorchestva, 1995), 86–91, 87–88.
20. Barskii, 293.
21. Ibid., 292.
22. Borodin, 90.
23. Ibid., 87.
24. Barbara A. Babcock, 'Arrange Me into Disorder: Fragments and Reflections on Ritual Clowning' in *Rite, Drama, Festival, Spectacle: Rehearsals Toward a Theory of Cultural Performance*, ed. John J. MacAloon (Philadelphia: Institute for the Study of Human Issues, 1984), 102–28, 103.
25. Borodin, 89.
26. On the cultural significance of narrating one's own 'mischief-making' activities (specifically among Russian males), see Nancy Ries, *Russian Talk: Culture and Conversation during Perestroika* (Ithaca: Cornell UP, 1997), 65–8.
27. Arthur Koestler, *The Act of Creation* (London: Arkana, 1989), 31.
28. See C. Banc's and Alan Dundes' collection of translated (mostly Romanian) jokes titled *First Prize Fifteen Years!: An Annotated Collection of Romanian Political Jokes* (Rutherford, NJ: Farleigh Dickinson UP, 1986).
29. A. V. Lunacharskii, 'O smekhe', *Literaturnyi kritik* (1935), 4: 3–9, p. 9.
30. Maksim Gor'kii, *Sobranie sochinenii*, vol. 27 (Moscow: Goslitizdat, 1953), p. 503, qtd. in V. M. Sidel'nikov, 'Ideino-khudozhestvennaia spetsifika russkogo narodnogo anekdota', *Voprosy literaturovedeniia*, vyp. 1 (Moscow: Universitet druzhby narodov im. P. Lamumby, 1964), 21–50, 22.
31. Andrei Nemzer, 'Desiat' bukv po vertikali', foreword, *Anketa*, by Aleksei Slapovskii (St. Petersburg: Kurs, 1997), 3–6, 3.
32. Petr Vail' and Aleksandr Genis, *60-e. Mir sovetskogo cheloveka* (Moscow: Novoe literaturnoe obozrenie, 1998), 142.
33. Boris Briker and Anatolii Vishevskii, 'Iumor v populiarnoi kul'ture sovetskogo intelligenta 60-kh – 70-kh godov', *Wiener Slawistischer Almanach* (1989), 24:147–70, 148.
34. Vladimir Elistratov, 'Argo i kul'tura', *Slovar' moskovskogo argo: Materialy 1980–1994 gg.* (Moscow: Russkie slovari, 1994), 592–699, 600.
35. Later, Rzhevskii was often depicted in encounters with another fictional character, Natasha Rostova from Tolstoi's *War and Peace*, Sergei Bondarchuk's famous screen adaptation of which appeared in 1966–67.
36. There is no consensus on the Chukchi cycle's origins. A recent television retrospective of Soviet history named 1972 as the birth year of the cycle, claiming it

was most immediately inspired by a popular song of that year by an indigenous singer from Chukotka. The chorus of the song went 'An airplane's good, but reindeer are better!' (Leonid Parfenov, prod., *Like Yesterday-71* [*Namedni-71*], NTV, 1999).

37. A. F. Belousov, 'Anekdoty o Shtirlitse', *Zhivaia starina* (1995), 1: 16–18, p. 16. The mini-series uses third-person voice-over narration frequently, especially to make Shtirlits' thoughts explicit to the viewer. The device is parodied often in the *anekdot* series, and indeed is one of the reasons the mini-series inspired such a flood of jokes in the first place.
38. On the status of the *anekdot* as a dramatic genre, see E.Ia. Shmeleva and A. D. Shmelev, 'Rasskazyvanie anekdota kak zhanr sovremennoi russkoi rechi: problemy variativnosti', *Fol'klor i postfol'klor: struktura, tipologiia, semiotika*, ed. S. Iu. Nekliudov, <http://www.ruthenia.ru/folklore/shmelev3.htm>, accessed May 29, 2001.
39. Walter J. Ong, *Orality and Literacy: The Technologizing of the Word* (London: Routledge, 1982), 3.
40. Vadim Lur'e, 'Zhizn', smert' i bessmertie Vasiliia Chapaeva', *Nezavisimaia gazeta*, 9 Feb. 1991, p. 8.
41. Evgenii Andreevich, *Kreml' i narod: Politicheskie anekdoty* (Munich: n.p., 1951), 15.
42. Rashit Iangirov, 'Anekdoty 's borodoi': Materialy k istorii nepodtsenzurnogo sovetskogo fol'klora', *Novoe literaturnoe obozrenie* (1998), 31: 155–74, 172.
43. M. A. Krongauz, 'Bessilie iazyka v epokhu zrelogo sotsializma' in *Znak: Sbornik statei po lingvistike, semiotike i poetike pamiati A. N. Zhurinskogo* (Moscow: Russkii uchebnyi tsentr MS, 1994), 233–44, 241.
44. Tat'iana Cherednichenko, *Tipologiia sovetskoi massovoi kul'tury: Mezhdu 'Brezhnevym' i 'Pugachevoi'* (Moscow: RIK Kul'tura, 1993), 10.
45. Ibid.
46. Sergei Romanov, *Usypal'nitsa: Biografiia sovetskikh 'tsarei' v anekdotakh* (Moscow: IRLE, 1994), 6.
47. Richard Schechner, 'Collective Reflexivity: Restoration of Behavior' in *A Crack in the Mirror*, ed. Jay Ruby (Philadelphia: Pennsylvania UP, 1982), pp. 38–9.
48. Susan Stewart, 'Some Riddles and Proverbs of Textuality: An Essay in Literary Value and Evaluation', *Criticism* 21 (Spring 1979), 2: 93–105, 99.
49. Schechner, *passim.*
50. An example of the use of literary allusion in political *anekdoty*: in her notebooks from the mid-1930s the writer Natal'ia Sokolova recorded an *anekdot* about the productions being staged at new Moscow theatres that season: at the Lenin Theatre, *Woe from Wit* (*Gore ot uma*); at the Stalin Theatre, *Don't Sit in Someone Else's Sleigh* (*Ne v svoi sani ne sadis*); at the Kalinin Theatre, *Ivan the Fool* (*Ivanushka-durachok*); at the GPU (later known as the KGB) Theatre, *Hunting for Pearls* (*Iskateli zhemchuga*) in the morning and *Guilty Without Guilt* (*Bez viny vinovaty*) at night (Natal'ia Sokolova, 'V zerkale smekha: Literaturno-teatral'nyi iumor pervoi poloviny 30-x godov', *Voprosy literatury* [1996], 3: 362–75, 374).
51. Bauman, 47.

52. See Daniel Rancour-Laferriere's *The Slave Soul of Russia: Moral Masochism and the Cult of Suffering* (New York and London: New York UP, 1995), a book-length discussion of Russian national masochism.

Chapter 17: Humour and Satire on Post-Soviet Russian Television

1. This applies above all to 'Khriun Morzhov', who by virtue of the dynamics of the programme tends to be given all the best lines. A search for 'Khriun' conducted on the site www.yandex.ru on 3 September 2001 produced 5415 responses.
2. These are the following: 'Pervyi Kanal', 51 per cent owned by the state, though until 2000 run by Boris Berezovsky, one of the so-called 'oligarchs', and since then effectively controlled from the Kremlin; 'Rossia' and 'Kul'tura', wholly owned by the state; TV-Tsentr, controlled by the Moscow city government; NTV, the largest private-sector channel; TV-6, a private-sector channel, controlled from 1999 to 2002 by Boris Berezovsky. NTV was until recently controlled by Vladimir Gusinsky's Media-Most group, but in April 2001 the station was taken over in controversial circumstances by Gazprom, previously a minority shareholder, but also a substantial creditor. After this takeover a number of leading figures and some programmes moved from NTV to TV-6. TV-6 was itself closed down after an obscure and complex law-suit in January 2002; its successor, TVS, owned by a consortium of oligarchs presumably acceptable to the president and his entourage, but staffed by many of the broadcasters from the former TV-6, started operating in June 2002. TVS was itself closed down in 2003.
3. A. Knyshev, quoted in L. Parfenov, E. Chekalova, *Nam vozvrashchaiut nash portret* (Moscow: Iskusstvo, 1990), 189. This is supported by the present writer's own observations made when studying at Rostov State University in 1970–71. The historical information about *KVN* is taken from the programme's official web-site (http://www.amik.ru/history61.asp and http://www.amik.ru/history86.asp#).
4. According to the web-site mentioned in note 3, Lapin, who was a member of the Supreme Soviet, had made an unsuccessful attempt to revive the programme in the 1970s in response to complaints from his constituents.
5. Iuliia Taratuta, '*KVN*: Kuplen? Tsenzurirovan? Mertv?', *Novaia gazeta,* 21, 26 March 2001 (Internet version: http://2001.NovayaGazeta.ru/nomer/2001/21n/n21n-s16.shtml).
6. Some attempts to reproduce *KVN* have been made among russophone communities outside the former Soviet Union (http://www.kulichki.com/KBH), and international games between Israel and the CIS were shown on NTV-International in May 2000.
7. http://www.amik.ru/history61.asp
8. http://www.nns.ru/Person/lesin; see also note 5.
9. Dmitry Khatarov, 'Vol'nodumie s nechelovecheskim litsom: Khriun i Stepan nanosiat otvetnyi udar', *Ezhenedel'nyi zhurnal,* 00 [sic], 22 November 2001 (Internet version: http://www.ej.ru/00-/particular/profile/index.html).
10. *Antologiia iumora,* NTV-International, 27 May 2001.
11. Galina Chermenskaia, 'Igra v budushchee', *Nedelia* (1990), 51: 15.

12. This includes the title of the programme, a word that has eluded most lexicographers and over which ATV's announcers were wont to affect great puzzlement. It is, in fact, an interjection accompanying the accomplishment of some artistic endeavour; see V. S. Elistratov, *Slovar' moskovskogo argo* (Moscow: Russkie slovari, 1994), 283. For the use of this word in an obscene rhyme see Tatiana Akhmetova, *Tolkovyj slovar': Russkii mat*, 2nd edition (Moscow: Kolokol-Press, 1997), 105.
13. See also Sergei Fomin, 'Igor' Ugol'nikov i konets rossiiskogo klassicheskogo televideniia', *Nezavisimaia gazeta*, 28 December 1991 (Available on the Internet at http://ugol.mnogo.ru/press/article66.html). For an English-language account of *Oba-na* see 'A Television Show to Laugh With, not At', *Moscow Times*, 16 October 1993 (available on the Internet at http://ugol.mnogo.ru/press/article41.html).
14. Or almost. What Ugol'nikov actually said was 'As for our fax, it's American, and unfortunately it answers in American: "Fax you" (sic).' Both obscenities were uttered in the edition broadcast on 23 March 1992.
15. I. Iuganov, F. Iuganova, *Slovar' russkogo slenga* (Moscow: Metatekst, 1997), 8. See also E. A. Zemskaia's introduction to the collective work *Russkii iazyk kontsa XX stoletiia* (Moscow: Iazyki russkoi kul'tury, 1996), 22–3.
16. Lev Gudkov, Boris Dubin, 'Ideologiia besstrukturnosti', *Znamia* (1994), 11: 166.
17. Contrary to what might be expected, Sub-tropicheskaia Rossiia is a real, if not entirely serious political movement, led by V. V. Pribylovsky (http://www.subtropiki.ru).
18. See also J. A. Dunn, 'From Soviet bloc to post-Soviet camp', *Rusistika* (1996), 13: 4–10.
19. *Kuranty*, 18 August 1995.
20. Examples of Shenderovich's work, including scripts for *Itogi* and his new programme *Pomekhi v èfire (Interference)*, can be found on his web-site (http://www.shender.ru).
21. Alla Bossart, 'Shutki v kompanii s durakom letiat nezametno', *Novaia gazeta*, 29 March 2001 (Internet version: http://2001.NovayaGazeta.Ru/nomer/2001/22n/n22n-s13.shtml).
22. There are no regular female characters, though Tatiana D'iachenko, one of Yeltsin's daughters, and Valeriia Novodvorskaia have been represented from time to time. Other women prominent in Russian public life, such as Irina Khakamada, have been ignored by the programme.
23. In the latter case most notably in an episode entitled 'Tarakan' ('Cockroach'), broadcast on 19 September 1999; this remains for the present writer the best and most succinct account of the Chechen conflict.
24. See J. A. Dunn, '*Kukly* and the Russian Language', *Rusistika* (1998), 18: 3–7. This is less true of the programme in the Putin era, perhaps in part because the new President has demonstrated that he really does speak like a criminal.
25. Viktor Shenderovich, *Kukly* (Moscow: Vagrius, 1996); *Kukly-2*, (Moscow: Vagrius, 1998). For the history of the early years of the programme see Viktor Shenderovich, 'Kukliada', *Znamia* (1998), 3: 169–88.
26. See for example the episode entitled 'V Chechniu! V Chechniu!' ('To Chechnya! To Chechnya!'), *Kukly-2*, 67–75.
27. The script for this episode is published in *Kukly-2*, 83–114.

28. The episode is described in 'Kukliada', 174–9; see also the self-referential episode 'Ne tiani rezinu!' ('Don't stretch the rubber'), *Kukly*, 145–51.
29. The term used for the policy of strengthening the power of the centre at the expense of the regions.
30. 'Bez menia kapustu ne zasoliat', *Moskovskie novosti*, 2000, 46, 20.
31. See also the views expressed by Grigoriev himself in an interview published in *Izvestiia* on 19 July 2002 (Internet version: http://izvestia.ru/tv/article21308).
32. It is noteworthy that when *Krokodil* published columns of non-political jokes, these were always described as being 'foreign' and the participants were given appropriately exotic names. By the same token many jokes which were essentially obscene or examples of verbal absurdity gained a political element by being placed in the 'Chapaev' or the 'Armenian Radio' series.
33. For a selection of scripts from this programme see *O. S. P. – Studiia: Teledenek* (Moscow: Veche, 1998).
34. Bossart, op.cit. She praises *Gorodok* (as does one of the present writer's informants), though not unreservedly. *Maski-shou* is worth a mention for having bequeathed its untranslatable name to the Russian language, this being the term used to describe those incidents where gangs of armed men, wearing masks and camouflage uniforms and purporting to represent one or other of the law enforcement agencies, cause mayhem in the premises of a company which has in some way or other offended the powers that be.
35. The scripts are published in Igor' Ugol'nikov, *Oba-na!*, Vagrius, Moscow, 1996, pp. 51–96.
36. Since there are clear references to the American hospital series *ER*, it is tempting to translate the title as *E II R*.
37. *Pesni s Fomenko*, NTV, 24 April 2000. Fomenko should not be underestimated: he has achieved the unique distinction of selling one of his programmes, the emphatically non-humorous *Èkstremal'nye situatsii (Extreme Situations)* to a commercial channel in Germany.
38. Dzhon Dann (J. A. Dunn), 'Vstrecha po doroge v ad? (Konvergentsiia evropeiskikh sistem SMI v èpokhu postkommunizma)', *Vestnik Moskovskogo universiteta*, Seriia 10 (Zhurnalistika), 2001, 3, p. 21.
39. See note 2. If the victims of these events regarded them as an attack on freedom of speech, supporters of the President preferred to describe them as straightforward business disputes. For an account of the NTV affair see Laura Belin, 'The Rise and Fall of Russia's NTV', *Stanford Journal of International Law*, 38, (2002), 1: 19–42; for different opinions on the TV-6 affair see http://www.grani.ru/freepress/quotes
40. *Za steklom*, shown on TV-6. The apparent resemblances to *Big Brother* did not escape the attention of lawyers acting for the producers of the latter programme.
41. 'Ot "Krokodila" do Khriuna', *Izvestiia*, 5 August 2002 (Internet version: http://izvestia.ru/politic/article22072).
42. Nigel Morris, '"Brass Eye": Ministers say no plan to interfere', *The Independent*, 31 July 2001, 5.